RELIGION AND CULTURE SERIES

Joseph Husslein, S.J., Ph.D., General Editor

THE CATHOLIC EASTERN CHURCHES

POPE PIUS X, PATRIARCH OF THE WEST AND SUPREME PONTIFF,
WITH THE LORD CYRIL VIII, PATRIARCH OF ANTIOCH,
and other members of the Melkite hierarchy

The
CATHOLIC
EASTERN
CHURCHES

By

Donald Attwater

The Church of Jesus Christ is neither Latin nor Greek nor Slav but Catholic; accordingly she makes no difference between her children, and Greek, Latins, Slavs, and members of all other nations are equal in the eyes of the Apostolic See.

—Pope Benedict XV

THE BRUCE PUBLISHING COMPANY
MILWAUKEE, WISCONSIN
London, 17 Red Lion Passage, W. C. 1

Nihil obstat:
    H. B. RIES,
        Censor librorum

Imprimatur:
    ✠ SAMUEL A. STRITCH,
        Archiepiscopus Milwaukiensis

July 22, 1935

TO

G. B. AND O. B.

WITH

GRATITUDE AND AFFECTION

PREFACE BY THE GENERAL EDITOR

Red Internationalism is working today at the overthrow of every government that is not its own. Its propaganda is carried on indiscriminately among men of every race. East and West are alike to it. Everywhere it is engaged in its one supreme work, with tireless energy and often heedless sacrifice, to create a world in which God shall not be known, and much less worshipped by any man.

Its wide-flung propaganda, diversified in a thousand ways and always skillfully adapted to racial temperament, is promoted from one single center of activity. Its work is executed with mechanical regularity according to the orders flashed from one central station. Any policy once decided upon by the small group in power, be it right or wrong, moral or immoral, is followed out with unquestioning obedience. This in fact is ultimately its one code of ethics, to promote effectively the red revolution.

Evidently, in the face of such a force, the faithful must be no less united, not indeed after the wrongful manner of the Communist and acting upon principles that are subversive to the social, moral, and spiritual order, but gathered in unity of legitimate purpose around Christ their King and His Vicar upon earth. East and West must henceforth form no barrier to Catholic co-operation.

But that this may be made possible it is not necessary that ancient forms of worship be reduced to one common sameness. Rather, reversing the Pentecostal miracle, let all continue to express in whatever different tongues and rites and liturgies, the same truth; offer the same essential Sacrifice; and praise in one accord the Trinity in Unity and Unity in Trinity.

That has been done within the Church of Christ, but evidently it will not suffice. In order that Catholics of all rites may perfectly co-operate with one another, they must learn to know each other correctly. Only so can they come to understand each other, and finally to appreciate the true worth of each other. Hidden today from the eyes of Western Catholics there lies a whole world of beauty, artistry, and sublime devotion in the liturgies of the Eastern churches, of whose very existence many are but vaguely aware. Still more deplorable, though natural enough under such circumstances, their minds are not seldom betrayed into misconceptions, misunderstandings, and possibly even false suspicions. This, indeed, is a sorry basis for that perfect, world-wide co-operation which present conditions make imperative.

And yet, who can blame the men and women of English-speaking lands for not understanding what they have practically had no opportunity to learn?

With the appearance of Mr. Attwater's book this excuse vanishes. For the diffusion of the required knowledge among all ranks of the faithful, whether clergy or laity, it will prove a helpful and effective aid. It is the only work of its kind in our language, presenting in a single volume a brief, popular, yet adequate exposition of the important points to be noted in the history, liturgy, rites, vestments, music, architecture, and other characteristics of the various Eastern churches in communion with the Holy See.

The name of the author should vouch by itself for the fact that this is an authoritative work. But to secure exactness the most rigorous precautions have been taken by him, to the extent of submitting his description of each rite to a priest of that rite for critical scrutiny. His own intimate relations with the clergy of these churches has made such a course possible. The material of his book, it may be added, is the result of keen study in this field ever since his stay in the Near East from 1917 to 1920.

As for the differences in languages, rites, and liturgy of the Eastern churches among themselves, and as compared with the Western church, let it be understood that all these divergencies but lend new charm to the incomparable beauty of the Bride of Christ where she stands at the right hand of her Spouse, in gilded vesture embroidered *with variety*. Harmony in variety is the plan of God's creation, and why should it not equally be the plan of His Church, one, without spot or wrinkle, a glorious Church, rich as a musical symphony in all the varying phases of her bewildering beauty!

One is the Sacrifice offered in all her many rites, one with the Sacrifice instituted by Christ at the Last Supper. Call it, as in the East, "the Holy Liturgy," or as in the West, "the Holy Mass," it does not matter. And what if the circumstances and the accessories of this transcendent Act differ—the supplementary prayers, the vesture of priests and ministrants, the song, music, and architecture itself of the place of worship— they are all but manifold and subtle varieties blended into one great and divine harmony, replete with the fervour of the Holy Spirit, and charming with its delights the ears of Heaven!

Nothing, in fine, is more earnestly desired by the Holy See than the creation of a better understanding among Catholics of all rites, and a more profound appreciation on our part of the meaning and value of the Eastern churches. This happy result Mr. Attwater's book is admirably calculated to bring about. It should be universally welcomed.

JOSEPH HUSSLEIN, S.J., PH.D.,
General Editor, Religion and Culture Series.

St. Louis University,
August 31, 1935.

INTRODUCTION

This book is meant to be a tiny contribution for English-speaking countries toward the fulfillment of the often-expressed wish of the present pope, His Holiness Pius XI, that Catholics of the Latin rite should become more familiar with the history, religious life, and present state of the Eastern church.

Though the expression "Eastern church" is often met, bearing various meanings, there is not in fact, and never has been, a single unified Eastern church corresponding to the Western church over which the Bishop of Rome rules as Patriarch as well as Supreme Pontiff. The "Eastern church" now consists of four unrelated divisions, of which the first two (*Nestorians* and *Monophysites*) are esteemed heretical and consist of six separate churches, two of them national; the third is schismatical (the *Orthodox*) and consists of some eighteen self-governing churches, most of which are national and in communion one with another; and the fourth division consists of nine fully organized churches and a number of groups, one in Catholic faith and morals and the communion of the Holy See, known as the *Catholics of Eastern rite*. It is with the last-named division that this book is concerned. Charity begins at home, and until we Latins learn more about the orientals of our own communion and (I regret to have to add) realize that they are every bit as fully and unequivocally Catholic as ourselves, and begin to act accordingly, it is not much use troubling our heads about all the millions of non-Catholic orientals, work toward whose reconciliation with the Holy See is such an outstanding activity of the present pontificate.

Successfully to present Catholicism to others needs that we should first ourselves realize Catholicism at its best and most authentic. A study, however slight, of the Catholic East contributes to this by emphasizing the variousness and all-embracingness of the Church, and helps powerfully to break down that exclusive occidentalism and Europeanism of which we Latin Catholics are so often, and not always unjustly, accused: a narrow particularism that is not compatible with Catholicity and is a formidable barrier for non-Catholics of other ancient civilizations.

I also hope that in a modest way this book may serve another purpose. "So far from being an obstacle," says that distinguished scholar and monk, Dom Fernand Cabrol, "the exact knowledge of facts is, on the contrary, of the greatest assistance to true piety." I include in these pages a considerable number of facts (which I have done my best to make exact) about the various aspects of Eastern religious life, and especially about its liturgical worship. There is no need to apologize for and explain the amount of space given to this last to those who appreciate the fundamental identity of true Christian life with the life of common worship, and who know how passionately the recent Roman Pontiffs have encouraged a "liturgical movement" in the Western church. The religious life of Eastern Catholics is far more centred in the Mass as a communal sacrifice and in the daily observances of the Church's year than is ours. We may therefore profit by a consideration of their example, and "be excited to a yet warmer love for the true Bride of Christ" by looking upon her "bewitching beauty in the diversity of her various rites" (Pope Pius XI).

This book makes no claim to be anything more than a popular work, an *oeuvre de vulgarisation*. The writer has had some personal experience of Catholic life in the Near East, but for the historical parts and accounts of more remote churches he has had to rely on the works and information of others, and has done no original research of his own. Some of the numerous books consulted are noted in the bibliographies that follow each section and further information about each of the churches concerned can be found in the general reference books mentioned at the end. These bibliographies are meant mostly for the general reader and so, except here and there, do not include technical works or those in more esoteric languages than English and French. The asterisk (*) indicates that the book is by a non-Catholic.

The perhaps rather daunting schematic arrangement of Chapters V to IX was imperatively necessary for the clear and orderly treatment of a very complex subject; for the same reason I gave up any attempt to treat the various groups in chronological order or according to ethnic or geographical affinities: to have done so would have resulted in the most complete confusion. I have instead primarily taken them in alphabetical order of liturgical families, and secondarily in the chronological order of the adherence of the different bodies to the Holy See. But on account of their importance the churches of the Byzantine rite are dealt with first, and for convenience their liturgical rite is considered before the people instead of afterwards as elsewhere; and it was found convenient for historical reasons to treat the ("pure") Syrians before the Maronites.

I have not attempted to be consistent in the transliteration or translation of foreign names—it seems impossible in all but erudite works. With practically no knowledge of tongues at my disposal, I have endeavoured to make respectable words out of them, without doing outrageous violence to any forms that are well known in English. To save constant repetitions, I may say here that, except in a few cases where I have been able to get later official information, all statistics are taken from the *Statistica con Cenni Storici . . . di Rito Orientale*, published by the Sacred Eastern Congregation at Rome in 1932. I cannot say how much I owe to this book, and must record my grateful thanks to its anonymous compiler: an anonymity easily pierced, and covering one to whom everybody interested in Eastern ecclesiastical affairs owes an incalculable debt.

As regards customs, ritual, etc., I have concerned myself only with typical Catholic usages, which do not necessarily hold good for non-Catholics of the same rite, though to a very large extent they are identical. Only occasionally do I note divergences under this head, though they are often implied by the context (e.g., when a Catholic body uses a Roman office translated into its own liturgical tongue).

The names used for the different groups of Catholic Easterns are those found in the above-mentioned official *Statistica*. They have the advantage of being clear and in accordance with past history and present fact; they have the disadvantage of often being different from what the people concerned call themselves or are called locally, especially in North America. The commonest colloquial name is "Greek Catholic," for any Catholic of the Byzantine rite; apart from the scientific inadmissibility of such a usage, it is unsuitable in a book like this because of the difficulty of distinguishing between Rumanian and Melkite and Greek and other "Greek Catholics." I suppose that within limits people are entitled to call themselves what they like; but a writer on the subject can hardly be expected to grapple with such atrocities as "Ruthenian-Greek-Roman Catholic"—which I have seen in an American paper!

Catholic orientals are sometimes called "Uniates." This word is derived from Latin *unio*, "union," through the Polish *unia* (Russian *unija*, Greek *ounia*), whereas the word for "union" is ordinarily *jednosc, soedinenie*, and *enosis* in those languages respectively. It was coined as a term of contempt by the opponents of the Union of Brest (p. 77), and for that reason alone its use by Catholics is to be deplored. It is always used in an offensive sense by non-Catholics and it is repudiated by those of whom it is used;[1] moreover, it is never found in official ecclesiastical acts at Rome or in such publications as the *Annuario Pontificio*. "Catholic of such and such a rite" is more trouble to say and write, but it is strictly accurate and void of offence or regrettable association.[2]

A word, too, about "rite." This term primarily means the words to be said and actions to be done in performing a given act of religion; e.g., the rite of Baptism. By extension it means a complete system of ritual and prayer to be used in the worship of God and the administration of the sacraments: so we have the Antiochene rite, the whole complex of prayers and

---

[1] It is rather as if an Eastern Catholic should insist on calling English-speaking Catholics "Romanists"—a term forever associated by us with the attacks of Protestantism.

[2] "United Rumanians," "United Syrians," and so on, is a convenient and harmless expression, very popular in French.

ceremonies originating at or associated with the city and patriarchate of Antioch. In time this gets modified, on the one hand into what we call the "Syrian rite" and on the other into the "Maronite rite."[3] Counting the several variations of the Latin rite as only one, there are ten rites in this last sense, and each one is represented by a body of Catholics using it today (and, with the exception of the Latins and Maronites, by much larger non-Catholic bodies as well). Each of these bodies is also called a rite, which in this sense is equivalent to "church" and includes the manner of organization, proper canon law, customs, etc., appertaining thereto. Every child of Catholic parents belongs in fact and in law, and every child of baptized non-Catholic parents belongs in fact or in law, to one or other of these rites. The word *rite* constantly occurs in these pages in one or other of all these senses: which one is meant should be clear from the context.

My grateful thanks are due for the help of the following: Count and Countess Bennigsen, the Rev. Edward Bowron, Stephen Gaselee, Mar Ivanios, Archbishop of Trivandrum, Father Gabriel Khury, Mgr. Mark Khuzam, Bishop of Thebes, the Jesuit Fathers of Beirut, Father Joseph Ledit, S.J., Prodott C. K. Mattam, Amba Jakob Muijser, the Friars Preachers of Mosul, Der Nerses Papasian, Father Costa de Beauregard, S.J., Dom Placid de Meester, O.S.B., Msgr. George Kalavassy; and to the editors and publishers of *Orate Fratres, Thought*, and the Catholic Truth Societies of London and Dublin for permission to reproduce matter contributed by myself to their publications. All the illustrations unless otherwise noted, are due to the kindness of the Prior and Convent of Prinknash, publishers of *Pax*.

DONALD ATTWATER

Feast of the Glorious Taking Up of Our
Illustrious Queen the Ever-maiden Mary,
Mother of God. August 15/28, 1934.

---

[3] The English technical word "use" ("*ad* usum *ecclesiae Sarum*") is obviously fitted for some of these sub-rites, e.g., the Maronite and the Ethiopic. Unfortunately it has become almost obsolete.

CONTENTS

The Italo-Greeks. The Ruthenians. The Podcarpathian Ruthenians. The Hungarians. The Yugoslavs. The Rumanians. The Melkites. The Greeks. The Bulgars. The Russians. Other Byzantine Elements.

The Copts (Egypt). The Ethiopians (Abyssinia).

LIST OF ILLUSTRATIONS

Chapter I

EAST AND WEST BEFORE THE SCHISM

EAST AND WEST BEFORE THE SCHISM

One of the most common misunderstandings about the Catholic Church is that it is uniform in all respects throughout the world. That is not true. The Church has unity, that is, there is only one true church and she is one in herself, and she has *uniformity of faith* in things divinely revealed, whether touching dogma or the principles of right conduct: these things are matters of absolute truth and therefore necessarily uniform. But beyond that, no. There is not and never has been any principle of uniformity in Catholicism that requires all Catholics to worship with the same liturgical forms, in the same language, to be subject to an identical canon law, to have the same customs and usages. And, in fact, they do not.

It is easy to see how the misunderstanding has arisen. Most American and western European Catholics never assist at any Mass but the Roman Mass in the Latin tongue, or come across usages with which they are not more or less familiar, or hear of discipline that differs from their own; pulpit, press, and private conversation all seem to assume (sometimes definitely say) that these things are and must be the same for all Catholics everywhere. And yet we have not to look very far to see that this seeming uniformity is fallacious. To mention only one thing, but the most important of all, the Mass: the prayers and ceremonies of the Mass as celebrated by a Dominican or Calced Carmelite friar are not exactly the same as those in the Roman Missal; nor are those of the Carthusian monks, nor those used in the archdioceses of Milan and Braga and

3

4 CATHOLIC EASTERN CHURCHES

Lyons, or at Toledo; while in many churches in Yugoslavia
the Roman Mass is celebrated in Slavonic.

It is true that the Mass is always and everywhere *one* considered as the Eucharistic Sacrifice: the true sacrifice of the
body and blood of Christ made present on the altar by the
words of consecration, the representation and renewal of the
offering made once for all on the cross of Calvary; and that
is what matters, and all that matters, essentially. But to say
that in every Catholic church Mass is celebrated with the same
prayers and ceremonies is *not true*. The Eucharistic Sacrifice is
one, the ways of offering it are *many*.

The varieties of the Latin Mass mentioned above are more
or less closely related to and resemble the usual Roman form.
But there are other Catholics, eight millions of them, distinguished as the Catholics of the Eastern rites, whose Mass is
altogether different in its prayers and externals from those with
which we are familiar, who are subject to different canon law,
who differ from us in almost every conceivable thing[1]—
always excepting faith and morals.

For some time after all the Apostles were dead the organization and liturgy of the Church were fluid. The unit was the
local church, the community of Christians in one place, whose
bishop, assisted by priests and deacons, "presided in the place
of God," as St. Ignatius the Godbearer says, over the faithful
of that locality. It was not long before certain important
bishops were exercising jurisdiction over other bishops, especially those whom they had themselves ordained and set over
some new Christian community.[2] This was the beginning
of "metropolitans" or "archbishops" and led later to the very

---

[1] They share their distinguishing features with 150 million other Eastern Christians, no longer Catholic. Father Janin, A.A., gives a good
account of them in *The Separated Eastern Churches* (London, 1933),
and there is a useful summary in the C.T.S. pamphlet *The Eastern
Churches* (London, 1934).

[2] The principle that a bishop has jurisdiction over the bishop whom he
consecrates is a very important one in ecclesiastical history, especially in
the East. The Pope as Patriarch of the West has the right to consecrate
all bishops of the Western church (a right which for obvious reasons
he does not exercise in person); the same with the other patriarchs.

important office of "patriarch" and the accompanying territorial division. The forms of worship and offering the Holy
Sacrifice differed from church to church and were in the
vernacular of the local faithful (e.g., Aramaic at first in Jerusalem, Greek at Antioch and Rome); gradually these forms
solidified into types or "families," those of the most important
churches becoming the norms for the lesser ones associated
with or dependent on them.[3]

From the earliest times a primacy of the see of St. Peter in
Rome was recognized by all other sees, and the next most
important bishops were those of Alexandria (whose church
was founded by St. Mark) and Antioch, where also St. Peter
had presided, and these were also the three chief cities of the
Roman Empire. After Constantine the Great had transferred
his capital to the east Constantinople soon climbed to the
second place of ecclesiastical honour. These four cities give
their names to the four chief types of Christian liturgy, which
with their variants are in use today. In the early centuries the
East played a preponderating part in Christian history and
thought (Greek was the language of the Roman church until
about the middle of the third century: Latin was first used for
liturgical purposes in Africa); the Greek Fathers and Doctors
not merely left an ineffaceable mark but were the fundamental
formative influences in the post-apostolic Church; the first
eight oecumenical councils were all held in the East and
were predominantly oriental in their constitution. For seventy-
five years in the sixth and seventh centuries almost every one
of the popes of Rome was a Greek: and there were others;
over twenty oriental popes in all.

Though of course it would not be true to say that the great
heresies of the early days of Christianity, Arianism, Pelagian-
ism, etc., disappeared without leaving a trace, only two of
them are still represented by existing churches, whose origins
were in the Christological controversies of the fifth century

---

[3] In the middle of the third century Firmilian, Bishop of Caesarea in
Cappadocia, remarks that the liturgical variety then existing made no
difference to unity.

which are known respectively as Nestorianism and Monophysism.

The condemnation by the Council of Ephesus in 431 of the teaching of Nestorius, Bishop of Constantinople,[4] gave rise to the separate heretical *Nestorian Church*, those members of which who have returned to Catholicism are called Chaldeans (see p. 228). Twenty years later an even worse loss was caused by Monophysism. This heresy, often called Eutychianism after Eutyches (d. *c.* 455), who taught an extreme form of it, is the doctrine that in Jesus Christ there is only one nature, His humanity being completely absorbed in His divinity and His body not of one substance with ours, which means that He was not really a man at all and His earthly life only an appearance. It arose from the opposition to Nestorianism, which was led by St. Cyril, Patriarch of Alexandria, upon whose death in 444 his successor Dioscoros hotly and unscrupulously took up the cause of the exaggerators. After six years of controversy and violence the Emperor Marcian convened a council, at which Pope St. Leo I's legates presided. It met at Chalcedon and, after deposing Dioscoros who refused to submit to the "dogmatic letter" in which, two years earlier, the Pope had defined the truth about the disputed matters, the bishops on October 22, 451, declared the Catholic Faith to be that in the one person of Jesus Christ there are two real, perfect, and complete natures, the divine and the human. Thus the Council of Ephesus was confirmed against Nestorianism, and Monophysism solemnly condemned. This resulted in the formation of the Monophysite churches, namely, the *Coptic* in Egypt, the *Syrian Jacobite*, the *Armenian*, the *Ethiopic*, and (indirectly and centuries later) the *Malabar Jacobite Churches;* minorities from all of these have since come back to Catholic unity (see. pp. 14; 150 ff.; 246).

---

[4] Nestorianism maintains that in our Lord there are *two* persons, God the Son and the man Jesus, and that Jesus alone was born of our Lady and died on the cross. The controversy raged round the representative word *theotokos*, Mother of God, a title which the Nestorians, of course, refused to recognize. Diodoros, Bishop of Tarsus, and Theodore, Bishop of Mopsuestia, rather than Nestorius, were the originators of the heresy.

For six hundred years after the Council of Chalcedon the Universal Church remained organized in five distinct parts, the patriarchates of Rome (or the West), Constantinople, Alexandria, Antioch, and Jerusalem. The West included roughly everything west of a line from the eastern end of Crete to Danzig (though the borders, especially Illyricum, were disputed with Constantinople), with the north coast of Africa; Constantinople had Thrace, most of Asia Minor and, at the very end of the period, Russia; Alexandria was reduced to the few Catholics left in Egypt and the lands south of it who were faithful to Chalcedon; Antioch ruled the similar but much larger Catholic remnant in Syria; Jerusalem had the small territory of Palestine and the Sinai peninsula. Each of these divisions was administratively independent of the other and appointed its own patriarch locally, and each had its own liturgy, discipline, and customs,[5] though ultimately what was left of the last three patriarchates became uniform with Constantinople, the imperial city. In those days there was more liturgical and disciplinary uniformity in the Catholic East than in the West; Constantinople much more than Rome has always tried to impose her own observances as a matter of principle. The four Eastern patriarchs recognized in the Bishop of Rome, as successor of St. Peter, a primacy of jurisdiction and a final court of appeal in doctrinal matters although the dogma of papal infallibility was not yet distinctly formulated and defined.

At that time one could speak of an Eastern and a Western part of the Church with more definiteness than now, and the difference was more than geographical and ritual (as it still is). It was temperamental, and there was a strong cultural division. Surprising as it may seem to us, Constantinople looked on western Europe as a land of barbarians—and not without reason. She, "the new Rome," was the heir of the glories both of Greece and Rome and, with all her glaring faults, a not unworthy one; she was, too, the bulwark of Christendom, staving off to the best of her ability the Arabs, Turks, and

[5] But a man did not necessarily have the same liturgy as his patriarch, e.g., the Pope ruled over Byzantines in *Magna Graecia* and Illyricum.

Mongols while the western countries were painfully hammering out a new order from the ruins of the Western Empire and the new barbarian peoples that occupied its lands.

Friction and ill-feeling between East and West were manifest at an early date; it was aggravated by Constantinople's rise to power, and her ambition was increased after the Arabs had overrun the other Eastern patriarchates and made them powerless;[6] on the other hand, it is admitted that Rome did not always act with discretion and in a spirit of conciliation. Temporary formal ruptures of communion became more and more frequent, till in 863 Pope St. Nicholas I decreed excommunication against Photius (who was, in the Pope's own words, "a man of great virtue and world-wide knowledge"), unless he gave up the see of Constantinople to its rightful occupant, St. Ignatius. Photius refused, and professed to condemn Nicholas on five charges, four of which arose from legitimate variations between Eastern and Western discipline; the fifth was the matter of the *Filioque* in the creed. On the death of his protector, the Emperor Michael III, in 867, Photius fell from power. But irremediable harm had been done; Greeks and Latins, East and West, had been brought into formal opposition. Mutual distrust and jealousy grew, and 186 years later, when the churches were enjoying "complete peace," the patriarch of Constantinople, Michael Cerularius, suddenly attacked Pope St. Leo IX. He impugned certain Western customs as unchristian,[7] closed all the Latin churches in Con-

---

[6] So early as 586 John IV the Faster assumed the title of "Oecumenical Patriarch," still borne by the patriarch of Constantinople.

[7] There was no mention at first of the *Filioque*, but that trouble too was in its origins more disciplinary and liturgical than dogmatic. The East has always attached more importance to matters of discipline and ritual than the West has. At this time all their traditional usages were esteemed of directly apostolic origin and were given a textual support from Holy Scripture (e.g., for fasting, Luke v. 33-35). Also they had a great aversion from "judaizing," hence their objection to *azyme* and the Sabbatine fast. In our own times Eastern Catholics received without demur the definitions of the Immaculate Conception and Papal Infallibility but raised endless trouble about the Gregorian calendar and the election of bishops (Melkites in 1857-60, Armenians and Chaldeans in 1867-79).

stantinople, and, in the course of the resulting controversy, struck the Pope's name from the commemoration in the Liturgy. After vain negotiations the papal legates solemnly excommunicated Cerularius and two of his prelates in the church of the Holy Wisdom on July 16, 1054. It was a solemn and awful moment when, just as the Liturgy was about to begin, Cardinal Humbert, Cardinal Frederick Gozelon, and Peter, Archbishop of Amalfi, passed through the crowded church, entered the sanctuary, and laid Pope Leo's bull of excommunication upon the altar. *"Videat Deus et iudicet,"* they exclaimed, and departed.

The Great Church of Constantinople itself was not (and never has been) excommunicated by the Holy See, but it separated from Rome and the other Byzantine patriarchates followed, thus forming what is now known as the *Orthodox Eastern Church.*[8]

July 16, 1054, is the most calamitous date in Christian history. It made the separation of East from West complete, and no subsequent reconciliation has been lasting or widespread enough to make any substantial difference. The unity of the Catholic Church is indefectible and remains formally resplendent; but materially it is maimed and weakened: the unhealed breach between Rome and the East is the biggest, saddest, and most significant among the divisions of Christendom.

---

[8] It appears that historically the epithet "Orthodox" distinguishes those Christians who accepted Chalcedon. See P. de la Taille in *Orientalia Christiana*, Vol. V, No. 21, February, 1926, p. 281. Latterly, Monophysite Copts, Jacobites, and others have taken to adding "Orthodox" to their names, which is confusing. Some Byzantines in communion with Rome call themselves "Catholic-Orthodox," quite reasonably. In the *berat* which the Sultan formerly gave to a newly elected Catholic Melkite patriarch he was called head of the *Rûm kathulik milleti*, of which the English equivalent is "Catholic Orthodox nation."

Chapter II

EAST AND WEST AFTER THE SCHISM

EAST AND WEST AFTER THE SCHISM

What would have been the position today had the schism of 1054 never happened or had the brief reunion patched up at the Council of Florence in 1439 been permanent? Other things being equal, there would now be some 482 million Catholics in the world (instead of about 335 million), of whom *one third* would be using the liturgy of Constantinople, in numerous languages, with communion in both kinds, a married parochial clergy, and all other their own customs, under their own patriarchs, subject to the Pope as *Supreme Pontiff*. But the schism *did* take place, and after 1054 those who had separated from Rome looked upon the Catholic Church as a European institution, Latin in its outlook, worship, and usages: as if Catholicism were synonymous with the Western church. And after the Council of Trent there was a greater and ever-increasing uniformity of worship, discipline, and administration.[1] Throughout the Middle Ages it was *almost* true to say that in every Catholic church the Mass was the Latin, western Mass. Almost, but not quite. There remained faithful to Rome a body of Christians of Greek blood in southern Italy and Sicily who kept their Greek liturgy and customs; there was in the Lebanon the larger body of Maronite Catholics, with their Syrian liturgy and customs; and after the First Crusade there was in Cilicia a number of Catholics of the Armenian rite who had returned to communion with the Holy See. This tiny minority of Catholic Easterns served providentially to preserve

---

[1] This, however, has been exaggerated by some critics.

the material Catholicity, the all-embracingness, the diversity-in-unity, of the Church of Christ.

There were two attempts at reunion with the Byzantine churches during the Middle Ages, both originating on the Eastern side and both prompted fundamentally by political considerations—though very worthy ones. The Emperors of Constantinople hoped by recognizing the Pope to encourage him to send a crusade that would draw off the Franks from their capital and drive the Saracens into the desert. The Patriarch Joseph I was not willing, so Michael VIII Palailogos shut him up in a monastery and sent representatives in 1274 to the second Council of Lyons who concluded a union with the Roman Church. But the people and clergy of Constantinople did not want it, it was never effective, and was formally repudiated by the Emperor Andronikos II eight years later. The story of the Union of Florence in 1439 is very similar, though with more important results. John VII Palailogos wanted help against the Ottoman Turks, who were at his very gates. This time the Patriarch of Constantinople, Joseph II, himself attended the council,[2] as well as representatives from other churches, and acts of reunion were effected on behalf of the four Orthodox patriarchs, the Katholikos of the Armenians, the Coptic Patriarch, some Syrian Jacobites, and one Nestorian bishop. In the case of the last four the union was never effective though it had important repercussions in the non-Byzantine East.

The "four points of the Council of Florence" which formed the basis of agreement with the Orthodox was their acceptance of the supreme primacy of the Pope, of the validity of the use of unleavened bread in the Eucharist, of the existence of Purgatory, and of the procession of the Holy Ghost from the Father and the Son.[3] In Russia the Great-Prince Basil II refused the union at once, but it was the remote cause of the reconciliation of the Kievan eparchies at Brest in 1595. In the patriarchates of Alexandria, Antioch, and Jerusalem it subsisted

[2] He died in Florence. His tomb may be seen in Santa Maria Novella.
[3] These four points were made the basis of the Rumanian reunion at Alba Julia in 1700.

for a time, and may, indeed, be said never to have died out in the second of them. At Constantinople it was not well received; but at the taking of the city by the Turks in 1453 the last Liturgy was celebrated in the church of the Holy Wisdom ("St. Sophia"), and the last Roman emperor, Constantine XII, died in battle, in communion with the Holy See. A few limited and local attempts at reconciliation are mentioned elsewhere in this book.

These efforts at reuniting Christendom failed primarily because they were not always undertaken from pure motives of love of God and concern for the good of religion. Moreover, the schism had gone hard and set on both sides, and despite the interest of Roman church authorities, much of the West was indifferent to the matter. In the East, on the other hand, the people and clergy as a whole were enthusiastic —against union with Rome. This was due more than anything else to the Crusades, particularly the Fourth. The Greeks did not forgive, they never have forgiven, the Westerners for sacking Constantinople, stealing their churches, murdering their emperor, and setting a Frank in his place (1204–1261); they resented and feared the haughty arrogance and domineering efficiency of Normans and Englishmen, and wanted to have nothing to do with either them or their church. In addition, time and again they had looked to their fellow-Christians in the West for help in their struggle against the oncoming tide of Islam; that help was rarely forthcoming and never effective.[4] At length, "Better," they said, "to be under the Sultan's turban than the Pope's tiara." They learned whether it was so or not.

Up to the time of the schism of 1054 there had never been any idea of uniformity in the Universal Church outside the necessary uniformity in faith and morals: such a notion would have been regarded as superfluous, impracticable, improper,

---

[4] Not always the Westerners' fault. But the only Western "powers" helping the Greeks at the last defence of Constantinople, the city that had conserved European culture through the barbarian dark ages, were a handful of men from the Papal States sent by Eugenius IV and five ships and seven hundred men from the Republic of Genoa.

and more than a little laughable. After that schism, as I have said, the Church quite accidentally took on to all intents and purposes an entirely Western, Latin, and more uniform complexion (though it must not be forgotten that in those days the Latin Mass varied in details almost from diocese to diocese).[5] This was greatly extended by the missionary activities of the sixteenth and seventeenth centuries. But at the very time when Spanish, Portugese, and French missionaries were carrying Catholic faith and Western practices to the heathen of the New World and the Far East, bodies of Eastern Christians nearer home began to return to the Pope's obedience. The first of these was led by the Nestorian katholikos John Sulaka in 1551. From that time onward there has been a continuous movement of orientals back to Catholic unity, generally a dribble of individuals but sometimes amounting to the small wave of an "hierarchical reunion," down to the reconciliation of Mar Ivanios and Mar Theophilos in India in 1930. It is with these Catholics and their few predecessors that this book is concerned.

When these people submitted themselves to the Holy See they kept their own forms of worship, church law, and religious customs. It must be clearly understood that this is not a matter of *concession* but of *right:* they as Catholics have as much right to their traditional and immemorial usages as we Latins have to ours.[6] To attempt to produce a universal uniformity in these things would be artificial, un-natural, un-traditional, un-Catholic; and it would not succeed. Moreover, their orders being, in general, valid, their prelates and priests were usually re-instated in the offices which they had held as schismatics. There were only two exceptions to this on a large scale, the Ethiopians and the Malabarese in the seventeenth century: both were disastrous and resulted in the loss of

---

[5] During the later Middle Ages there were in England and Wales alone the "uses" of Sarum, York, Hereford, and Bangor, to say nothing of those of the religious orders.

[6] No doubt in the abstract the Holy See could impose the Latin rite on, say Byzantines—and could impose the Byzantine rite on Latins. It is as likely to do the one as the other.

several million people to the Church. Both these tragedies were due to too close a dependence of missionary clergy on a "Catholic power" (Portugal) and to the disregard by European prelates (who were ignorant and frightened of oriental ways) of the instructions of Rome that these people's lawful customs were not to be interfered with.

Since then the Holy See has made it perfectly clear time and again that the Church is Catholic and not specifically Latin or European. In his bull *Etsi pastoralis* in 1742 for the Italo-Greeks, Pope Benedict XIV declared that they were to keep to their own rites, recognized the ordination of the married, and ordered that no precedence was to be based on rite; certain provisions that implied privileges for the Latin rite were abrogated subsequently. In the following year he addressed a decree, *Demandatam caelitus*, to the Melkites, in which he forbade them to alter their liturgy or to become Latins without Rome's express permission. In 1755 the same Pope issued an encyclical, *Allatae sunt*, to the missionaries in the Near East. Herein he traced the consistent attitude of the Holy See in this matter from the eleventh century onwards, and set out legislation based on the text "We desire most intensely that all people should be Catholics but not all Latins," reminding those whom he addressed that their function was to support and help the local indigenous Catholic clergy and not to boss them. Pope Pius IX emphasized the same things in his appeal to the schismatic orientals, the encyclical *In suprema* of 1848.

In 1893 the International Eucharistic Congress was held in Jerusalem and at it the Eastern element predominated. It marks a new era in the history of the Catholic East, of which the first important fruit was Pope Leo XIII's constitution *Orientalium dignitas* in 1894.[7] Among other things, this emphasized that all rites are on exactly the same footing religiously and canonically; moreover, it decreed that any Latin priest who

---

[7] This Pope did a pleasing thing toward our separated Eastern brethren in 1882. He substituted the title "titular bishop" for "bishop *in partibus infidelium*" because some of the sees *i.p.i.* again had Christian populations, though not in communion with Rome.

should persuade an Eastern Christian to adopt the Latin rite should by that very fact incur suspension from his sacerdotal functions. Any non-Catholic who becomes a Catholic must adhere to the rite to which he canonically belongs: without a rescript from the Holy See an American or western European convert to Catholicism cannot become a Byzantine, an ex-Orthodox Russian cannot become a Syrian, and so on (*Codex Juris Canonici*, canon 98).[8]

That is the law, but it is well known that it is not everywhere administered in its full rigour,[9] and that is one of the reasons why non-Catholic Easterns insist that "Rome wants to turn them all into Latins." The relative insignificance of some of the Eastern churches and the obscurity of the individuals who compose them, right and proper soil wherein Christianity may flourish, produce a result very marked among the smaller ones and apparent in its degree in all of the Eastern churches—some dissidents who wish to return to Catholic unity, especially if they be persons of some culture or position, or if, on the other hand, they be extremely poor and downtrodden, ask to be, and are, allowed to join the Latin rite. Numbers of orientals, whether Catholic or to be reconciled, and even bodies of non-Christians living among Catholics of Eastern rite (e.g., Alauite villages in Syria) do this. Why? Spiritual reasons? Undoubtedly, sometimes and in part. But there are other reasons, the existence of which the Latin missionaries admit but do not enlarge upon: material reasons. The Latin rite stands for European civilization and influence, for its attractive ideas of progress, for prestige, education, commerce, pseudo-Parisian clothes, for being "in" with the Franks; Eastern rites are looked down on as being for mere peasants: too often, nay, ordinarily, Latins accept rather than oppose such wrong views. I have shown that all rites and those who belong to them are equal in the Church: but in

---

[8] In 1933 a Japanese convert was received into the Church in Poland as a Byzantine; presumably converts from such countries as Japan and China have a certain freedom of choice of rite.

[9] Even still one meets and hears of cases of most improper pressure being applied to induce orientals to "turn Latin."

practice they are often, accidentally but inevitably, nothing of the sort—and it is the *Latin rite* that always gains from the misfortunes of its brethren and European missionaries accept and encourage, not always overtly or even consciously, that situation. It is an appalling sight to see little Syrian children marching through the streets, dressed in immaculate little French suits, each with a tricolour in his hand, and singing "Je suis chrétien" (it would be no less appalling were the suits, flags, and words English). "But," it is often asked, "can't an oriental save his soul in the Latin rite?" That is the crux, and when one answers "Of course he can, and does" the objector thinks there is no more to be said. But there is, a whole lot of things, and one is, over and above "saving souls" and the perfectly clear mind of the Holy See on the matter: *what about the quality* of the souls to be saved?

The perfection of a man resides in this, that he lives in accordance with the laws, general and particular, of human *being*. And the Church as Church, and especially the Holy See of Rome itself, has never lost sight of the fact that a particular law of an Eastern Christian is that he practises an Eastern rite: otherwise he is to that extent an oriental *manqué*. There is an analogous state of affairs in the country where I used to live, where people give up their own Welsh language because it has not the social prestige or commercial value of English. A Welshman who does that has spoiled his perfection as a Welsh human being, as a soul to be saved. Just so, only more so, a Syrian or a Copt who turns Latin. *Inglese italianato, diavolo incarnato* expresses the same idea in more forcible terms. The Italianized Englishman, the Welshman who loses his Welsh, the oriental westernized, whether in ecclesiastical rite or in manners, can get to Heaven all right, but surely when they get there they begin with shame (if there were shame in Heaven) to take the lower place—below plain Harry Brown, below the Merioneth shepherd, below the illiterate Maronite peasant. I need hardly add that this consideration has nothing to do with the virtue of patriotism or the disorder of political nationalism. Of late years Rome has tended to become more strict in her insistence that people shall stick to their own rite, and the adequacy of the reasons of those who desire a dispensation to change it more strictly examined. Increasing numbers of Latins are allowed to do so in order that they may work as priests or nuns among their Eastern brethren.

It is one thing to "belong" to a rite and quite another to "frequent" it. Latin Catholics are not only at liberty but strongly recommended by the Holy See to frequent the churches of Eastern Catholics, and vice versa, so that they may learn more about one another and strengthen the bond of mutual charity. Not only that, but the Code of Canon Law expressly lays down (canon 866) that a Latin Catholic may receive Holy Communion in a Catholic Eastern church out of devotion (and not merely in case of necessity), even if to do so involves receiving in both kinds. The only restriction in this matter is that "Easter duties" and the last sacraments should be received if possible in one's own rite. Marriages should be performed according to the rite of the groom, and the bride is free to adopt her husband's rite either permanently or until widowhood. Children follow the rite of their father (unless he be a non-Catholic), even if through error or in emergency they have been baptized by a priest and with the ceremonies of another rite.

Several popes from Gregory XIII onwards made tentative efforts to establish at Rome some sort of congregation or permanent commission to deal with oriental affairs. Eventually, in 1862, Pius IX erected a congregation "for Eastern Rite business," as a department of the Sacred Congregation for the Propagation of the Faith. This was found inconvenient and the association with *Propaganda*, whose concern is primarily with the heathen, recognized to be unfortunate, and in 1917 Benedict XV set up a new and independent Sacred Congregation for the Eastern Church (whose name has apparently been recently altered to "the Sacred Eastern Congregation").[10] Of this congregation the prefect is always to be the reigning Pope in person, and its personnel in 1934 consists of a cardinal secretary and sixteen other cardinals, an assessor and a *sostituto*,

---

[10] In the *motu proprio* of erection the Pope made use of the words printed on the title page of this book.

and 42 expert consultors (a number of whom are orientals), together with the usual officials. This congregation is competent in all matters arising out of the Eastern rites whether persons, discipline, or divine worship are in question, even those which in matter or person also affect Latins. There is also since 1929 a commission to deal with the codification of Eastern canon law; fourteen of the Eastern churches have delegates on this body. The very first canon of the Roman *Codex Juris Canonici* says that it does not bind the Eastern churches except when it deals with matters which from the nature of the case affect them also (viz., canons 1, 98, 542, 622, 782, 804, 864, 866, 881, 955, 1004, 1099).

In 1917 Benedict XV created the Pontifical Institute for Eastern Studies ("The Oriental Institute"), which is now one of the autonomous institutions of the Pontifical Gregorian University and is under the direction of the Society of Jesus. Its ordinary course is of two years, and it is open to all Eastern clergy (whether Catholic or not) and to Latins who are going to work in the East. Its professorial body is extraordinarily strong (twelve nationalities are represented on it) and includes eight professors of Eastern languages, that of Turkish and of Islamic religion being Mgr. Paul Mulla, an Ottoman convert from Islam.

Chapter III

THE EASTERN CATHOLICS

THE EASTERN CATHOLICS

The position today of the former Eastern church, then, is that the overwhelming majority of Christians belong to the schismatic Orthodox churches; a minority belong to the old heretical Nestorian and Monophysite churches (their originating heresies seem now to be material only); and another minority is Catholic. These are divided into Catholics of the Byzantine rite, subdivided into ten separate groups, chiefly ethnological; of the Alexandrian rite, in two independent bodies (Copts and Ethiops); of the Antiochene rite, in three bodies (Syrians, Maronites, Malankarese); of the Armenian rite; and of the Chaldean rite, in two churches (Chaldeans proper and Malabarese). They together represent a proportion of twenty-six non-Latin Catholics to every thousand Latin Catholics, and of about 56 Catholic Easterns to every thousand non-Catholic Easterns.

After all that I have said there should be no need to emphasize that these Eastern Catholics are as fully and completely members of the Church as are we Latins: they are not an inferior kind or a sort of halfway house to Rome, but just plain Catholics, as were St. Athanasius, St. John Chrysostom, St. Basil, St. Gregory Nazianzen, St. Gregory of Nyssa, St. Ignatius of Antioch, St. Cyril of Jerusalem, St. Cyril of Alexandria, St. John the Damascene, St. Ephrem the Syrian, St. James of Nisibis, St. Gregory the Wonderworker, St. Gregory the Illuminator, St. Theodore the Studite, St. Antony the Abbot—none of whom celebrated the Roman Mass or said their prayers in Latin.

It is sometimes said that Catholics of Eastern rite have a horrid tendency to go into schism when they can't have their own way. Before making such a judgment it is desirable to acquaint oneself with the Eastern point of view and to study the traditional relationship between Rome and the East. From the very fact that they are orientals they have never been, and are not now, in such close touch historically and juridically with Rome as we of the West. We do not realize how many of *our* relations with the Holy See are in its patriarchal and not its papal capacity; the Pope is our Patriarch as well as Supreme Pontiff and so is bound to mean more in practice to an American or a Frenchman than to a Syrian or Russian. Some people have tried to make capital out of the fact that the Eastern bishops at the Vatican Council supported the party who regarded a definition of the Pope's infallibility as inopportune. That proves nothing; a loyal Catholic was perfectly entitled to think it inopportune; thousands did. Those bishops had solid reasons for fearing the effect of such a definition on the non-Catholic Christians of the East. Time has proved that they were right: just as time has proved that the reasons in favour of defining the Pope's infallibility were right too. And what was the upshot of the Council? Papal infallibility was defined to be an article of faith and was at once accepted throughout the Catholic East: it was *in the West*, especially in Germany, that some Catholics went into schism rather than accept the decree of the oecumenical council.[1] And as a matter of sober history some of the Eastern Catholic bodies, e.g., the Melkites, have loyally suffered as much during the past three hundred years for their allegiance to the Holy See as any one of the Latin churches has been called on to do. I am not concerned to deny that there has been a number of schisms among the orientals[2] —some of them are referred to elsewhere in this book—but

---

[1] In our own day we have seen a schism among the Latin Czechs—to name no others. In this matter of schism we Latins cannot afford to take a "superior attitude."

[2] I do not refer to such common incidents as ecclesiastics and others becoming Catholics and then returning to schism soon after. These are easily explained by their grossly inadequate "reasons" for reconciliation in the first instance. It is on sound historical grounds that the submission of dissident prelates to Rome is often regarded with a prudent scepticism.

they were rarely, if ever, concerned with any matter fundamental to Catholic Christianity. And, though nothing can justify the sin of schism, it can sometimes be explained, and we do well to bear in mind that these little, oppressed bodies of Eastern Catholics have centuries of neglect, persecution, and inculpable separation from the Center of Unity behind them; and that, to a small, depressed, and sometimes ignorant people who, rightly or wrongly, think they have a legitimate cause of complaint, schism must often appear to be the only weapon of defence against a powerful and well-equipped authority. In his splendid book on the Italo-Greeks and Melkites Dr. Adrian Fortescue, after pointing out what irritations and injustices have been suffered by Catholics of Eastern rite through the disregard by local Latins of the instructions of the Holy See, says, "The really wonderful thing about them is . . . their magnificent loyalty to the Catholic ideal. It is the right sort of loyalty, to an ideal, not to a person. They have no more personal devotion toward Italian cardinals and the monsignori of the Roman congregations than we have in the North. What they care for is the one united Church of Christ throughout the world, and the Holy See as guarding that unity . . ." (*The Uniate Eastern Churches*, p. 23). The Eastern Catholics are neither favourers of schism, as their Catholic critics assert, nor yet groaning under the yoke of Rome, as so many non-Catholics fondly imagine.

Of all the matters for discussion arising out of the Eastern Catholics and their customs, none are more frequently debated than those of clerical marriage and the "hybridization" of rites.

The custom of a celibate clergy has become so firmly rooted in Western Catholic consciousness, its economic, administrative, and social advantages have been so amply demonstrated, and the spiritual qualities accruing from this willing asceticism are so resplendent, that we are prone to forget that it is not an evangelical precept and that it took a thousand years for it to become general in the West. In the East, whether before or after the schism, clerical celibacy was never the rule for the lower clergy. There the normal law is that a married man may be ordained to the diaconate and priesthood and retain his wife; he may not be married after receiving the diaconate or, if his wife dies, marry again; bishops must be single or widowers, and for that reason were formerly invariably chosen from among the monks. Of all the so-called peculiarities of the Easterns this is the one that seems most troublesome to Latins—this and communion in both kinds! Some time ago I had to read a paper on the Eastern rites to a Catholic audience, and afterwards a lady, wife to a well-known Irish man of letters, came up and told me that as I had spoken without disapproval of married priests I could not possibly be a Catholic. I protested that I was. Not a *Roman* Catholic, then. Yes, a Roman Catholic. At last my chairman, who happened to be a bishop, persuaded her that I really was in communion with the Pope of Rome and the Bishop of Cork, so she said as a parting shot that "nothing would induce *her* to go to confession to a married priest." I could think of no more devastating reply than that she was not likely to be asked to.[3] Another woman of my acquaintance, of a quite different class, simple but very intelligent, who had heard that there were married Catholic priests somewhere in the world, was quite distressed: that none of our clergy were under any circumstances allowed to have wives was for her apparently the ultimate proof of the truth of Catholicism. A well-known Catholic "intellectual" once admitted to me that he could not reconcile himself to the idea of a married priest; he was conscious that his attitude was unreasonable and all against his own instincts, and he must try and get over it. I think those three examples about cover the average Latin reaction to this subject. Now, we must do better than that, and help others to do better than that, if we are to produce a more sympathetic atmosphere and state of mind where orientals are concerned. An unmarried clergy is one of the great achievements of Western Christianity and there is not the remotest chance of the Latin church altering

[3] I may note here that a Syrian priest told me that in parts of his country people would not go to confession to an *unmarried* priest. In other parts the opposite is true.

its law in this matter; nor, for an indefinitely long period, will the Eastern churches to any considerable extent alter theirs. Without doubt the ultimate ideal being aimed at is general clerical celibacy among the orientals as well, but only one Eastern body (the Malabarese) as yet has the full Western discipline,[4] and the Church is not likely to favour any *strict* application of that discipline to the East at large, for the simple reason that it would be a further barrier raised against reunion of the dissidents. We Latin Catholics must make up our minds that any and every mass reunion of orientals will bring more and more married priests into the Church and we must face the fact that there is no *essential* inconsistency between holy orders and marriage. We must, however, admire the austerity involved in the voluntary renunciation of marriage and appreciate the heightened spirituality which this asceticism for God's sake has brought to the Western clergy; we know what an advantage celibacy has been in spreading the gospel in foreign missions and in many aspects of parochial work at home; we realize how much this selfless renunciation has done to raise the priesthood in the eyes of the Faithful. But on the other hand, whatever accidental difficulties may be involved, the fact that a priest has received one more sacrament than usual does nothing to derogate from his sacerdotal dignity. The popular Latin attitude is not only unreasonable—it may easily become uncharitable. In places where there are married Eastern Catholic clergy, America, for example, this attitude of their Latin brethren is extremely distressing and embarrassing to those priests—and to their wives and children.[5] If we can do something to modify that attitude of mind among people in our own country we shall have done a work of charity and some-

---

[4] The disciplines in force among Catholics of various Eastern rites are noted in the following chapters. About 50 per cent of the 8,000 secular priests are married. As a general thing, *all* non-Catholic secular priests are married before ordination.

[5] A Byzantine priest who had to minister to his people in a European city told me with tears in his eyes that his Latin neighbours, clerical and lay, made him feel like a criminal because he had a wife and children. "And," he added, "the Holy Father himself has blessed my family."

thing that will help to encourage non-Catholic Eastern clergy to come into the Church.

"Hybridization" is the modification of Eastern liturgies, customs, and modes of thought by undiscriminating adoption of foreign practices and submission to foreign influences; as these practices and influences mostly come from the West it is also called "latinization," but occasional examples of small hybridisms from one Eastern rite to another are to be met with. Another term, "uniatism," has recently come into use to designate this process by which Catholics of Eastern rites tend to become de-orientalized, neglecting the study of the Eastern Fathers and the early Councils, adopting Western disciplinary customs, forms of popular devotion, and ascetical treatises to the exclusion of their own, adapting themselves to a European or alien outlook, and accepting liturgical hybridism. In spite of the fact that the Church is opposed to this process, especially since the constitution *Orientalium dignitas* of Leo XIII, most of the Catholic Eastern churches have suffered more or less from it, some of them very badly. Sometimes it is due to what can only be called "Latin aggression," as when in 1636 the Bishop of Paphos in Cyprus descended upon the Maronite colonies in his diocese and arbitrarily insisted that they should give up using wooden altar "stones" and administering communion in both kinds, that they should put holy-water stoups in their churches and kneel throughout the Liturgy, and other things entirely foreign to their customs; quite often it is due to the orientals themselves many of whom, long subject to the Turks or other tyrants, have a strong sense of inferiority and think that anything from the West is essentially superior, or else they want to flatter and please their European benefactors; and much of it is due to the well-meaning efforts of Western, but particularly French, missionaries and nuns, who sincerely believe that a more or less tactful process of latinization is in the best interests of the orientals: some of them apparently could not imagine that pure Eastern customs were best fitted to the needs of Easterners, that they were really as legitimate as those of Rome, and they seem to have thought that the Popes were inadequately informed about Eastern affairs. There has been in our day a strong, but not complete, reaction against hybridization.[6]

And this is well, for such innovations make the most notice-able external difference between schismatics and Catholics of the same rite and so come to be improperly identified with Catholicism itself, which becomes in consequence in worse odour than ever among the dissidents, who are greatly attached to their own legitimate customs and fear to lose them if they submit to the Holy See.[7] Hybridization, so often condemned at Rome,[8] is a grave stumbling-block to reunion, and it is in effect a practical identification of Catholicism solely with the Western church—the false idea that Eastern Catholicism is essentially an inferior or only half authentic article, and that the more it is made to resemble the Latin church the more "really Catholic" it will be. Moreover, the ancient Christian liturgies are works of art, the supreme works of art, manifesta-tions of the religious, social, and cultural life of Christian communities over long centuries, and to tinker with them, to

---

[6] An example of how strong it is at Rome: In 1934 the Administrator Apostolic of the Copts asked the Sacred Eastern Congregation for per-mission to translate into Arabic for use in his rite the Latin formula for blessing the five-fold scapular. It was refused, the Holy See having directed that if the Copts wanted to use scapulars they must be blessed in a way more conformable with their own rite. The prayers and works required to gain the Jubilee of the Redemption indulgence varied in every rite (S. C. O. April 3, 1934).

[7] Among cultured non-Christians as well as among the Christians of the East the greatest obstacle to the acceptance of Catholicism nowadays is its apparent exclusive Occidentalism and Europeanism. What the Hindu refuses is not the Christian faith but its European trappings and civilization and modes of thought, says Dr. H. C. E. Zacharias in *Renascent India*, and he relates the horrified indignation of an Indian Catholic at "the impious alliance between the missionaries and the for-eign powers in China." It is a small but significant step that the present Pope has forbidden the building of churches in Gothic or other European styles in China.

[8] Those occasional papal pronouncements that seem to approve "latin-izing" are either the result of special local circumstances (e.g., the Italo-Greeks in the sixteenth century, Kholm in 1874) or, if compared with earlier and later decrees, are seen to be advancing stages in the non-latinizing policy.

spoil their integrity by borrowing from alien cultures, is unworthy of the Catholic mind: it is not in accordance with that variety, inclusiveness, and local perfection and fittingness which are marks of the Church as the universal ark of salvation.[9]

What these external differences between West and East in worship and discipline are, will be found set out in some detail in the chapters which follow, but a few general observations may usefully be made here, especially as regards that which matters most—the Mass. And first of all, orientals do not, in their own languages, call it "Mass." That word in its primary and original sense means the complex of prayers and ceremonies, words and actions, *as used in the Western church*, which, said and done with the requisite intention by a minister validly ordained to that end, effects the Eucharistic Sacrifice. Orientals call it "the Divine Liturgy" or "the Offering."[10] Things should be called by their proper names, and so in this book "the Liturgy" means the Eucharistic Sacrifice in one or other of its Eastern forms, unless the context obviously requires the more extended meaning of the word.

Eastern Liturgies are on the whole more primitive in type than the Roman Mass, which underwent a good deal of alteration during the fifth–sixth century: they are longer, their *tempo* is slower, their material expression more ample and their atmosphere more "mysterious" than in the Latin Mass; their language is more artless, less refined and scholarly (but not less theologically accurate); a later but very notable characteristic is a tendency to ritual purely for the sake of its symbolism: they lack the straightforward simplicity to which we are accustomed. In them the deacon has an important part,

---

[9] From this point of view a case can be made out for the long-established modifications of the Italo-Greeks (and in a lesser degree of the Ruthenians), as being now assimilated and historically proper to them. Cf. the 800-year-old "latinisms" of the Armenian rite.

[10] Cf. the Celtic languages, which have no word for *Missa*. Irish *An t-Aifreann*, Welsh *yr Offeren*, Cornish *an offeren*, Scots *an aifrionn*, are all equivalent to the Greek *Anaphora* and Syrian *Kurbana*, "Offering" or "Sacrifice."

and is the only sacred minister necessary to the celebrant at a solemn Liturgy; particularly is it his business to form a link between celebrant and people by means of litanies and, especially in the Byzantine and Armenian rites, in a sense to direct the proceedings as a sort of glorified master of ceremonies for both priest and people, so perpetuating the primitive diaconal charge of the congregation.

What we call "low Mass" is a comparatively late development of Christian worship; in the Western church solemn Mass is the normal Mass still (though we often forget this). In the East it is not only the normal but a sung Liturgy is the usual and ordinary way of celebration. All Catholic Eastern rites now provide for "low Mass" on week days, but in only some of them is the form systematized.[11] No Eastern Liturgy has any "proper of the saints" or "season" as we understand it; only the scriptural lessons and certain chants and verses are variable, according to the feast or time. On the other hand, all of them (except the Armenian and Malabarese) have a number of alternative *anaphoras*, that is to say, different "canons of the Mass,"[12] which are used interchangeably on certain occasions, somewhat after the manner of our proper prefaces. The celebrant's voice can be heard by all throughout the church, *especially* at the words of consecration, except, of course, that when the deacon or choir are chanting he speaks in a low voice. "Low Masses" are supposed likewise to be said aloud, but this is one of the matters in which admiration for Roman prestige has often led to an unreasoning and unnecessary adoption of Roman customs.[13] Organs are not customary

---

[11] Some time ago I assisted at an unsung Byzantine Liturgy twice within a short period: one celebrated by a Melkite, the other by a Russian. If I had not known beforehand, I could not have told what Liturgy the Melkite was celebrating, and it was not recognizably the same as that of the Russian, who even as it was, chanted certain parts of it, notably the words of consecration.

[12] Strictly speaking, the part of the Roman Mass from the beginning of the preface to the postcommunion corresponds to the Eastern *anaphora*.

[13] There is nothing intrinsically sacred about an inaudible canon of the Mass. It has been general in the West since the tenth century.

in Eastern churches, though unhappily they are now sometimes heard.[14] The *Gloria in Excelsis Deo* does not figure in
any Eastern Liturgy, and the Creed of Nicaea-Constantinople
is the only one used liturgically.

Orientals have to a large extent conserved the true Christian
tradition of *standing* at public prayer (kneeling is proper only
to penitential seasons, and sitting, to them, a sign of laziness
or even disrespect), and in general there are few or no seats
in their churches (except in Western countries); women, too,
are very often accommodated apart from men.[15] There is no
principle against vernacular liturgical languages in the Catholic Church and many Easterns assist at the Liturgy in their
daily tongue; others understand the language used rather
better, I suppose, than we understand the English of Chaucer,
and a minority make use of a quite dead language.[16] Unless
"latinized," orientals do not genuflect but bow profoundly
(as in the West until relatively lately, and still liturgically
among Carthusians, Dominicans, and Calced Carmelites), and
all Byzantines, Catholic or not, make the sign of the cross with
the thumb and first two fingers *from right to left*, as all
Christians probably did in earlier times.

Other notable customs normal to the East are the use of
leavened bread for the altar (as for centuries in the West),
the reception of communion in both kinds together (as at

[14] It is doubtful if organs are really more than *tolerated* in the Latin
rite.

[15] The Code of Canon Law considers that desirable for us, too. See
canon 1262, § I.

[16] Articles are often written to explain to Protestants why the Western
church continues to use a dead language for her services, in which great
stress is laid on the practical advantages that accrue, such as uniformity
of celebration and fixity of meaning. This is quite right, but must not be
overemphasized, because the Church has never insisted on a uniform or
non-vernacular language. The ultimate reason for having a special liturgical language is its consonance with the nature of Christian worship:
the Mass is a sacrifice, in the first place an act to be done (*actio*), not a
prayer to be said, and it is done in and with the proper hieratic forms,
of which the hieratic language is one. The vestments are another; they
are simply the proper clothes for the purpose, handed down through
the ages: symbolical meanings attached to them are a mediaeval addition.

Rome till the fourteenth century), Baptism by immersion and Confirmation given immediately after by the priest, and the forbiddance of statues in the churches—except under Latin influence, only pictures, wall-paintings, and mosaics are allowed; this appears to be a backwash of the Iconoclasm controversy of the eighth and ninth centuries, but on the other hand the great veneration accorded to these *eikons* is a most notable characteristic of Eastern religious life.

Oriental Catholics have retained far more than ourselves the notion of religious worship as a social and corporative act centred in the Holy Sacrifice, but they had no extra-liturgical *cultus* of the Blessed Sacrament until it was introduced from the West, and the degree of it varies from rite to rite and even within the same rite. Latins are naturally surprised, even shocked, by the apparent indifference sometimes shown by orientals to the presence of the Blessed Sacrament. The surprise is not all on one side; their veneration is directed rather toward the whole sanctuary as the holy place of God, for the Host in the tabernacle is very far away, "on the throne of the Lord, surrounded by all the holy ministers, by all the angels, and by all the saints." They sometimes remind us that the efficacy of the Eucharist as a sacrifice is bound up with the act of the Mass, and as a sacrament with the act of eating with faith. We excite devotion by displaying the Blessed Sacrament, theirs is aroused by its very hiddenness. Both attitudes are permissible, both true, both Catholic; and so with other divergences that we continually meet.

While all Liturgies are identical theologically and are fundamentally identical in structure, there are nevertheless differences between the celebration of the Mass of the West and of the Eucharistic Liturgies of the East that go deeper than accidental differences of languages, of forms of words, of actions, of music, of ceremonial dress. But, like many deeper things, they are more easily "felt" (I do not mean merely by a comparison of resulting emotions; the mind, too, can "feel") than understood and expressed in words. One deep difference has been illustrated thus by Dr. Andrew de Ivanka (*Irenikon*, Vol. IX, No. 5, p. 420): "Whoever has had occasion to assist at an Eastern Liturgy, even if only in the little church of some Ruthenian country parish, and has been struck by the intimate participation and inspired collaboration of even the most simple peasants in the wonders of the Liturgy, that perfect *ensemble* of teaching, prayer, and sacred action, he alone is able to estimate the treasure of doctrine, lived faith, and encouragement to religion of which Catholics in the West are deprived." "Intimate participation" and "inspired collaboration" in the teaching, prayer, and sacred action of the Liturgy certainly hardly describe the usual relation between western Catholics and the Mass.

It is undoubtedly true that the disposition and temperament of peoples have profoundly affected the spirit and form of their Liturgies. We commonly take it for granted that lay people do not in any degree influence such matters. It is a mistake. Their influence is not expressed corporately or juridically, that is all. The Holy Spirit of God, concentrated in the bishops of His Church, is also diffused among *all* her members; and that Spirit is not gainsaid or without effect merely because we are unconscious or forgetful of it. For instance, the definition of the conception of our Lady free from the state of original sin was not the work of a body of theologians; it was the expression by proper authority of what the *whole* Church knew by faith to be true. And so the needs and natures and graces of the people at large, clergy and laity, help to mould our forms of corporate worship, even within the limits of the same technical "rite." Nobody present at a Russian Liturgy could suppose himself to be in a Greek church, or would mistake a Maronite for a Roman Mass (though their vestments and church appointments are both alike); nay, one assisting at Mass in Brittany or Naples could be pardoned did he not recognize the same act and form of worship he had seen in a Catholic church in a London suburb. Some orientals, without external necessity and for purely spiritual reasons, habitually frequent Latin churches, and the reverse process is far from unknown. Such exceptions serve to emphasize the part of temperament in determining Liturgy. On the other hand, liturgy also influences people, and thus there is produced a continual action, interaction, and tension—and without tension there is no human life.

The variousness of human temperament has had its profound and legitimate effect on religious life and worship no less in the East than in the West. The oriental, for instance, in general prefers an interior process before, often at the expense of, external discipline, juridicism in all its forms is foreign to him, his note is "passivity" rather than "activity." It is significant that the sacraments are administered by deprecatory forms, "The servant of God N., is baptized . . . ," "May God, through me, a sinner, forgive thee. . . ." Confirmation is received passively by babes, there is no explicit contract between the parties to a marriage, the monk does not "make his profession" but "receives the habit." Western man has his mystics and contemplatives, but in general prides himself on being a "practical fellow"; among the Slavs, on the contrary, preoccupation with efficiency and order is little esteemed, and mysticism, in a broad sense, is the heritage of all. Holiness to them definitely means contemplation, and the complete recluse is the practical as well as the abstract ideal of a holy man. Orientals have been accustomed in a large measure to leave the obligations of religion and morality to the individual conscience, rather than to make them the subjects of positive law. For example, the obligation of public worship. All that Eastern canon law has to say about it is that a Christian living in a town who absents himself from church for three Sundays running shall be deprived of communion (canon 80 of the Council *in Trullo*, canon 11 of Sardica). Most Catholics have now adopted some form of the Western legislation, together with the general principle of dispensation, which again is quite foreign to the East. The lack of a system of recognized dispensation does not necessarily operate in favour of the individual supplying a lax one for himself, as the following anecdote, related to me by a French priest who had worked among Byzantines, shows. An old Catholic woman of that rite found the Lenten fast very trying and her parish priest (trained under Western influence) offered to dispense her. "You cannot dispense me from the law of God," said she.

"Then the bishop can." "No. He cannot." "Then I will go to the Pope for you." "His Holiness would be better employed fasting himself than by releasing an old woman from it," was the reply, not intended disrespectfully. In this connection it is to be noted that, whatever the practice may be, the theoretical standard of physical asceticism is far more exacting in the East than in the West (except in the matter of clerical marriage).

The Eastern religious temperament is indeed radically different from the Western, but is not therefore in itself at variance with Catholicism, which is not tied to any one temperament or mentality. It is true that Western prestige and the Roman genius for centralization, acting involuntarily (and contrarily to official legislation) on relatively small bodies, have tended to make of the Catholics of Eastern rite a religious and cultural hybrid. Nevertheless, these Catholics continue to display the spiritual and religious characteristics proper to them as orientals, and among the more recent groups there is a strong consciousness of the need to maintain their orientalism integrally for the Church's sake as well as their own. The Christians of both West and East have suffered and tended to develop one-sidedly through being deprived, for nine hundred years, of each other's contribution to philosophy, theology, general culture, and Christian life, and the balance can never be redressed from one side only. It was "as a member of the true and venerable Orthodox Eastern or Greco-Russian church" that the great philosopher and theologian Vladimir Soloviev on February 18, 1896, declared that he recognized "as the supreme judge in matters of religion . . . the apostle Peter, who lives in his successors and who did not hear our Lord's words in vain."

Catholicism, universality, is not a matter of numbers, and the whole body of Eastern Catholics, relatively small though it be, is a very important part of the Catholic economy. Without them, the Universal Church would appear perilously like what so many of its opponents assert it to be—a product solely west-European in religious culture, disposition, and history. Of all people we Catholics of the Latin rite should glory in these Catholics of Eastern rite, as the late Dr. Adrian

Fortescue said, for "they are an exceedingly important factor in our concept of the universal Church; they are our great palpable argument that the primacy of Rome is more than patriarchal rights over part of the Church. Indeed, in some ways, it is just they who save the whole situation, from our point of view. . . . The fact that vast numbers of the members of the Eastern patriarchates have gone out of the Church altogether, distressing as it is, does not affect the legal position. . . . In spite of the many heresies and schisms which at various times have robbed each patriarchate of its members, the constitution of the Catholic Church remains what it has always been, not one patriarchate with one rite, but the union of East and West, differing in rites, having in many cases different details of canon law, but united in the profession of the same faith and in conscious inter-communion" (*op. cit.*, pp. 27, 28). That position is safeguarded by the Eastern Catholics.

There is another thing. It is a charge often made against the Church, and it is a charge to which intelligent people today are very sensitive, and rightly so, that she stretches the necessary uniformity of revealed truth, faith, and morals, to cover other things; that she has no real regard for the variations in human mentality, temperament, and culture. The words and actions of many individual Catholics give colour to this accusation; even a great and learned publicist like Mr. Belloc, when he reiterates that "the Faith is Europe and Europe is the Faith" is saying something which, if taken at the foot of the letter (as all ordinary people take such sayings), would make of the Church a large European sect: on this showing, Ireland, for instance, must be imperfectly Catholic and imperfectly civilized, for she was never submitted to the rule of the Roman Empire or bathed herself in the waters of the Mediterranean basin! If this charge of desiring, or even tending, to impose an unhuman, unnatural uniformity on the human people whom God has made diverse were true, it would be a very serious, nay, a fundamental fault in the Church (which is impossible). On every page of this book it is demonstrated that this charge is false. "The Church is not Latin or Greek or Slavonic; it is Catholic": and Catholicism includes *everything* that is not in any way sinful or in any way erroneous. Just as there is nothing secular but sin, so there is nothing foreign to Catholicism but error, ugliness, and disaccord with right reason. The prevailing Latin uniformity of the Church today is simply the result of historical events: it might just as well have been Greek; in another two thousand years it may be Chinese. Catholicism is the religion of variety, the variety displayed by seventeen hundred million people (or however many there may be in the world), and the best and simplest proof of this is the variousness of divine worship as used by Catholics, the fact that the Mass is one but the ways of celebrating it are many.

Chapter IV

THE BYZANTINE RITE:
LITURGY AND CUSTOMS

THE BYZANTINE RITE:
LITURGY AND CUSTOMS

The Byzantine rite[1] is the name given to the system and forms of worship and administration of the sacraments proper at first to the Church of Constantinople (Byzantium) and her dependencies. After the defection of the monophysites Constantinople gradually imposed her own liturgy on the faithful of the other patriarchates, and by the end of the thirteenth century the Melkites of Alexandria, Antioch, and Jerusalem had abandoned their own ancient usages in its favour. The Byzantine rite is therefore now used by the whole of the Orthodox Eastern Church and by many Catholics, and is the most widely spread rite after the Latin; it is followed by (nominally) 150 million Christians, of whom seven millions are Catholics.

The Byzantine rite has not the uniformity of the Roman use of the Latin rite, even among the dissidents. Catholics observe it with varying degrees of uniformity, whose deviations from the Constantinopolitan or Russian norms seem to be in corresponding ratio to the size of their body: e.g., the Greeks, Russians, and Bulgars preserve exact liturgical purity while the Ruthenians have introduced all sorts of modifications, many of them from Western sources. The account given here follows in general the typical Greek or Russian observances, the principal modifications being noted later when dealing with the people concerned.

---

[1] It is often called the "Greek rite." See page 49.

Church buildings. The system of building whose characteristic and essential feature is a dome covering a space which
is square, and whose prototype is the great church (now a
museum) of the Holy Wisdom ("St. Sophia") at Constantinople, spread all over the Byzantine religious world, much
modified from place to place by local and national characteristics. The interior appearance of a Byzantine church is sufficiently well known. Its chief characteristic is a solid screen,
covered with pictures (*eikons*, and therefore called the *eikonostasis*), before the altar and hiding the sanctuary (*bema*);
this is pierced by lateral and middle ("holy") doors. Greek
screens are usually lower than Russian ones. Among the Ruthenians these doors are never shut and the screen is generally
of openwork (I have seen it so in several Melkite churches).[2]
The stone altar stands away from the east wall (apsidal),
beneath a canopy on four columns (*ciborium*); it is square,
flat, and plain, with a flat crucifix, two or more candlesticks,
and the gospel-book upon it; the Blessed Sacrament is reserved
in a small tabernacle or hanging pyx, but is not the subject
of exterior *cultus* to anything like the same degree as in the
West. To the north and south respectively, sometimes in separate apses, are altar-like tables, the *prothesis* and *diakonikon*.
In the nave there are normally no seats, except around the
walls, or statues, but *eikons*, each with its lamp, are numerous.
Men and women should properly be separated. The stalls for
the choir are in front of the *eikonostasis*, though there is often
a mixed choir occupying a decently screened gallery. There
is sometimes an ambo on the north side in front of the screen
and there is always one or more *proskynetaria*, small sloping
desks on which the *eikon* of the saint or mystery of the day
is exposed for veneration: the faithful cross themselves and
bow three times and kiss it. In cathedrals the bishop's throne
is in the apse behind the altar and there is another as well as
an episcopal stall on the south side of the choir. Open "side

---

[2] It is said that some Byzantine churches in North America have no
screen, as some in south Italy and Syria certainly have not. I suppose this
is temporary, due to lack of funds, for the *eikonostasis* is really now a
liturgical necessity of the rite.

THE RUTHENIAN CHURCH OF ST. BARBARA
AT VIENNA

(*Byzantine Rite*)

Beginning of the Liturgy

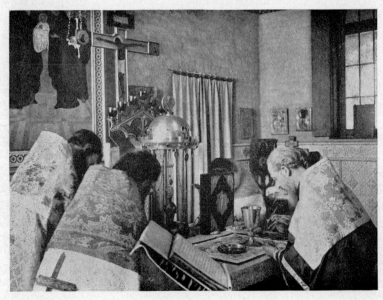

The Consecration
THE BYZANTINE LITURGY

altars" are an innovation; strictly speaking, if there is more than one altar each should have its own *eikonostasis*, etc., forming as it were a separate church (*parekklesia*). Larger churches have a closed porch (*narthex*) extending the whole width of the west end, with three ("royal") doors into the nave, containing the baptismal font.

Vestments correspond more or less to the Roman ones and have the same origins, but they have evolved into quite different shapes. The deacon wears a long, ungirdled, wide-sleeved tunic (*stikharion*), white or dark red and often embroidered; his stole (*orarion*) is a long narrow strip of silk, worn over the left shoulder with the back end hanging to the ground and the front carried under the right arm and over the left shoulder (Greek) or hanging down back and front over the left shoulder (Russian). A priest puts on first a *stikharion*, plainer than the deacon's and with narrow sleeves (in some places Catholic clergy substitute an alb for it); then the *epitrakhelion* or stole, in one piece with a loop at the top to go over the head, the *zone* (girdle), like a belt, the *epimanikia*, oversleeves or cuffs (unconnected with our maniple), and lastly the *phelonion* or chasuble, a long, full, bell-shaped garment, sometimes cut away up to the chest in front. The vestments are usually white; there is no regular sequence of liturgical colours, except among the Ruthenians. A bishop wears the *sakkos* (rather like a dalmatic) instead of the *phelonion* and a diamond-shaped ornament (*epigonation*) depending at his right side (cf., the Pope's *subcinctorium*). He also wears the crown (*mitra*) instead of the priest's *kalemaukion* (see p. 46), the *omophorion*, like a long, wide *pallium*, the pectoral cross, and two *enkolpia* or *panagia*, round or oval medallions suspended from the neck bearing images of our Lord and His all-holy Mother. The episcopal crown or mitre is rather like the papal tiara, derived in shape from the imperial crown, and the pastoral staff, shorter than the Western crozier, ends in the form of two serpents facing one another. Other episcopal insignia are the *khazranion*, a straight ebony walking-staff,[3] and the *mandyas*, a processional

---

[3] A similar staff is carried by the bishops of Spain.

garment not unlike a blue or purple cope but longer and fastened at the lower hem as well as at the neck.

The principal articles of clerical ordinary dress are the black *rason*, a loose, wide-sleeved gown, and the *kalemaukion*, a cylindrical hat about six inches high with a flat brim at the top, rather like an inverted top-hat. Minor clerics and Russian priests wear it without a brim, bishops and monks cover it with a black veil falling on to the shoulders (a few bishops have this veil white). Russian priests often wear a pectoral cross. Byzantine bishops do not normally wear rings, but all the Catholic hierarchs do so. The beard and long hair were formerly most strictly *de rigueur* for all Byzantine clergy, but the latter is going quickly out of fashion in many places and even clean-shaven bishops and priests are now not unknown.

Liturgical books. In most Eastern rites the offices are arranged in a number of separate books, each containing only those parts required by individuals, e.g., celebrant, deacon, choir, as in the West before about the eleventh century. The chief Byzantine books (by no means uniform in arrangement) are the *Typikon*, a perpetual kalendar with full instructions for carrying out the office; the *Eukhologion* which is, roughly, a compendium of missal, ritual and, among the Greeks, pontifical; the books of the Gospels and Epistles; the *Horologion*, containing the common parts of the daily offices and certain proper hymns, etc., of the Eucharistic Liturgy; the *Triodion*, *Pentecostarion*, and *Parakletike* or *Oktoekhos*, choir-books forming a sort of "proper of the season" of both Mass and Office; the *Menaia*, one volume for each month, have the proper parts of the Divine Office for all fixed feasts, including the "historical lessons" for saints' days; and the Psalter.

Numerous Catholic editions of these books have been published in various places according to local requirements, the typical Greek editions by the Propaganda Press at Rome. The best Orthodox editions were for long those of the Phoenix Press at Venice. The Orthodox books differ from ours practically not at all and in fact are used by some Catholics, e.g., the Russians, with such necessary modifications as the addition of the Pope's name to the diptychs. A very fine edition of these books according to Melkite usages is being published by the Fathers of St. Paul at Harisa in the Lebanon. The *Horologion* appeared in 1928. A typical Slavonic edition is being undertaken at Rome.

Altar-vessels and bread. These are the chalice (*poterion*); the paten (*diskos*), larger and deeper than the Western paten, with a rim and sometimes a foot; the *asteriskos*, made of two pieces of metal crossed and bent into two semicircles, sometimes with a small star hanging at the intersection, is put over the paten to prevent the veil touching the holy Bread;[4] the lance, a knife for cutting the altar-bread; the spoon, often with two small prongs projecting from the bowl, for giving Communion; and a small piece of sponge (*mousa*) sewn up in red silk, used for several purposes, including that of the Western "purificator." There is a small silk veil each for chalice and paten and a larger one (*aer*) to cover them both.

During celebration of the Liturgy the altar table is covered by an *antimension*, a piece of linen or silk about eighteen inches square on which are embroidered or painted instruments of the Passion, etc.; sewn into it is a tiny bag containing relics. It must be consecrated by a bishop. Strictly speaking it is not required on a consecrated altar but is now always used, together with a "corporal" (*eileton*) of linen. The ordinary altar coverings are a linen cloth which hangs down on all sides and a silk or velvet one above it which may be coloured and embroidered.

The Eastern thurible has shorter chains than in the West and incense is offered by swinging these chains from their ends, with one hand. The *ripidion* or *hexapterygon* is a flat metal disk, representing a cherub's head surrounded by six wings, mounted on a shaft in such a way that it can be made to revolve on its axis. These are carried in processions and on pontifical occasions; their original use was to keep flies from

---

[4] A similar thing is used to cover the paten when Holy Communion is brought to the Pope when he celebrates pontifically.

the holy things during the *anaphora* but the deacon now generally waves a veil instead.[5]

Bishops make use of a hand-cross to give certain blessings, as do Ruthenian and Russian priests, and some episcopal benedictions are given with a two-branched candlestick (*dikerion*) in the left hand and a three-branched one (*trikerion*) in the right.

The Byzantine altar-bread (*prosphora*) is a flat round cake of leavened bread about 1½ inches thick, stamped in the middle with one or more square "seals" containing a cross between the letters I C X C N I K A ("Jesus Christ conquers"); on the left is a square with a triangle, called "the all-holy" because it is set aside as a commemoration of our Lady; and on the right three rows of three triangles for the choirs of angels and the saints. The portions of the Host that are to be reserved are all "anointed" with a drop of the sacred Blood; before administration to the sick or from the tabernacle (*artophorion*) it is dipped into unconsecrated wine.

Music. The music of the Byzantine rite varies from country to country, and in some large churches polyphony of a bad Western type is now heard, sometimes with the additional innovation of an organ. The traditional Greek liturgical chant is enharmonic with varying intervals between the notes, and as the modes are continually changing even in the same melody there is a singer appointed to sing the dominant (*ison*) throughout, changing it as the mode changes. This music requires an incredible skill of voice and accuracy of ear, for it abounds in quarter-tones and other strange intervals, but the result to Western ears is a barbarous and arbitrary wailing until one learns to recognize its strange beauty.

In Slav churches, on the other hand, the singing is immediately attractive to Westerners. Russia is, or was, the land of church polyphony *par excellence*. After a varied and complex history Russian church music came into its own during the nineteenth century. Rimsky-Korsakov solved the problem of how best to harmonize the old Muscovite chants and his

---

[5] They were formerly used also in the West and have survived in the papal *flabella*.

work was taken up by A. T. Gretchaninov, Rachmaninov, P. P. Chesnokov, and A. D. Kastalsky, with results in which some people find a far more *religiously* satisfying quality than in the musically greatest efforts of the classical polyphonists of the West.

Liturgical languages. The Byzantine is sometimes called the "Greek rite," because that was its original language, but it is characteristic of it that linguistic uniformity is not required and the numbers who use it in ancient Greek are relatively few; among Catholics, very few, only the "pure" Greeks and Italo-Greeks in fact. Church Slavonic (*Staroslav*) is now its principal language, and it is also celebrated in old Georgian and modern Rumanian, Magyar, and Arabic.[6]

THE EUCHARISTIC LITURGY

The Byzantine rite has two *anaphoras*, or rather, Liturgies, that of St. John Chrysostom for ordinary use and that of St. Basil for Sundays of Lent (except Palm Sunday), Maundy Thursday, Holy Saturday, the vigils of Christmas and the Epiphany, and St. Basil's feast, and a Liturgy of the Presanctified (called "of St. Gregory Dialogos," i.e., Pope St. Gregory the Great) for every day in Lent except Saturdays and Sundays; in practice this last is often sung only on Wednesdays and Fridays, the other week days of Lent (except Saturday) then having no celebration. The Liturgy of St. Chrysostom is simply a modification of the Liturgy of St. Basil, which in turn is a shortened edition of the early Liturgy of the Church of Constantinople, derived through Caesarea from the primitive uses of Antioch and Jerusalem; in the opinion of Dom Moreau they together form the most authentic expression of the Church's original liturgical tradition. Unlike practically all other Eastern *anaphoras*, those of Basil and Chrysostom have probably some association with the saints whose names they bear. St. Basil is said to have shortened and

---

[6] And by the Orthodox in many tongues, including Japanese, Chinese, and, in some American churches, English. A Byzantine priest may celebrate in any of the approved liturgical languages he chooses, subject to local legislation.

"edited" the Liturgy of Caesarea, and his version was further modified (only slightly in the pre-anaphoral part: the ceremonies are identical) by St. John Chrysostom.

Concelebration by several celebrants together, all consecrating the same bread and wine, is very common among Byzantines. The senior in dignity officiates aloud at the altar, the others all saying the prayers in a low voice. Any number of priests, of priests and bishops, or of bishops alone, may thus celebrate together; each one so doing offers the holy sacrifice really and truly and may accept an offering therefor.[7]

Catholic Byzantine clergy celebrate "low Mass" on week days but there is no uniform version of the Liturgy adapted for this purpose, except among the Ruthenians.

At the hour for celebration the priest and deacon, in their ordinary clothes, say certain prayers before the doors of the *eikonostasis* and then go within to the *diakonikon* to vest. When they are vested they wash their hands, saying Psalm xxv. 6–12, and go to the *prothesis* for the preparation (*proskomide*). The priest cuts up one or more altar-breads with the "lance," arranging the pieces in a certain order on the paten in honour of our Lord, our Lady, the saints, the living, the dead, etc., the deacon pouring wine and a little water into the chalice; the offerings are then incensed and covered up. Each action of the priest is directed by the deacon and accompanied by appropriate words, thus:

Deacon: "Let us pray to the Lord. Sir, strengthen."
Priest: "And the star came and stood above where the child was." (He puts the *asteriskos* above the holy bread.)
Deacon: "Let us pray to the Lord. Sir, make beautiful."
Priest: "The Lord hath reigned, he is clothed with beauty, the

---

[7] This practice has gone out in the Western church since about the thirteenth century, but survives at the ordination of priests and consecration of bishops. In commemoration of the Council of Nicaea Pope Pius XI presided at a concelebration of the Byzantine Liturgy in St. Peter's on November 15, 1925. The concelebrants were six bishops (two Rumanian, one Italo-Greek, one Melkite, one Jugoslav) and a dozen priests. The creed of Nicaea was sung in Greek, Slavonic, Rumanian, and Latin, the last by the Pope himself.

Lord is clothed with strength and hath girded himself."
(He censes a veil and puts it over the bread.)

Deacon: "Let us pray to the Lord. Sir, cover up."

Priest: "Thy glory, O Christ, has covered the heavens, and
the earth is full of thy praise." (He censes another veil
and puts it over the chalice.)

Deacon: "Let us pray to the Lord. Sir, shelter."

Priest: "Shelter us under the shadow of thy wings; drive away
every foe and adversary. . . ." (He censes the *aer* and puts
it over all, and censes all.)[8]

After further prayers the deacon censes the sanctuary and
church, and then comes to the celebrant at the altar saying,
"It is time to sacrifice to the Lord. Reverend sir, give me a
blessing. . . . Pray for me. . . . Remember me . . . ," and each
time the priest blesses him. The deacon then goes and stands
outside and facing the holy doors,[9] which are open,[10] and the
Liturgy proper begins.

After a blessing the deacon recites a litany, the great
synapte, the two sides of the choir answering alternately *Kyrie
eleison* to each petition:

"In peace let us pray to the Lord." "*Kyrie eleison.*"

"For the peace from on high, and for the salvation of our
souls, let us pray. . . ." "*Kyrie eleison.*"

"For the peace of the whole world, for the good estate of
all the holy churches of God, and for the unity of all, let
us pray. . . ." "*Kyrie eleison.*"

[8] My quotations from the text of the Liturgy of St. John Chrysostom
are, in the main, taken from the excellent translation made by the
Benedictine dames of Stanbrook and published by Messrs. Burns, Oates
& Washbourne (London, 1926).

[9] This is his normal place, his function being precisely to be a link
between the celebrant and the people. If there be no deacon the priest
has to sing or say everything with the help of a lay cantor. A priest
may not officiate as a deacon.

[10] The times at which these doors are open or shut vary accordingly
as Greek or Russian customs are followed; e.g., the Greeks open them at
the priest's blessings, Russians do not. Neither system is completely set
out here.

And so on, for the patriarch or other ordinary, the sovereign, the city, the harvest, the sick, etc., ending with a commemoration of our Lady. Then the choir sings the first antiphon, of psalm and hymn verses and invocations, according to the day, the deacon recites the little *synapte* (one petition and the commemoration of our Lady), and the priest says *secreto* the prayer of this antiphon, singing the last words, "For thine is the kingdom," etc., aloud, the choir answering "Amen."[11] There is a second antiphon in exactly the same way, and a third with its prayer. After the second antiphon is sung the *Monogenes*, a hymn written probably by Severus of Antioch (d. 536):

> "The only-begotten Son, the Word of God, being immortal and wishing to take flesh in the womb of the holy Mother of God, the ever-virgin Mary, for our salvation, became man without change. Thou wast crucified, O Christ our God, trampling on death by thy death; O thou, thyself one of the persons of the Holy Trinity, who art glorified with the Father and the Holy Spirit, save us."

Then comes "the little entrance."

Preceded by the cross, lights, and *ripidia*[12] and followed by the celebrant, the deacon, holding the book of the gospels against his forehead, leaves the sanctuary by the north door. They stop in front of the holy doors and the priest says inaudibly the prayer of the entrance:

> "Lord and master, our God, who has established in Heaven the orders and armies of angels and archangels to minister to thy glory, grant that with us there may enter those holy angels who with us serve and glorify thy goodness. . . ."

---

[11] An *ekphonesis*. This is the common ending to inaudible prayers throughout the Liturgy (cf., the conclusion of the "secret" in the Roman Mass).

[12] Though these are really pontifical accessories the Greek custom is to use them ordinarily.

BYZANTINE BISHOP GIVING A SOLEMN BLESSING
(Mgr. Gregory Hajjar, Melkite Bishop of Akka)

CONCELEBRANTS OF A SLAV-BYZANTINE LITURGY IN WESTMINSTER
CATHEDRAL, ENGLAND

On the extreme left, the Deacon

Deacon: "Sir, bless the holy entrance."

The priest blesses it inaudibly and kisses the gospel-book, which the deacon then lifts up, saying, "Wisdom! Stand!" and they re-enter the sanctuary while the choir sings:

"Come let us adore and bow down before Christ. Save us, O Son of God, who didst rise again from the dead, we who sing to thee Alleluia," and other verses.

Then is sung the *Trisagion:*

"Holy God, holy Strong One, holy Deathless One, have mercy on us (three times). Glory be to the Father and to the Son and to the Holy Ghost, now and for ever, world without end. Amen. Holy Deathless One, have mercy on us."

The deacon comes to the doors and, as though to encourage the singers to further efforts, exclaims "Strength!" (a Greek custom only) and they sing the first part again. Meanwhile the celebrant has prayed secretly for forgiveness of sins and recites the *Trisagion* with the deacon. Then the epistle is chanted by a lector or layman (in Catholic churches sometimes by a subdeacon), outside and facing the holy doors. While the choir sings alleluia and psalm-verses, the celebrant says a prayer, "O Lord and lover of men, irradiate our hearts with the pure light of thy divine knowledge and open the eyes of our mind to the understanding of thy gospel teaching," etc., and the deacon censes sanctuary and people. Then he takes the gospel-book, is blessed, and sings the gospel from the ambo or elsewhere and afterwards is blessed again and returns the book to the celebrant. Then before the holy doors he recites a litany for all sorts and conditions of the faithful, the choir answering *Kyrie eleison* and the celebrant saying secretly the corresponding prayer with the *ekphonesis;* then in the same way the litany for the catechumens, after which they are dismissed: "All the catechumens, go out! Catechumens, go out! Let not any of the catechumens—!" But of course, there are none now, or if there are, they do not

go. At this point the celebrant unfolds the *eileton* and spreads
it upon (or under) the *antimension;* he then says the two
prayers of the faithful and a long prayer for purity of conscience secretly; the deacon enters the sanctuary, and the
Cherubikon is intoned:

> "We who mystically represent the cherubim, who sing to
> the life-giving Trinity the hymn of *trisagion,* let us now
> lay aside all worldly cares, that we may receive the King
> of the universe who comes escorted by unseen armies
> of angels. Alleluia. Alleluia. Alleluia."

While the choir is singing this very slowly with a break in
the middle, the priest censes the altar and people and the great
entrance is made. The deacon, holding the paten and bread
above his head and the priest, bearing the chalice, preceded by
the cross, lights, and *ripidia,* leave the sanctuary by the north
door, go to the middle, and in at the holy doors, repeating
aloud one to the other: "May the Lord remember us all in
his kingdom, always, now and for ever, world without end."
(This famous liturgical rite has been cut down by the Ruthenians.) The vessels and gifts are put on the altar, the veils are
removed, and they are incensed. The deacon comes before
the holy doors, which are now shut, and recites a litany
(*Choir:* "Grant it, O Lord!") while the celebrant offers the
bread and wine. At a pontifical Liturgy and at concelebration
the officiating clergy here exchange the kiss of peace; ordinarily the priest kisses the *aer* covering the gifts and the deacon
the cross on his stole; he then cries an ancient warning: "The
doors! the doors! Let us attend with wisdom!" and the Creed
of Nicaea is recited (sung by the choir in Russian churches)
by the senior cleric present aloud and the rest to themselves,[13]

---

[13] It is incumbent on no Catholics of Byzantine rite to add "and the
Son" in the creed unless its omission would cause scandal. In fact, most
of them say it—but not in the church of the Greek College at Rome,
and it is not in the official liturgical books printed in Rome. This need
cause no surprise; the function of the liturgical creed is not to give a
list of all our articles of faith.

the celebrant meanwhile fluttering the *aer* over the holy things. The *anaphora* "of our father among the saints John Chrysostom" now begins:

Deacon: "Stand we well, stand we with fear. Let us attend to offer the holy offering in peace." (The holy doors are opened.)

Choir: "The mercy of peace, a sacrifice of praise."

Priest (facing the people): "The grace of our Lord Jesus Christ, the love of God the Father, and the fellowship of the Holy Ghost, be with you all."

Choir: "And with thy spirit."

Priest: "Lift up your hearts."

Choir: "We have, to the Lord."

Priest (turning to the altar): "Let us give thanks to the Lord."

Choir: "It is right and just."

The holy doors are shut and covered. The celebrant says the invariable preface secretly, and while the choir sings the *Sanctus* and *Benedictus*, goes on with a short prayer direct to the words of institution.

". . . Who . . . giving thanks, blessing, sanctifying and breaking, gave it to his holy disciples and apostles, saying (aloud and raising his right hand; the deacon indicates the bread) *Take, eat, this is my Body broken for you for the forgiveness of sins.*" (*Choir:* "Amen.") "In like manner after he had supped, saying (aloud as before) *Drink ye all of this, this is my Blood of the new testament, shed for you and for many for the forgiveness of sins.*" (There are no genuflections or elevations[14] but a profound prostration.) *Choir:* "Amen."

Priest (secretly): "We therefore, remembering this saving precept . . ." etc., ending aloud "In all and for all we offer thee thine own of what is thine own," followed at once by the invocation of the Holy Ghost (*epiklesis*):

---

[14] But among the Russians the deacon (or priest) lifts up the chalice and paten (with his hands crossed) while the *anamnesis* is said.

". . . send down thy Holy Spirit upon us and upon these gifts here present."

Deacon: "Sir, bless the holy bread."

Priest: "✠ And make this bread the precious body of thy Christ."

Deacon: "Amen. Sir, bless the holy chalice."

Priest: "✠ And that which is in this chalice, the precious Blood of thy Christ."

Deacon: "Amen. Sir, bless both these holy gifts."

Priest: "✠ Changing them by thy holy spirit."

Deacon: "Amen. Amen. Amen. Reverend sir, remember me, a sinner."[15]

The holy Gifts and the altar are incensed while the choir sings a hymn of our Lady, the priest blesses bread with the Sacred Host, and the holy doors are opened; the deacon reads the names of the dead from a tablet, the priest commemorating our Lady, St. John Baptist, the saint of the day, and all the departed, and then the living, adding aloud:

"Remember in the first place, O Lord, our sovereign pontiff Pius, Pope of Rome (our blessed patriarch N.), and our bishop M.; preserve them to thy churches in peace, in health, in honour, in length of days, faithfully dispensing thy word of truth."

The deacon goes back to his place before the holy doors (now shut) and recites a litany for spiritual gifts and the fruit of the sacrifice, ending with the Our Father said aloud by the priest, with the doxology "For Thine is the kingdom and the power and the glory, Father, Son, and Holy Ghost, now and for ever and world without end. Amen."[16]

The doors are opened, the priest says privately two prayers before communion, the deacon exclaims: "Let us attend!" and the priest elevates the sacred Host saying, "Holy things

---

[15] According to the dissident Orthodox, the consecration is not achieved until this invocation of the Holy Ghost has been pronounced.

[16] Not, therefore, a Protestant innovation, as is so often ignorantly supposed!

to the holy."[17] The choir sings: "One only is holy, one only is Lord, Jesus Christ in the glory of God the Father. Amen," followed by a hymn. The doors are shut and the priest breaks the Host into four parts saying: "Broken and distributed is the Lamb of God, Son of the Father, who is broken but not divided, ever eaten and never consumed, and who sanctifies those who partake." He puts one particle into the chalice and the deacon adds thereto a little warm water (*zeon*), a symbol of "the fervour of faith, full of the Holy Ghost."[18] Then he communicates himself with a particle of the Host and gives the other into the hand of the deacon, which he consumes standing behind the altar. Likewise with the Chalice, of which each drinks three times.

When the hymn which the choir is singing is ended the holy doors are opened and the deacon, standing thereat, lifts up the chalice covered by its veil, exclaiming, "Approach with fear of God, with faith and love." Each lay communicant, standing before the priest, receives a particle of the holy Body steeped in the precious Blood, drawn from the chalice in the spoon which is put into his mouth. The words of administration are: "The servant (handmaid) of God, N., receives the precious and all-holy Body and Blood of our Lord God and Saviour Jesus Christ for the forgiveness of his (her) sins and life everlasting. Amen." Meanwhile the choir sings:

> "Make me this day a sharer in thy mystic supper, O Son of God. For I will not reveal thy mysteries to thy enemies, nor like Judas give thee a kiss, but like the thief I say to thee: Remember me, O Lord, in thy kingdom."

---

[17] This elevation, common to all Eastern Liturgies, has nothing essentially in common with the elevation at the consecration in the Latin Mass, though some rites (e.g., the Maronite) have modified it to approximate to Roman usage. The mediaeval errors whose propagation made the Western elevation desirable did not penetrate to the East. It is rather the "little elevation" at the end of the Roman canon.

[18] But originally probably a precaution against the contents of the chalice freezing in the mountains of Cappadocia.

Priest (blessing the people): "✚ O Lord, save thy people and bless thine inheritance."

Choir: "We have seen the true light, we have received the heavenly Spirit, we have found the true faith worshipping the undivided Trinity, for he hath saved us."

The celebrant now incenses the Chalice, makes a low bow, then takes and holds it up before the people saying, "Blessed be our God always, now and for ever, world without end." *Choir:* "Amen." He carries it to the *prothesis*, while the deacon prays aloud: "Stand! Having received the divine, holy, spotless, immortal, heavenly, life-giving and awful mysteries of Christ, let us give due thanks to the Lord."

Choir: "*Kyrie eleison.*"

Deacon: "Help, save, pity and protect us, O God, by thy grace."

Choir: "*Kyrie eleison.*"

Deacon: "Having prayed that this whole day may be perfect, holy, peaceful and sinless, let us commend ourselves, each other, and our whole life to Christ our God."

Choir: "To thee, O Lord."

Priest: "For thou art our sanctification, and we give glory to thee, Father, Son and Holy Ghost, now and for ever, world without end."

Choir: "Amen."

Priest: "Let us go forth in peace."

Deacon: "Let us pray to the Lord."

Choir: "*Kyrie eleison.*"

The celebrant, standing before the image of our Lord on the *iconostasis*, says aloud a prayer, full of scriptural allusions, for the Church, and afterwards blesses the people, saying:

"✚ The blessing of the Lord and his mercy come upon you by his grace and love towards man, always, now, and for ever, world without end."

Choir: "Amen."

Priest: "Glory to thee, Christ, O God, our hope, glory to thee."

Lector: "Glory be to the Father, . . . Amen. *Kyrie eleison* (three times). Reverend sir, bless!"

The priest turns to the people and says the dismissal (*apolysis*), invoking the prayers of our Lady, St. John Baptist, the apostles and martyrs, St. John Chrysostom, the saint of the church and the day, etc., the people answering "Amen."

The blessed bread (*antidoron*) is now distributed,[19] while the deacon at the *prothesis* consumes what is left of the holy Things. The celebrant unvests in the sanctuary.

THE DIVINE OFFICE

The Byzantine divine office (*Akolouthia*) has eight "hours," corresponding to those of the Roman Breviary, but its composition is entirely different. The psalter is sung through every week and there is a large number of rhythmic hymns. The office is exceedingly long, and when sung takes about eight hours altogether; Catholic priests are bound to recite privately only as much as they conveniently can.

Mesonyktikon (midnight-office) in its ordinary form consists of the *Trisagion*, Our Father, Nicene Creed, with psalms, prayers, and *troparia* (hymns), and a final litany. It is not sung on certain days. *Orthros* (Matins and Lauds) has in addition to psalms and hymns a litany, the *Magnificat*, the day's reading from the *Menaion*, and a gospel on Sundays and feasts, when an amplified form of *Gloria in excelsis Deo* is sung. After this office on a great feast those present are anointed with oil from the lamp burning before the *eikon* of the day. The offices of the First, Third, Sixth, and Ninth Hours each have three psalms, prayers, and hymns, and sometimes short additions called *mesoria*. *Hesperinos* (Vespers) begins the liturgical day, as with us. It is divided into three parts, of which the second contains the "hymn at the lighting of lamps," *Phos hilaron*,[20] which is the centre to which all parts of the office

[19] Another practice dropped by the Ruthenians. It is the Greek usage to bless it; in most churches the bread is what remains of the *prosphora* after the preparation, simply hallowed by its original use.

[20] There is a good translation by Keble of this lovely hymn in *Hymns Ancient and Modern*, No. 18. The tune given to it there is good, too.

converge; it ends with the Song of Simeon, *Trisagion*, Our Father, and the *troparion* of the day and a prayer to our Lady. Normally *Hesperinos* is sung in every Byzantine church on Saturday evening. *Apodeipnon* (Compline; literally "after supper") is extra long during Lent and is joined to the night-office to form the vigil service of Christmas and Epiphany. Ordinarily it consists of three psalms, Nicene creed, *Trisagion*, Our Father, and a hymn for the day.

The short hymns of this rite are generically called *troparia*, and are composed of syllabic lines, based on the tonic accent; they are of frequent occurrence throughout the offices. Each strophe is properly a *troparion*, of which several make up an *ode*, the rhythm and melody following that of the first *troparion* (the *hirmos*). Nine odes, having reference to the scriptural canticles, make a *kanon* (three in Lent, *triodion*). There are numerous classes of *troparia*, e.g., a *theotokion* is in honour of our Lady, a *kontakion* refers to the feast of the day, an *apolytikion* precedes the dismissal, etc.

The Sacraments[21]

Baptism. After three exorcisms, renunciation of Satan is made and the Nicene Creed said by the sponsor, the effect of which is to make the child a catechumen. Then the priest incenses the baptistery, the deacon says a litany, and after several prayers the priest blesses the water and oil. Then he anoints the child on the forehead, chest, back (each twice), ears, hands, and feet, and afterwards plunges it three times into the font, saying, "The servant of God N., is baptized in the name of the Father. Amen. And of the Son. Amen. And of the Holy Ghost. Amen." Psalm xxxi is sung three times and a hymn, while the priest puts the baptismal garment on the child. He then proceeds to confirm it.

Confirmation. The child is anointed with holy Chrism on the forehead, eyes, nostrils, mouth, ears, chest, hands, and feet, with the words "The seal of the gift of the Holy Ghost. Amen" at each anointing. Priest and sponsor with the child

---

[21] The word "mystery" is used instead of "sacrament" throughout the East.

A BYZANTINE BISHOP ENTHRONED

Mgr. Cyril Kurtev at his consecration as Titular Bishop of Briula at San Clemente in Rome, 1926

Courtesy of La Bonne Presse

A BYZANTINE ARCHBISHOP
Vested in Crown, Sakkos, and Omophorion

then walk round the baptistery, singing, "Thou who hast been baptized in Christ hast put on the vesture of Christ. Amen." An epistle (Rom. vi. 3–11) and gospel (Matt. xxviii. 16–20) are read, and the rite ends with a short litany.

Penance. The penitent and confessor stand before an *eikon* of our Lord, and after certain prayers (including the psalm *Miserere*) the penitent confesses his sins. Then he kneels and the priest prays for the penitent's pardon and gives him absolution in a deprecative form, "May God, through me, a sinner, forgive thee. . . ." But among the Slavs the form is "May our Lord and God Jesus Christ through the goodness and depth of his love for men forgive thee all thy sins, my child N. And I, an unworthy priest, by the power that he has given me forgive thee and absolve thee from all thy sins in the name of the Father. . . . Amen." A penance is then imposed.

Most Catholic Byzantines have approximated this office more closely to the Roman usage, and administer the sacrament in a confessional-box.

Eucharist. See page 57; also pages 90 and 115.

Extreme Unction. The Byzantines and all other orientals call this sacrament simply "Holy Anointing." It theoretically requires the ministration of seven priests, one for each anointing, but the sick must usually be content with one, who gives them all. Seven candles are lit, the priest incenses the room and those present, and blesses the oil. The sick person is anointed on forehead, eyes, nostrils, mouth, ears, chest, hands, and feet, a passage from the gospels being read before each anointing. The words of administration are: "O holy Father, physician of souls and bodies, who hast sent us thine only Son, our Lord Jesus Christ, who cureth every sickness and saveth from death, heal thy servant N., from every bodily and spiritual ill that afflicts him and fill him with healthy life by the grace of thy Christ."

Holy Orders. The orders of the Byzantine rite are reader, subdeacon ("minor"), deacon, priest, bishop ("major"). For the ordination of a deacon the candidate is led to the altar before the communion during the Liturgy. The bishop blesses him; then he kneels down, and the bishop lays his right hand on the candidate's head, invoking the Holy Ghost: "The grace of God, that always strengthens the weak and fills the empty, appoints the most religious subdeacon N., to be deacon. Let us then pray for him that the grace of the Holy Ghost may come upon him." He then vests him with the *orarion* and hands him the *ripidion*, exclaiming *Axios!*, "He is worthy!" which the assistants repeat, three times. The ordination of a priest is similar, he being vested in the *phelonion* and given the chalice; this takes place after the "great entrance." After the consecration the bishop gives a particle of the sacred Host to the new priest, who holds it in his hand until "Holy things to the holy" is sung. The episcopate is likewise conferred by laying on one hand and invoking the Holy Ghost; two co-consecrators are of course required. It is to be noted that there are no anointings in any of these ordinations.

Some deacons remain in that order all their lives, and Eastern archdeacons are deacons, not priests.

Marriage. This office varies but little from country to country and has strongly influenced the corresponding services in non-Byzantine churches of the East.

Before they leave their house, bride and groom are blessed by their parents with *eikons* of our Lord and his all-holy Mother. The wedding ceremony itself consists of two parts, the betrothal and the blessing. The groom waits near a small table set before the *eikonostasis* and the bride comes to him up the church, preceded by a small boy carrying an *eikon*, while the choir sings a hymn, "Come, O dove, from Zion." The priest gives each party a lighted candle, incenses them, and blesses them three times. Then, after prayers for conjugal fidelity and with further blessings, rings are mutually exchanged three times: "The servant of God N., joins him (her) self with the servant of God M." This ends the betrothal.

While the choir sings Psalm cxxvii, the priest leads the couple to the table, before which a silken carpet is spread. Then, having ascertained the free consent of each, he brings two crowns of metal and precious stones from the sanctuary. With these he blesses groom and bride twice, and puts them on their heads, saying, "The servant of God N., is crowned

with the servant of God M., in the name of the Father," etc.
A passage from St. Paul's letter to the Ephesians (cap. v; cf.,
the Roman nuptial Mass) is read and the gospel of the wedding
at Cana, and the choir sings the Lord's Prayer while the
married couple drink thrice from a cup of blessed wine. The
priest joins their hands, which he covers with his stole, and
leads them in procession three times round the cross and
gospel-book on the table while the choir sings three hymns.
The ceremony ends with a prayer that invokes the memory and
virtues of Abraham and Sara, Isaac and Rebecca, Jacob and
Rachel. Some Eastern marriage rites require an explicit declaration of contract from the parties, others do not.

Calendar. The reformed annual calendar put forward by
Pope Gregory XIII in 1582, and at once adopted by most of
western Europe except England and Wales, Scotland and Ireland, took a long time to get any foothold in the East. None
of the dissident Orthodox churches began to accept it before
1924, and few Eastern Catholics before the beginning of the
nineteenth century. Even now, though most of the different
Catholic bodies have received it, a majority of the individuals
are following the old Julian calendar because that is the
custom of the numerically superior Ruthenians. According
to the Julian reckoning, fixed feasts fall thirteen days after
the corresponding day by the Gregorian reckoning, and the
two Easters and feasts depending thereon coincide about only
one year in every three.

The Byzantines have no liturgical cycles corresponding to
those of the Roman church year, but the period from the
Sunday "before Septuagesima" to the Saturday after Whit-
sunday (*triodion* of Lent and *triodion* of Easter) stands apart
from all the rest in importance. Many Sundays are named
after the gospel which is read: Sunday "of the Prodigal Son"
(Septuagesima), "of the Paralytic" (third after Easter), etc.
Certain feasts are preceded by vigils, of which the "greater
vigils" extend over several days (e.g., five before Christmas),
and there are likewise periods corresponding to the Western
octave, which last from three (e.g., Sunday "of the Man Born
Blind"—fifth after Easter) to nine days (e.g., Epiphany). An

interesting observance is the feast called a *synaxis*, assembly, when the people meet together to honour those saints connected with the mystery celebrated on the previous day, e.g., of SS. Simeon and Anne on the day after the Purification of our Lady. The ecclesiastical year begins on September 1.

Feasts. These may be divided into "great," "lesser," "little," and what we should call "commemorations." Easter stands all by itself, and the two Sundays and three week days before and the Sunday after are all in the class of "great" (Greek usage). The feasts of saints celebrated naturally vary from country to country; e.g., the calendar used by the Catholic Melkites has about 100 ancient feasts of all sorts in common with the Roman Church, some of them on different dates. The chief more recent modifications among most Catholics are the addition of Corpus Christi and the Sacred Heart, and increased solemnity given to St. Joseph (on the Sunday after Christmas) and to the Child-begetting of the Mother of the Mother of God, i.e., the Immaculate Conception, on December 9.

Among the special Byzantine observances are the feast of Orthodoxy (first Sunday in Lent), celebrating the triumph of orthodox veneration for holy images over Iconoclasm in 842; the Three Holy Hierarchs (SS. Basil, Gregory Nazianzen, and John Chrysostom), on January 30; the foundation of Constantinople (May 11); our Lady of Kazan (July 8); the Miracle of our Lady at Miasene (September 1); and many feasts of the just of the Old Dispensation (Joseph, David, Elias, Josue, the Three Children, Job the Great Athlete, the Ancestors of the Messias, etc., and a general feast which includes Adam and Eve). The Exaltation of the Cross on September 14 is a specially solemn day. The number of "holydays of obligation" varies; the Melkites have 30 (in addition to Sundays), including St. Nicholas, St. George, and St. Elias.

Penitential seasons. Eastern fasting, like many other of their religious usages, is the observance proper to monks gradually extended to the people at large (but by custom more than by law, cf. p. 65), and it is notoriously severe. For centuries the pious faithful made it a point of honour to keep the fasts,

BYZANTINE MOSAICS AT FLORENCE

St. Gregory Theologos

Christ the King (Pantokrator)

SEVENTEENTH-CENTURY SERBIAN EIKONS

and many still do; but conditions of modern life (to say nothing of religious cooling) make it increasingly difficult to do so. Among Catholics, the new conditions have been met in some places by canonical legislation, generally approximating to Western observances; in others, local customs are in process of evolution.

There is only one word, *nesteia*, to designate both fasting and abstinence and it is rather difficult to distinguish between them. Among the Greeks, fasting involves one meal only and that after sunset; strict abstinence forbids meat, milk, eggs, fish, oil, and wine; mitigated abstinence allows oil and wine, and sometimes fish: this is according to the old canons and customs, which envisaged strict fasting every Wednesday and Friday and in Lent, and abstinence on from 50 to 90 other days! But for the Catholic Melkites, for example, the second synod of Ain Traz in 1835 directed that fasting should consist of complete abstinence from food, drink, and tobacco until noon; afterwards anything may be eaten without limit of quantity, except meat, eggs, and milk. Their fasting days are five before Christmas, four before Epiphany, all Lent except Saturdays and Sundays and the Annunciation, and three other days. The same synod defined abstinence to extend to meat, eggs, and milk. It is obligatory for ten days before the fast of Christmas, twelve days before SS. Peter and Paul, fourteen days before the Assumption, on the solemnities of the Beheading of St. John Baptist and Holy Cross, and every Wednesday and Friday. But there is no fasting or abstinence during paschal-time and at certain other seasons, and even the above regulations are modified from place to place, apparently with no particular authority.

General observations. The Catholic Byzantines have taken up the use of Western "devotions," rosary, stations of the cross, etc., in varying degrees. Among their own observances is the Akathistos Hymn, an office in honour of our Lady which is sung liturgically at certain times and much used privately as well. Holy water (*hagiasma*) is in use to a limited extent and it is solemnly blessed in the baptismal font (and sometimes in rivers or the sea) at the Epiphany, in commemoration of our

Lord's baptism. Houses are blessed on the first day of every month, grapes or apples on the Transfiguration, and flowers, especially sweet basil, on the two feasts of the Cross. The custom of blessing and eating corn-cakes (*kolybes*) in memory of the dead is unquestionably a pagan survival. On Good Friday a figure of our Lord is laid on an ornamental bier (*epitaphion*) with flowers, spices, and grave-clothes (the "Burial of Christ"). In the evening it is carried in procession round and out of the church, sometimes through the streets (the "Funeral of Christ") and then laid on the altar or in the middle of the church while *troparia* modeled on the last five verses of Matthew xvii are sung.

BIBLIOGRAPHY

de Meester: *The Divine Liturgy of . . . John Chrysostom.* Greek and English texts (London, 1926).

Sembratovitch: *The Divine Liturgy of . . . John Chrysostom.* Translated from the Slavonic (Detroit, 1932). Translations of other Byzantine offices are published by Williams & Norgate of London.

Moreau: *Les Liturgies Eucharistiques* (Brussels, 1924).

*Holloway: *A Study of the Byzantine Liturgy* (London, 1934).

Couturier: *Cours de Liturgie Grecque-Melkite.* 3 vols. (Paris, 1912–1930).

Salaville: *Liturgies orientales* (Paris, 1932).

Stoelen: *L'Annee Liturgique Byzantine.* Russian usage (Amay, 1928).

McNabb: *The Akathistos Hymn* (Ditchling, 1934).

*Hamilton: *Byzantine Architecture and Decoration* (London, 1933).

Bréhier: *L'Art byzantine* (Paris, 1924).

Couturier: *Syllitourgikon.* Responses of the choir and other music in European notation (Paris, 1925).

Schwarz: *Le chant ecclésiastique byzantin de nos jours* (In *Irénkon*, X, pp. 225, 235; XI, p. 168. Amay, 1933–4).

*Gogol: *La liturgie méditée* (Amay, 1934).

Chapter V

CATHOLIC CHURCHES OF THE BYZANTINE RITE

CATHOLIC CHURCHES OF THE BYZANTINE RITE

1. THE ITALO-GREEKS

General Ecclesiastical History

The Italo-Greeks, more accurately called now Italo-Greek-Albanians, or even Italo-Albanians, are the only orientals who have been in communion with Rome since before the Eastern schism; they therefore have an historical interest out of proportion to their numbers and present importance.

For several centuries before the birth of Christ Hellenic colonists had made Sicily and southern Italy predominantly Greek: the provinces of Calabria and Apulia are known historically as *Magna Graecia*. From at least the second century after Christ there were Christian communities in these parts, and the present inhabitants regard their churches as apostolic foundations (Acts xxviii. 11–14).[1] The first seven hundred years of their ecclesiastical history are full of difficulties, but it seems certain that, after the superseding of Greek by Latin in the liturgy at Rome about the middle of the third century and the crystallizing of different liturgical rites, Roman and Byzantine usages existed side by side in southern Italy and

---

[1] Pope St. Agatho (d. 681) was a Sicilian Greek, and Pope St. Zacharias (d. 752) a Calabrian Greek.

Sicily; and there is no doubt that all bishops of these Christians were under the direct jurisdiction of the Bishop of Rome.[2]

About the year 732 the Iconoclast Emperor Leo III, the Isaurian, began forcibly to subject these Greek districts which Justinian had joined to the Eastern empire to the Patriarch of Constantinople, and metropolitan sees were erected at Naples, Syracuse, and elsewhere. To avoid disputes the Popes accepted the situation. But the conquest by the Normans of southern Italy, begun in 1017, and then of Sicily (at that time in Saracen hands), removed the possibility of these Greek churches following Constantinople into schism in 1054, and they came again under the immediate jurisdiction of the Pope, as they have ever since remained.[3]

But the influence of the Normans and the increasing Latin element was not favourable to the Greek Catholics; several of their eparchies (dioceses) were suppressed, whole parishes turned Latin, the numerous monasteries became decadent. By the beginning of the fifteenth century the Byzantines were on the verge of extinction, and an influx of refugees from Constantinople after 1453 did not do much to save them. Then for a hundred years there came colonists from Albania, following the alliance of Scanderbeg with Ferdinand I of Naples. Some of the immigrants were Latins, some Byzantines, and these saved their dying rite in Italy.[4]

As there were by now no Byzantine bishops in Italy, the Albanians were subjected to the local ordinaries, who encour-

---

[2] Liturgical rite has essentially nothing to do with patriarchate. The notion that all subjects of the same patriarch should have his rite is partly a result of the aggressive "uniformizing" of Constantinople. The Pope was patriarch of Byzantines in Illyricum as well as metropolitan of those in *Magna Graecia*. The great Archbishop of Canterbury, St. Theodore, was a Greek monk of Calabria; when Pope St. Vitalian appointed him in 664 to rule over us Latins he had to "change his rite" —and his style of hair-dressing (see Bede's *Ecclesiastical History*, IV, 1).

[3] At a council held by Pope Urban II at Bari in Apulia in 1098 certain Italo-Greek bishops threw doubt on the procession of the Holy Ghost from the Son (*"Filioque"*). They were confuted by St. Anselm, Archbishop of Canterbury.

[4] Pope Clement XI (1700–21) was a descendant of one of these Albanian families, which had settled in the Papal States.

aged, sometimes forced, them to turn Latin. (To the average
Western bishop of those days, Eastern subjects were a nuisance,
and at least suspect of heresy all the time! That orientals
have as much right to their "peculiarities" as Latins have to
theirs did not occur to them: the Popes, indeed, seem to have
been the only ones who never lost sight of this.) Moreover,
there was difficulty in recruiting and training their clergy,
though the Greek College at Rome was open to them, so that
the rite disappeared in Apulia and decreased fast elsewhere.
An Oratorian priest, George Guzzetta, started an Albanian
community at Piana in Sicily in 1716 and a seminary at Palermo
in 1734; during the century or so of their existence these
Byzantine Oratorians did much good work but were handi-
capped by their insistence on the Western principle of clerical
celibacy; the seminary is still in being. There was a seminary
for Calabria at Ullano from 1732 till 1860. Pope Clement XII
authorized the consecration of a bishop, who should ordain
priests but have no jurisdiction, for Byzantines in Calabria,
and one for those of Sicily was appointed by Pius VI.

Meantime, in 1742, Pope Benedict XIV issued the constitution *Etsi pastoralis*, which was a sort of compendium of canon
law for the Greeks and Albanians: their rites and customs are
to be kept, their privileges are confirmed, no Latin ordinary
is to interfere with their lawful usages or invite them to become
Latins, and a Byzantine vicar general must be appointed; the
Latin rite has no precedence as such over the Byzantine:
"before God there is neither Greek nor Jew nor barbarian
nor Scythian, for all are one in Christ." The effect of this was
to restore self-respect to the Greco-Albanians and put a brake
for the time being on their cultural and ecclesiastical decay;
moreover, *Etsi pastoralis* paved the way for other and more
far-reaching papal pronouncements on the true place of orientals in the Catholic economy.

PRESENT STATE

Italy. In 1919 Pope Benedict XV constituted a separate
eparchy for the Byzantines of Calabria, with its see at Lungro,

Mgr. John Mele being the first and present bishop. Though it is not in his jurisdiction, mention must be made of the church built for the Greek colony at Leghorn in 1605; the priest here is now a Melkite and his hundred parishioners are mixed Melkites, Italo-Greeks, and Italo-Albanians.

Sicily. At present the Sicilian Albanians are still subject to the Latin ordinaries of the place, who have Byzantine vicars general; but there is an ordaining bishop attached to the Panormitan seminary.

Parochial clergy. These make their studies in the "little" seminary founded by Pope Benedict XV at the abbey of Grottaferrata, at the Palermo seminary founded by Father Guzzetta, and at the Greek College in Rome.[5] Although surrounded by Western influence for so many centuries the Italo-Albanian priests have retained their right to marriage, and out of sixty about fifteen are married. The use of the traditional Greek clerical costume has been restored indoors and for formal occasions; most rectors of churches call themselves protopopes, i.e., archpriests.

Religious institutes. Both in the earlier and later Middle Ages the centres of Byzantinism in southern Italy were the numerous monasteries. To arrest their decline, Pope Gregory XIII in 1579 united them all into a congregation on the model of the Benedictine one of St. Justina of Padua; unfortunately it was also joined to the Spanish Basilian Order, a purely Western institute (founded 1559; now extinct), and this hastened the decay in Italy by a prolonged process of voluntary latinization; the houses were Greek almost only in name. Rodotà, the first ordaining bishop for Calabria, could still speak in 1758 of 43 struggling oriental monasteries "where once there were about a thousand"; today there are none left at all, with the distinguished exception of Grottaferrata and its dependencies.

About the year 980 a Greek abbot, St. Neilos of Rossano, and his monks fled before the Saracen raids on Calabria and,

---

[5] The direction of this college has been entrusted to the Benedictines since 1897. The monks adopt the Byzantine rite while employed there.

having long enjoyed Benedictine hospitality at Monte Cassino, established a monastery at Grottaferrata in the Alban hills in 1004. Here, at the very gates of Rome, there have been Greek monks ever since, a living witness that the Catholic Church is not solely a Latin institution. The history of the abbey has been eventful and troubled, and its Byzantinism not always above reproach. But Pope Leo XIII instituted a reform in this respect, and the Greek rites and observances are now restored almost in their integrity.

The community has at present fourteen hieromonks and nine monks, mostly Italo-Albanians. In addition to the "little" seminary for their rite, they conduct a printing establishment and an orphanage. In 1920 they took over the old monastery of Mezzoiuso in Sicily and made it a novitiate for the training of monks for apostolic work in Albania itself and later on Greece,[6] while in 1932 a daughter-house was started near Lungro.

There are some fifty Byzantine Sisters of several congregations engaged in teaching and other good works in Calabria and Sicily.

The Faithful. There are now only twenty villages of Italo-Greek-Albanians in Italy and six in Sicily where the Greek observances are maintained; the chief are Lungro, San Demetrio Corone, Piana dei Greci, and Palazzo Adriano. The people are all peasants, rather poverty-stricken in Italy, more prosperous in Sicily. There are 35,000 of them in the one country and 15,850 in the other, of whom a fair proportion (here and there whole villages) speak a somewhat debased Albanian as their usual language. A Greek dialect is still spoken in certain villages of Terra d'Otranto; there is evidence that it is derived primarily from the Greek of ancient times and not from later Byzantine colonists. It seems unavoidable that they should all in time become completely italianized and be absorbed into the Latin rite—but that time is still a long way off.

---

[6] The dissident Orthodox Greeks are rather proud of Grottaferrata and sympathetic toward its monks, because it was founded *before the schism* and has an unbroken Greek tradition.

OTHER JURISDICTION

United States. There were very large emigrations of Italo-Greeks at the end of the nineteenth century, mostly to the states of New York and Pennsylvania. Many of these were lost to the Church for lack of priests of their rite. The first priest was sent from Palermo in 1904, and he opened two churches in New York. There are no statistics of their number in U. S. A. today. Fifteen years ago they were said to be 20,000, but there has been a tendency greatly to overestimate the number of Catholic orientals in America.

PARTICULAR CUSTOMS

As their history would lead us to expect, the liturgy of the Byzantines underwent very serious modifications during the course of time in southern Italy, but in Sicily it was much better observed. These innovations have to a considerable extent been corrected and in most churches the Greek rite is now observed with a very fair degree of fidelity. They use the excellent books printed at Rome. But as the churches are nearly all too poor to afford *eikonostases*, and as statues, side-altars, etc., have been admitted into them, there is not much to distinguish them from the Latin churches. The Italo-Greeks adopted the Gregorian reckoning with the Catholic West in 1582, the first Easterns to do so. They have modified the Constantinopolitan calendar by celebrating certain feasts (e.g., All Saints, All Souls, St. Joseph) on their Roman as well as their Byzantine dates and by the addition of more modern feasts, e.g., Corpus Christi, the Sacred Heart, our Lady of the Rosary, St. Anthony of Padua, St. Francis of Paula. Confirmation is separated from Baptism and conferred by a bishop, and absolution is given in the Roman form. Pope Benedict XV restored the privilege of confirming to priests in the eparchy of Lungro but the reform has not yet been effected.

Their church music is a traditional version of that of Constantinople, and in some churches Albanian hymns are still sung (unhappily, organs have been introduced into their churches in America). As is natural, Benediction of the Blessed Sacrament and all the other "popular devotions" of the West have long been known among them.

BIBLIOGRAPHY

Fortescue: *The Uniate Eastern Churches* (Italo-Greeks and Melkites), (London, 1923).

Gaisser: *I canti ecclesiastici italo-greci* (Rome, 1905).

Rossini: *Canti tradizionali delle Colonie Italo-Greco-Albanesi* [the melodies made chromatic] (Birmingham, 1926).

2. THE RUTHENIANS

"Ruthenian" is the official ecclesiastical descriptive term for certain bodies of Catholics of the Byzantine rite found in Polish Galicia, Podcarpathia (Czechoslovakia and Hungary), and the Bukovina (Rumania), with colonies in North America and elsewhere. They all belong to one race, the same which inhabits the soviet socialist republic of the Ukraine and the Polish provinces of Volhynia and southern Polissia.

The Ruthenians are Slavs and, moreover, they may be justly regarded as the original Russians. After the fall of their great city of Kiev in 1240 to the Mongols the centre of state power gradually shifted to Moscow, and eventually the Muscovites, who were much less purely Slav than the people of the southwest, reserved for themselves the name of Great Russians and called the others Little Russians.[7] A third element, the White Russians, is now mainly confined to the regions of Poland around Grodno and Vilna and the corresponding part of Russia. Each of these three Russian elements has its own language, descended from a common tongue that was spoken by them all before the twelfth century.

During the nineteenth century considerable cultural self-consciousness arose among the Ruthenians or Little Russians, which by the end of the Great War developed into an acute nationalism. That is no concern of mine here, and I mention it for only one reason: a manifestation of this nationalism is to refuse the name Ruthenian, because that is what their foreign governors, Poles, Hungarians, etc., call them. They call themselves Ukrainians.[8] However, so far as the Catholics are concerned "Ruthenian" is still their official *ecclesiastical* desig-

---

[7] In the West the Russians were first called Ruthenes and then Muscovites.

[8] Historically, this is the far less noble and significant name of the two. *Ukraine* only means "the borderland" or "marches."

nation, and so I employ it in this book, varying it by "Ukrainian" when it seems convenient to do so: I use both terms without any political significance whatsoever.

GENERAL ECCLESIASTICAL HISTORY

St. Vladimir, the apostle of Russia, was a Northman and his capital Kiev, "the God-protected mother of Russian cities," was in the heart of what is known now as "the Ukraine." For two hundred and fifty years it was the political and ecclesiastical centre of Russia, and the chief hierarchs continued to call themselves Metropolitans of Kiev for two hundred years after they had resided at Moscow. Accordingly, for all this time from 988 until the Metropolitan Isidore had to flee from Moscow in 1443 after promulgating the Union of Florence, the religious history of the Ruthenians was the same as that of the Russians in general (see pp. 125-126).

In 1458 Pope Pius II nominated a monk called Gregory to be metropolitan of Kiev, and by arrangement with Casimir IV of Poland he was allowed to exercise jurisdiction over the eight eparchies of the Kiev ecclesiastical province that were then under the control of Poland and Lithuania.[9] This lasted only till the beginning of the sixteenth century, when they slipped back into schism. During the second half of that century the Jesuits came to Vilna, Yaroslav, Polotsk, and elsewhere and at once set themselves to work for the definitive reunion of the Ruthenian bishops and their flocks, the leading spirits being Father Peter Skarga (d. 1612) and Father Anthony Possevino (d. 1611). At length in 1595 Michael Ragoza, Metropolitan of Kiev, and the bishops of Vladimir, Lutsk, Polotsk, Pinsk, and Kholm met at Brest-Litovsk in Lithuania and petitioned the Holy See to admit them to its communion, and on December 23 the reunion was solemnly proclaimed in the hall of Constantine at the Vatican. Only the bishops of Lwów (Lemberg, Leopol) and Przemysl stood out.

At once the enemies of the union, led by these two bishops

[9] Kiev and the part of Little Russia west of it was under the political suzerainty of Poland and Lithuania from the middle of the fourteenth century till 1686.

and Prince Ostrozhsky, began a violent opposition, but happily
Ragoza (d. 1600) was succeeded by two energetic and capable
prelates, the second of whom was an outstanding figure in
Ruthenian church history, Joseph Benjamin Rutsky, a convert
from Calvinism. While he occupied the throne of Kiev (1614–
1637) the bishop of Polotsk, Josaphat Kuntzevitch, was slain
out of hatred of the faith in November, 1623; he had been
known as the "thief of souls," and fourteen years later his
chief opponent Melety Smotritzky himself became a Catholic.[10]

In 1620, encouraged by the dissident Patriarchs of Constantinople and Jerusalem and aided by Protestant sectaries, a
dissident hierarchy was set up side by side with the Catholic
one, and eventually in 1632 the attacks of the Zaporozhsky
Cossacks of the Dnieper forced the Polish king, Ladislas VII,
to recognize it; in the following year the city of Kiev was lost
to the union, the famous Orthodox theologian, Peter Mogila,
becoming its metropolitan. There followed a period of pressure
and persecution from schismatic Cossacks, Lutheran Swedes,
and Mohammedan Tartars that ended only with the election
of John Sobieski to the throne of Poland in 1674. In 1692 the
Bishop of Przemysl brought his flock into the Church, in 1700
the Bishop of Lwów did the same, and in 1702 another dissident bishop; schism had now practically disappeared from
Polish territory. The metropolitan continued to have the title
of Kiev but lived at Radomysl, in the Ukraine.

At this time the Ruthenian Catholics must have numbered
about twelve millions, but during the seventeenth and eighteenth centuries practically the whole of the nobility and the
bigger landowners (*boyary*) became polonized and passed to
the Latin rite, in spite of a decree of Pope Urban VIII in 1624
that forbade them to do so. This divided and greatly weakened
the faithful, most of whom had been reduced to serfdom by
the Poles, for the trials that were to come.

From early in the eighteenth century Russia began more and
more to interfere with the internal affairs of Poland, and in
1772 there began that process known as "the partition of

---

[10] St. Josaphat was canonized in 1867 and his feast extended to the
Western Church by Pope Leo XIII in 1882. We keep it on November 14.

Poland," which was concluded in 1795.[11] The fate of the Ruthenians varied according to the power into whose hands they fell. Russia eventually got back all the territory in which there were any Ruthenians, except Galicia, and it soon became apparent that the government's intention was to obtain control over and then suppress those Catholics who were not Latins. Catherine II and Alexander I reduced the Ruthenian episcopal sees to three, monasteries were closed, and churches handed over to the Orthodox. After the Polish insurrection of 1831 more repressive measures were taken, a treacherous Catholic, one Joseph Siemashko, was nominated to the episcopate by Nicholas I and, on the death of the faithful Metropolitan Bulgak in 1838, this man induced the two remaining bishops to sign, and over 1,300 clergy to assent to, an act of union with the schismatic state Church of Russia. The remaining clergy and very many of the lay people refused to follow them, so the government resorted to open force: Catholic baptisms and weddings were forbidden and Orthodox priests intruded into the churches; all religious houses were shut and their goods confiscated; those who resisted were flogged or exiled to Siberia, and 160 priests were degraded and imprisoned in remote monasteries. The Ruthenian Catholic church was dead in Russia. Only in the Kholm district, which was ceded by Austria in 1815 and was less severely dealt with, did it linger on till 1875 and even a few years longer, during which some Jesuits ministered to the Ruthenians at the peril of their lives.[12] When Nicholas II granted religious toleration in 1905

[11] As we have seen, the *Ruthenian part* of the then Poland (Galicia, Volhynia, and part of the present Ukrainian republic) together with White Russia (where there were many Ruthenians) was indubitably Russian.

[12] This grievous persecution was not primarily religious, but arose from the notion that every subject of the Russian state must be a member of the Russian church. The Latin Catholics of Poland also were persecuted, but their Catholicism was not regarded as so iniquitous because they were not Russians or regarded as "perverts from Orthodoxy." Nevertheless that Russia did not otherwise or in general oppress the Ukrainians is shown by the fact that, while Jews, Poles, Lithuanians, and Great Russian sectaries emigrated wholesale, Ukrainians did not: they were quite "at home." Ukrainian emigration was from Austria-Hungary, a foreign land.

over 300,000 of these ex-Catholics and their children returned
to the Church, one third of whom were *Uporstvujushchie*,
"Obstinates," old people who for thirty years and more had
refused to attend the Orthodox churches; but as Catholic
Byzantines were still illegal they had to become Latins. The
new Catholics in Volhynia (see p. 76) are also descendants
of the Ruthenians who were forcibly "decatholicized" during
the nineteenth century.

THE GALICIAN RUTHENIANS

The story of the Ruthenians of Galicia,[13] who came under
the sway of Austria, is a less unhappy but far from satisfactory
one. There were (apart from Kholm, which was to go to
Russia in 1815) two episcopal sees, Lwów and Przemysl (the
last two sees to join the Union of Brest are the only ones that
have survived), now under different civil rule from their
metropolitan, which caused difficulties. The Holy See solved
them in 1807 by making Lwów an archiepiscopate and uniting
with it the old metropolitan see of Galicz, which had been
revived a few years before. Two of the occupants of this
see have been elevated to the cardinalate, Mgr. Michael Levit-
sky in 1856 and Mgr. Sylvester Sembratovitch in 1895.[14] It
was not till 1885 that the huge eparchy of Lwów was reduced
in area by forming a new one from it, Stanislawow.

Under the rule of the Austrian emperors the Ruthenians
had full religious liberty; serfdom was abolished in 1848 and
in 1860 Galicia was given a measure of civil autonomy and its
own assembly. The Ruthenians, having lost their natural
leaders by polonization, were all peasants, but from the middle
of the nineteenth century a cultured and enterprising middle
class began to develop and an *intelligenzia* made its appearance. For this they had to thank their married clergy, from

---

[13] The term "Ruthenian," without qualification, generally refers to
these.

[14] Very few orientals have been made cardinals. The office is radically
in relation to the local church at Rome: that is why they are called
"Cardinals of the Holy Roman Church." They elect the bishop of
Rome—who is as well supreme pontiff of the Universal Church, *ex
officio* and *iure divino*.

A CHARACTERISTIC WOODEN UKRAINIAN CHURCH IN POLISH GALICIA

The Most Reverend Mgr. ANDREW SZEPTICKY,
Ruthenian Archbishop of Lwów and
Metropolitan of Halicz

(*Byzantine Rite*)

whose children this new class was chiefly recruited. The Ruthenians were jealous of their former overlords the Poles, and the ill-feeling of the Poles was aggravated by the later policy of the Austrian government, which favoured the Ruthenians in order to counterbalance Polish influence and fostered the "Ukrainian movement" as a political move against Russia. On the other hand, the Ruthenians themselves were not of one mind politically: at the time of the outbreak of war in 1914 they were divided into five parties.

Their subsequent troubles did much to unite them. First they were suspected of pro-Russianism, and many were interned with considerable brutality, including 300 of the clergy. General Brusilov captured Lwów on September 3, 1914, and again many were interned or deported to Russia, this time on suspicion of being pro-Austrian and to conciliate the Poles. Also full liberty was given to Orthodox clergy to cross the Podhorze and the Bug and do what they could with the Catholic Ruthenians. In circumstances in which there was so much, humanly speaking, in favour of schism, the solid Catholicity of the Ruthenians was well vindicated. Only 29 priests turned Orthodox, and of these 27 were chased from their cures by their flocks; among the 1,800 Ruthenian parishes of Galicia the state Church of Russia was able to establish only about one hundred temporarily in communion with itself.

At the end of 1917 a Ukrainian republic was proclaimed at Kiev and in October, 1918, a Western Ukrainian republic at Lwów, whereupon Poland assumed sovereign authority over the whole of Galicia. From November, 1918, the Ruthenians and the Poles were at war and, like all civil wars, the struggle was pursued with detestable bitterness and unscrupulosity on both sides. It is difficult to avoid the conclusion that a deliberate attempt was made by the Poles to cut off the supply of Ruthenian clergy and cripple the resources of Ruthenian culture: all three seminaries and two monasteries were closed, libraries pillaged and burned, printing presses carried off; Catholic Polish troops sacked churches of their fellow-Catholics, cast down *eikons*, desecrated vestments and vessels, and even treated sacrilegiously the Blessed Sacrament. It is not surprising if certain Ruthenian priests of Tarnopol so far forgot their Christian duty as to "preach in their sermons the extermination of the Poles," as the Polish government, whether truly or not, alleged. The Ruthenian resistance was short-lived, and from January to October, 1919, while Poland was fighting Russia, Galicia was occupied by bolshevist troops nearly to the gates of Lwów. Eventually, in 1923, in consideration of a promise (never fulfilled) by the Poles to give the Ukrainians an autonomous constitution, the Conference of Ambassadors confirmed Eastern Galicia as a province of Poland.

It is not difficult to imagine the results of these events—two deportations, two military invasions, and a civil war—on the Ukrainian people and the Ruthenian church; their marvelous recovery is due in the first place to the activity and ability of their metropolitan, Mgr. Szepticky, who has laboured day and night under the most trying difficulties both of the situation in itself and of obstacles deliberately put in his way. As an example of the one, the sixty priests in the deaneries of Rogatin and Drogobitch in 1913 had by execution, deportation, and natural decrease been reduced to five in 1920; of the other, from the beginning of the civil war the metropolitan was interned in his house by the Poles and not completely at liberty for over twelve months.

But history has left a terrible heritage of ill-will between Latin Poles and Byzantine Ruthenians, which the relations between them during the past ten years have only intensified. Not all the leaders are of the character and spirituality of Mgr. Szepticky on the one side and Mgr. Henry Przezdziecky, Bishop of Podlachia, on the other,[15] and such outrages as Marshal Pilsudsky's "pacification" of 1930 can lead only to fresh disasters among these Catholic peoples.

---

[15] See, for example, his pastoral letter on *L'Oeuvre de l'Union en Pologne* (Warsaw, 1932).

PRESENT STATE

Organization. The Ruthenians of Galicia form a single ecclesiastical province containing, in spite of their numbers, only three eparchies, viz., Lwów, Przemysl (with the added titles of Sanok and Sambor), and Stanislawow. The archbishop's full style is "Archbishop of Lwów, Metropolitan of Galicz, and Bishop of Kamenez, Primate of Lodomeria," and the see has been occupied since 1900 by Mgr. Andrew, Count Szepticky.[16] By the concordat entered into between the Holy See and Poland in 1925 it was enacted that in future these sees when vacant shall be filled by nomination from Rome, subject to the Polish government's approval of the nominees. Each Ruthenian see has a chapter of canons, as in the West. (Such chapters are unknown to Eastern canon law.)

Parochial clergy. The great seminary of Lwów was founded in 1783 and has had a very fruitful career; it entered on a new phase of much promise and importance in 1931, when it was erected into an academy of theology in fulfilment of the university aspirations that it has always had. At present there are in the seminary 220 theological students and 120 juniors. The other two eparchies also have seminaries, both established at the end of the eighteenth century. The Ruthenian College at Rome was erected by Pope Leo XIII in 1897, the Emperor Francis Joseph of Austria providing a generous subsidy. It was at first confided to the Jesuits but was handed over to the direction of the Ruthenian Basilian monks in 1904. It houses about 50 students. Others go to Innsbruck University and to the *Augustineum* at Vienna. Of the 2,600 secular priests, 80 per cent are married, but the celibate ideal is beginning very slowly to gain ground; this has an important economic aspect, for while, as has been said, a married clergy has in the past been a source of strength to Ruthenian religion and culture,

---

[16] Both religiously and civilly this revered hierach has been to his countrymen what the late Cardinal Mercier was to his. See an article by the present writer "A Protagonist of Church Unity and Ruthenian Culture" in *Central-Blatt & Social Justice*, Vol. XXV, Nos. 4–6 (Saint Louis, 1932).

nevertheless the burden of a family is often very grievous to pastors in the poor rural parishes that predominate. Of the 1267 parishes of Lwów, 482 do not have a resident pastor.

Each bishop has an *archdeacon* (who, contrary to Eastern custom, is a priest) among his officials, and there are numerous *deans* in charge of districts (the Byzantine name for such, archpriest or protopope, has been dropped). The diaconate, as among most Catholic Byzantines, is invariably a step to the priesthood and not a permanent office even in the monasteries. Roman titles of honour are conferred on the Ruthenian clergy, resulting in some very surprising prelatical costumes. Ordinary clerical dress is a black cassock and a round cap rather lower than the Russian brimless *kalemaukion;* the *rason* has been given up, and secular priests are often indistinguishable from Latins; most of them are clean-shaven, at any rate in the towns and in America.

Religious institutes. The most interesting monastic body not only in Galicia but among all the Catholic Eastern churches is the *Studites*, of whom a brief account will be found on pages 264–266. They are, however, less in the public eye than the more numerous and old-established "Basilians," to whom the Ruthenians owe so much. At the time of the Union of Brest there was a number of monasteries among the Ruthenians, and within the next twenty years St. Josaphat Kuntzevitch and Joseph Benjamin Rutsky had inaugurated a reform at the monastery of the Holy Trinity at Vilna. In 1617 this was organized as a congregation, with a superior general and a form of organization based on that of the Society of Jesus—already the monastic idea was being superseded. Before the suppression by the Emperor Nicholas I in 1832 there were 96 Basilian monasteries in Lithuania, Russian Poland, and the Ukraine, and by 1882 what little remained of the Ruthenian Order of St. Basil in Galicia was in dire need of reform, after having been for long the backbone of the Ukrainian clergy. In that year Pope Leo XIII entrusted the work to the fathers of the Society of Jesus, who carried it out with efficiency and thoroughness, beginning at the monastery of Dobromil whence it spread to the other houses. But the Ruthenian Basilians became in the process exactly like a Western religious congregation and, beginning as monks, have now become, in fact if not in name, clerks regular, though they are bound to choir-office. They take vows, temporary or solemn, and each religious is either a priest or a "lay-brother"; the last named must know some useful trade. In this capacity the Ruthenian Basilians have done a very great pastoral and educative work among the Catholic Ukrainians, especially in the country districts, and have carried their activity overseas to the Americas. They have 23 monasteries, 127 priests, 167 clerics, and 171 lay-brothers, and are now known officially as the *Basilians of St. Josaphat*. Their abbot general (*archimandrite*) lives at Rome and there is an abbot provincial (*protohegumenos*) for each of the three Galician provinces, for Podcarpathia, for North America, and for Brazil; the local superior is an abbot (*hegumenos*).

They have abandoned the traditional monastic dress of the East and wear a black tunic with hood, belt, and cloak (*mandyas*), and their choir-office is recited, not sung.

In 1913 Mgr. Szepticky introduced some *Redemptorists* from Belgium into his eparchy, from whom have sprung a Byzantine vice-province of that congregation; its Polish houses number four, with some thirty priests.

There are about a thousand Ukrainian nuns in Galicia, all engaged in active works of charity (except a few Studites). Three hundred of them are Basilians, and the rest belong to other local congregations.

The Faithful number about 3½ million in Galicia, more rather than less. At least 90 per cent of them are peasants, and they are people of outstanding intelligence, cultural activity, and farming ability among the huge block of peasant peoples that stretches from the Pindus mountains to Danzig and from the Black Sea to Tirol. They have remained faithful to communion with Rome throughout the generations of subjection to Polish and polonized Ruthenian landlords under the Polish and Austrian kingdoms, and during the years of oppression and persecution by the Polish republic since the Great War.[17]

In spite of its violent discouragement the people still habitually use the language now called Ukrainian (across the border in Russia their Orthodox brethren have adopted it for the Liturgy); it is, as I have said before, cognate with Russian, both being variations of a common tongue, evolved since the twelfth century.

OTHER JURISDICTIONS

United States. From 1879 there have been emigrations of Ruthenians to the United States, both from Galicia and Podcarpathia (see pp. 76 ff.; 94). The first priest to be sent was Father Ivan Valansky, who in 1886 opened the first Catholic church of the Byzantine rite in America, at Shenandoah, Pennsylvania. The number of immigrants increased rapidly and in 1907 Pope Pius X appointed a bishop of their rite for them, not, however, as ordinary but as an auxiliary to the local Latin bishop.

The arrival of numerous Byzantine Catholics in the country was naturally fraught with difficulties. Not only did they bring with them all their own political and national rivalries (e.g., between Galicians and Podcarpathians)—this was perhaps to be expected; but they also had a very bad reception, or none at all, from their Latin brethren in the United States. It is difficult to write of this matter in measured terms, so I will quote the words of the late Andrew Shipman, of New York: "These Ruthenians have continued to practise their ancient Greek-Slavonic rites and usages . . . strange to the Catholic accustomed only to the Roman Rite, and [they] have made [the

---

[17] To grasp the full religious import of this it must be remembered that the Poles also are Catholics. It is a matter of which little is known in English-speaking countries. The persecution has been well documented by Emil Revyuk in *Polish Atrocities in the Ukraine* (New Jersey, 1931). If, as it is not impossible, a day comes when the Ukrainians of Poland break off and associate themselves with the Ukrainians of Russia, either as an atheist soviet republic or as a dissident Orthodox state, then at least some, and a heavy part, of the responsibility for that tragedy will rest on those Poles who have been Poles first and Catholics afterward.

Ruthenians] *objects of distrust and even active dislike*" (italics mine). A curious interpretation of Catholicism, both as a word and as a religion![18]

The question of a celibate secular clergy has for long been one of the chief difficulties. The bishops of U. S. A. found the presence of married priests embarrassing, and the apostolic letter *Ea semper* of 1907 decreed that only celibate Ruthenian priests should be admitted or ordained in North America. This, and other innovations in their customs, was strongly resented, the Orthodox made the most of them, and 10,000 Ruthenians joined the dissident Russians. Eventually the Holy See withdrew the prohibition of married priests in the United States (though no married men may be ordained there) and otherwise modified *Ea semper*, but further legislation by the decree *Cum data* in 1929 has again caused trouble.

In 1924 the Ruthenians were put under the direct jurisdiction of two bishops of their rite, one for the Podcarpathians and the other for the Galicians. The last-named number 244,000 with 87 priests and 95 churches or chapels, and their bishop, Mgr. Constantine Bohachevsky resides at Philadelphia, which is the principal Ruthenian district. They have a dozen churches in New York and its vicinity, St. George's on East Twentieth Street being the first; St. Michael's and St. Nicholas's at Yonkers and SS. Peter and Paul's in Jersey City are fine examples of Russo-Byzantine church buildings. There is a junior seminary in Connecticut, and four houses of Basilian nuns.

Canada. Ruthenian emigration to Canada began in the nineties of the last century, chiefly from Galicia. The first church, SS. Vladimir and Olga's, was opened at Winnipeg in 1900, with a Slovak pastor, Father Damascene Polivka, but the dearth of clergy was so chronic that for a time (and still in a measure) the emigrants were a prey to Protestant and other

---

[18] This attitude is not a thing of the past. I have heard Ruthenian Catholic priests from U. S. A., well-bred, cultured men, complain bitterly of the way they are treated there in general by the clergy and lay people of the Latin rite. I have a letter before me at this moment, giving grievous particulars: it is dated last year (1933).

proselytizers. The first priests to come to the rescue, at the instance of Mgr. Langevin of Saint-Boniface, were French-Canadians and Belgian Redemptorists (Father Achille Delaere was their moving spirit), who soon were allowed to adopt the Byzantine rite. In 1913, at the instance of Mgr. Szepticky, the Holy See appointed a bishop with personal jurisdiction over the Ukrainians of Canada, but the shortage of clergy has continued to be so great that the religious state of the people is still far from satisfactory. The rule against married priests means, practically, that only widowers and monks can be sent from Europe and the supply of American-born priests is insufficient, while in general the attitude of the Canadian Latins is as unhelpful as in the United States. The Ukrainians "are not worth saving" is the opinion of some Catholics expressed to Mr. W. L. Scott, K.C., of Ottawa!

There are 300,000 or more Ruthenians in Canada, mostly farming in Alberta, Saskatchewan, and Manitoba, though there are numbers in Montreal and other cities, with only 57 priests to look after them. Of these, 20 are Basilian monks, whose monastery is at Mundare in Alberta, and eight Redemptorists, who have establishments at Yorkton and Ituna in Saskatchewan. There are 270 churches and chapels, of which only 34 have resident priests: the holy Liturgy is celebrated in half of them only about four times a year. The bishop, Mgr. Basil Ladyka, lives at Winnipeg; he has established a "little seminary," and some 30 students are preparing for the priesthood in various Latin seminaries. Much good work is being done by nuns of various congregations, who number about 150.

Both in Canada and U. S. A., there is considerable literary activity among the Ukrainians, newspapers are published in their language, and those who have been able to avail themselves of "higher education" have done so well as strongly to confirm the high opinion of Ukrainian abilities that is current in Europe.

Brazil and Argentine. There are 52,000 Ruthenians, mostly in the state of Parana in Brazil, with 13 priests, of whom seven are Basilian monks. The 15,000 of the Argentine have only

UKRAINIAN CHURCH OF ST. NICHOLAS,
AT CHICAGO, ILLINOIS
(Jurisdiction of Mgr. Constantine Bohachevsky,
Bishop in Philadelphia)

UKRAINIAN CHURCH OF THE ALL-HOLY MOTHER OF GOD,
AT MARION HEIGHTS, PENNSYLVANIA

(Church built by Mr. Peter H. Bryll; the screen painted
by the late Father Gleb Verchovsky)

one or two priests. They are all under the jurisdiction of the local bishops, subject to special regulations of the Sacred Eastern Congregation.

Elsewhere. The 62,000 Catholic Ruthenians of the Bukovina, formerly subject to Austria, are now incorporated in the Rumanian eparchy of Maramures, in charge of a special vicar general.

The few thousand Ruthenians scattered in other parts of the world are unprovided with churches, except at Vienna, where there is the fine baroque church of St. Barbara, taken from the suppressed Jesuits in 1775 and made the chapel of an ecclesiastical college for Ruthenians and Rumanians by the Empress Maria Teresa. It became a parish-church for Byzantines in 1784 and has had a very eventful history. A seminary was attached thereto from 1852 till 1892, and this *Barbareum* gave 400 priests to the several Catholic Byzantine bodies of the Austro-Hungarian Empire. At one time during the Great War the parish priest was giving spiritual and material help to 15,000 refugees of his rite who had fled to Vienna.

PARTICULAR CUSTOMS

So considerable are the modifications introduced into the Byzantine liturgy (which in ordinary speech they refer to as "the Divine Worship") by the Ruthenians in the past two hundred years that some people have been misled into the error of regarding their version as a quite separate rite. While none of these innovations were necessary, and some of them definitely undesirable, it is to be noted that some points of divergence from standard Russian usage so far from being innovations are precisely those observances which were swept away by the Patriarch of Moscow, Nikon, in the seventeenth century, whereby the great schism of the Starovery was caused.[19]

The chief alterations made in the Liturgy (particularly by

[19] Mgr. Szepticky has reconciled a number of these "Old Believers" to the Catholic Church, and given them a large chapel at Lwów, where all their traditional ritual customs are observed.

the Synod of Zamosc in 1720) are: the amice and alb are worn
in place of the *stikharion;* the Latin paten and purificator are
used instead of the *diskos* and sponge, and *ripidia* have disappeared; after the *proskomide* the holy doors of the *eikonostasis*
are opened and so remain throughout the Liturgy; the order
of some of the chants is altered; the procession at the great
entrance is cut down; the words *i ot Syna (Filioque)* are
added to the creed and reverences are made at "his only Son"
and "was made man"; at the consecration a bell is rung; hot
water is not put into the chalice before communion, nor
blessed bread distributed; the people receive the Blessed Sacrament in both kinds from a spoon, but kneeling; there is an
equivalent of *Domine non sum dignus* before communion and
two washings of the fingers have been introduced; the book
is moved from side to side of the altar at "low Mass"; the
vessels are left on the altar till the end of the Liturgy; and
there is a sequence of liturgical colours for vestments, elsewhere unknown in the East. A deacon is rarely seen assisting
at the Liturgy except in cathedral and monastic churches,
and then he is generally a priest, and he wears dalmatic and
alb (ungirdled) instead of a *stikharion.* Concelebration only
takes place on certain pontifical occasions, with the inevitable
result of the appearance of side altars in large churches.

In the bull *Apostolatus officium* by which Pope Benedict
XIII confirmed the acts of the Synod of Zamosc there was a
note of warning against spoiling the integrity of the Byzantine
Liturgy, and in approving the *typikon* (constitutions) of the
Studite monks in 1923 the Sacred Eastern Congregation declared: "It is the wish of this Congregation that the monks
observe the Byzantine rite in all its purity, getting rid of
all the alterations whatsoever in use among the Ruthenian
people and sanctioned by the Synod of Zamosc." It is one
of the objects of those monks to encourage the restoration of
liturgical purity among the people, but unfortunately the
clergy are attached to the old ways as "our tradition." It is a
great pity, for more reasons than one; Ruthenian "hybridization" is continually used as an argument to prove that "Rome

does not really respect the Eastern rites" and to dissuade dissident orientals from becoming Catholics.

For the administration of the sacraments (especially Penance) and other rites, the Byzantine offices have been freely interpolated with prayers translated into Church-Slavonic from the Roman books, without a shadow of necessity, and the propagation of Western "popular devotions" leads sometimes to fantastic results. The one Eastern usage above all that the Ruthenians ought to have got rid of they have preserved: the Julian calendar. This unhappy observance has a still more unhappy reason—it is still further to differentiate themselves from their secular enemies, the Poles. Their strong objection to going to a Latin church even when no other is available (noticeable in America) is largely due to the same reason: the behaviour of the Poles has made them suspicious and hostile toward all Latin Catholics. Infinitely regrettable—but more understandable than the attitude of Latin Catholics toward Ruthenians.

A number of less ancient Western feasts have been introduced into Galicia, sometimes with altered date: e.g., Corpus Christi, the Holy Trinity, the Sacred Heart, the Seven Sorrows of our Lady. Among the holydays of obligation are St. Josaphat, "the Martyr of Unity," St. Vladimir, and his two sons SS. Romanus and David (Boris and Gleb). The Russian habits of fasting have been modified, but the Eastern identification of fasting and abstinence is retained. Ukrainian racial feeling has happily ensured the preservation of their most lovely church music. Like most Catholic orientals the Ruthenians now make use of the Western form of rosary, but their version of the Hail Mary is different and includes a mention of the mystery pertinent to each decade.

BIBLIOGRAPHY

Likovsky, *Union de l'Eglise romaine conclue à Brest en 1596* (Paris, c. 1898).

Guépin, *Saint Josaphat et l'Eglise gréco-slave.* 2 vols. (Paris, Poitiers, 1897-8).

Korolevsky, *Le Metropolite André Szeptyckyj* (Grottaferrata, 1920).

*Tiltman, *Peasant Europe* (London, 1934).

Delaere, *Mémoire sur les tentatives de schisme . . . des Ruthènes de l'Ouest canadien* (Quebec, 1908).

Scott, *The Ukrainians: our most pressing problem* (Toronto, c. 1930).

*Rudnitsky, *The Ukraine and the Ukrainians* (New Jersey, 1922).

3. THE PODCARPATHIAN RUTHENIANS

GENERAL ECCLESIASTICAL HISTORY

Probably since the year 1339, certainly since the middle of the fifteenth century, there has been a large settlement of Little and White Russians on the southern side of the Carpathians, in what was formerly Hungarian territory and is now part of Czechoslovakia (Podkarpatska Rus). In 1652 most of these people were led by their clergy into communion with the Catholic Church, a monk named Peter Rostoshynsky, who had received consecration at schismatic hands, being recognized as their bishop (Union of Ungvar). Very troublesome conflicts of jurisdiction arose between the successors of Rostoshynsky, the Latin primate, and the Ruthenian metropolitans north of the Carpathians. These were resolved in 1771, when Pope Clement XIV, at the request of Queen Maria-Teresa, erected the Ruthenian eparchy of Mukachevo (Munkacs), subject to the primate of Hungary.

After the war of 1914–18 these Ruthenians came under the rule of Czechoslovakia, and a serious schism broke out in 1920. Within three years seventy villages, involving 100,000 people, had turned Orthodox. The cause was fundamentally racial and cultural. These people insist that they are Russians (as they are), and their experience is that the effect of the policy of the local Catholic authorities, civil and religious, has been to make them Magyar or Slovak; moreover the priests had got culturally and socially out of touch with their peasant flocks. These same priests were entirely loyal to Catholicism, and the schism has been to a considerable extent mended.

PRESENT STATE

Organization. There are two eparchies of Podcarpathian Ruthenians, Mukachevo and Preshov, their bishops being suffragan to the Latin Archbishop of Esztergom (Gran); those still domiciled in Hungary form an administration apostolic under an episcopal exarch at Miszkolcs. The two cathedrals have chapters of canons.

Parochial clergy. These are trained in the college of their rite at Uzhorod (Ungvar) or in Latin seminaries. They are mostly married, and a French observer who knows them well characterizes them as "well-instructed, affable, of a real Christian spirit . . . worthy of all respect, of simple habits free from pretensions and 'bossiness' "; but the priesthood tends as it were to pass from father to son and to form a sacerdotal caste.

Religious institutes. There are three small monasteries of *Basilians of St. Josaphat* (see above), and two small houses of Byzantine *Redemptorists*.

The Faithful are nearly all peasants, very self-sufficient and particularist, but sincerely religious. They have been called the "poorest peasants in Europe," but they are fortunate in this respect, that the attitude of the Czechoslovakian government toward them is very much more just and benevolent than that of the Poles toward their brethren across the mountains in Galicia. They number 578,000. Czechoslovakia is 80 per cent Catholic, with about 150,000 Orthodox, including the Podcarpathian schismatics.

OTHER JURISDICTIONS

United States. Of the 553,000 Catholic Ruthenian emigrants in the U. S. A., 309,000 are Podcarpathians, and they played the predominant part in the troubles referred to on page 87, being particularly tenacious for their married clergy. In 1924 the Holy See gave them a bishop of their own, subject to the delegate apostolic at Washington, whose cathedral is at Homestead, Pennsylvania. He has 144 priests, who serve 176 churches. The present bishop is Mgr. Basil Takacs.

Canada. The Podcarpathian Ruthenians of Canada and elsewhere are organized with their Galician brethren (p. 87).

Particular Customs

The particulars already given of the modification of the Slav-Byzantine rite in Galicia apply also to the Podcarpathians. This was precisely one of the elements in the schism of 1920, and steps are now being taken to remedy these just grievances by a restoration of liturgical purity. It is hoped that the movement will spread to the United States, where the "superior" attitude of Latin Catholics has helped to encourage orientals to imitate their practices, regardless of their suitability to the Eastern religious temperament. The Podcarpathians sedulously maintain general congregational participation in the liturgical singing, their traditional music being a particularly lovely variation of that of the Galician Ruthenians.

BIBLIOGRAPHY

Vassili, "The Podcarpathian Schism" in *Pax*, Nos. 147 and 150 (Prinknash Priory, 1934).

4. THE HUNGARIANS

GENERAL ECCLESIASTICAL HISTORY

The so-called Hungarians of the Byzantine rite are in fact Ruthenians from the Carpathians and some Rumanians who, living in the middle of the great Hungarian plain, have lost their own languages and become almost completely magyarized. For long they were divided between five Ruthenian and Rumanian eparchies, till in 1912 Pope Pius X, to the satisfaction both of the faithful concerned and of the Hungarian civil authorities who feared the influence of foreign bishops, united them all into the new eparchy of Hajdudorog. After the war of 1914–18 over half of the parishes concerned were returned to the jurisdiction of Rumanian bishops on the formation of the kingdom of Great Rumania.

PRESENT STATE

Organization. The Bishop of Hajdudorog is a suffragan of the Latin Archbishop at Esztergom. His cathedral is at Hajdudorog, but he lives at Nyiregyhaza where he has another episcopal church, with a chapter of canons. Aspirants for the priesthood are trained in the general Ruthenian seminaries.

The Faithful. Even since the dismemberment of the eparchy in 1919 its subjects are still numerous, 142,000, mostly peasants. The rest of the Catholics of Hungary are Latins; there are 24,000 dissident Orthodox.

PARTICULAR CUSTOMS

The Byzantine rite is used according to the hybridized version of the Ruthenian liturgical books. But having lost their own language, the people of Hajdudorog found difficulty in maintaining their congregational singing in Staroslav, and a movement arose to substitute Magyar (Hungarian) as their liturgical language. Translations of hymns, etc., and then of the Liturgies were made, and these were adopted without authorization in a number of churches. In 1912 Greek was authoritatively imposed for all liturgical services and three years were given for the change to be effected. For several good reasons this has not taken place (e.g., Greek—and Byzantine chant— is even more difficult for the people to learn than Staroslav); accordingly, Magyar is now used in all churches, with the approval of the bishop. For those services not yet translated, the singers continue to do as best they can with Staroslav. In the 1920 edition of the Liturgies the Greek text of the *anaphoras* is printed parallel with the Magyar.

5. THE YUGOSLAVS

GENERAL ECCLESIASTICAL HISTORY

The small body of Catholic Yugoslavs of the Byzantine rite is made up of a nucleus of croatized Serbs to which other elements have been added. When Matthias Corvinus, King of Hungary, recaptured Bosnia from the Turks he established on the border military colonies of refugee Serbs of the Orthodox Church. They nominally came into communion with Rome, but it was not made real until 1611, when their bishop, Simeon Vretanji, was recognized by Pope Paul V as Byzantine vicar of the Bishop of Zagreb. He lived at the monastery of Marcha, a great centre for Serbian reunion, of which there was some talk at this time, many Serbs having fled into Hungary from the Turks. After a troubled period the Serbs of Croatia were given a diocesan bishop by Pope Pius VI in 1777; his see was at Krizevtsi, under the primate of Hungary.

During the eighteenth century there was a migration of Podcarpathian Ruthenians to the southwest, and another of Galicians to Bosnia and Slavonia at the end of the nineteenth; there are also some Rumanians and Bulgarians from Macedonia in this heterogeneous collection, held together by the Catholic faith and their common Eastern rite.

PRESENT STATE

Organization. The Bishop of Krizevtsi, who is now a suffragan of the Latin Archbishop of Zagreb, has jurisdiction over all Catholics of Byzantine rite in Serbia. His cathedral has a chapter of four canons.

Parochial clergy are formed in the seminary of Zagreb (founded 1685), which is directed by Basilian monks. The parishes are arranged in archpresbyterates or deaneries. Most of the clergy are married.

Religious institutes. There are three *Friars Minor* of the Byzantine rite working in this eparchy. They wear the *rason* over the brown Franciscan tunic and cord, with *kalemaukion* instead of the hood. The *Basilian nuns* are represented by four convents with 26 religious.

The Faithful total 41,600 souls, among whom Ruthenians are most numerous and the Serbs next. The last-named call themselves Croats and speak their tongue; the other elements all conserve the language of their respective countries of origin. The people are nearly all peasants. There are 5½ million dissident Orthodox in Yugoslavia, and rather more Latin Catholics.

PARTICULAR CUSTOMS

The common liturgical language of these people is church Slavonic. They observe the Byzantine rite and usages in, on the whole, a high degree of purity.

BIBLIOGRAPHY

Picot, *Les Serbes de Hongrie* (Prague, 1873).
Simrak, *Graeco-Catholica Ecclesia in Yugoslavia* (Zagreb, 1931).

6. THE RUMANIANS

The Rumanians are descendants of the "veterans of Trajan," colonies of Romans chiefly from Illyria and Italy planted by him in the province of Dacia at the beginning of the second century of the Christian era; fusing with the Thracian natives, they gave rise to a new people, predominantly Latin in language and characteristics but modified by Greek, Slav, and other influences.[20]

The first Dacian Christians were of the Latin rite (according to some, St. Niketas of Remesiana was one of their evangelizers), and so remained until they were conquered by the Bulgars in the ninth century. Then they were subjected to Byzantine bishops, who imposed their own rite, and in due course the Rumanians were drawn into the schism of Constantinople. For long the Rumanians were dependent on the prelates of the Bulgarian and other churches; it was not till the fourteenth century (when Rumanian principalities independent of Turks, Hungarians, and Poles began to be formed) that three separate metropolitans were given to Valachia and Moldavia. Latin missionaries were active from the thirteenth century, attracted particularly by the pagan Kumans in the Danubian plain, and dioceses were erected; but the majority of these Catholics turned Orthodox or Calvinist at the time of the Reformation. Damianos, the Moldavian metropolitan, signed the act of union at the Council of Florence, but it was not acceptable to most of his church and he and his successor had to seek refuge in Rome. In accordance with a decree of the Fourth Lateran Council, the Rumanians of Transylvania (the Ardeal), which had been conquered by the Hungarians under the king St. Stephen in the eleventh century,

---

[20] Rumanian is almost an Italian dialect.

CATHEDRAL OF ORADEA MARE, RUMANIA

(Byzantine Rite)

BYZANTINE AND LATIN CLERGY IN PROCESSION IN RUMANIA

A Byzantine Bishop is carrying the Blessed Sacrament, covered, in a Ciborium

should have been given vicars of Eastern rite by the Latin bishops of the conquerors; this was not done, however, and they gradually fell away. After the Council of Florence St. John of Capistrano rallied 30,000 of them to the union, but it lasted only about 25 years. The Protestant Reformation wrought havoc in Transylvania both among Latins and Orthodox, who became "Calvinist by creed, Eastern by certain externals." There was even a Calvinist "superintendent" for the Orthodox, and resisters were persecuted by their Hungarian and German masters. But in 1687 the Emperor Leopold I of Austria drove the Turkish overlords from this province, and the Jesuit chaplains of his army set themselves to deal with the religious situation.

THE CATHOLIC RUMANIANS

In 1697 the Orthodox metropolitan of Alba Julia, Theophilus Szeremy, moved by the reasoning of Father Ladislas Baranyi, S.J., called a synod which signed an act of union with Rome. Within a few weeks Mgr. Theophilus was dead, not without suspicion of having been poisoned by Calvinists. In the following year Athanasius Angelus Popa was consecrated bishop for Transylvania at Bukarest, where he was solemnly warned by the Orthodox patriarch of Jerusalem, Dositheos (who was visiting Rumania), of the dangers of Protestantism. Mgr. Athanasius took the advice to heart—but not in a way Dositheos intended. On arrival at Alba Julia he got into touch with Father Baranyi, and in a few weeks had signed, together with 38 protopopes (deans), a profession of faith and a declaration of desire to become "members of the Holy Catholic Church of Rome."[21]

---

[21] It must be noted that this reunion was not entirely inspired by disinterested conviction of the truth of "Roman claims" and abhorrence of schism: not entirely, and perhaps not even primarily. Fear of Protestantism and need of protection therefrom were apparently the principal motives of both Mgr. Theophilus and Mgr. Athanasius. Such unsatisfactory features have been at the root of many "reunions," and must be faced and taken into consideration. Sometimes the reunion is spoiled thereby *ab initio;* at other times, as in the case of the Rumanians, the reunion nevertheless works out well and becomes permanent.

The bishop and archpriests had stipulated that their "discipline, church ritual, Liturgy, fasts, and customs remain unchanged; if not, neither do our seals bind us."[22] Assurance was given of this, and in 1701 the union was finally confirmed at Vienna and Athanasius solemnly enthroned. Thus 1,500 priests and 200,000 other Rumanians were brought into communion with the Holy See.

The Calvinists were furious and the Orthodox no less; there was an outbreak of violence. For a time the union was in great danger, but the Jesuits came to the rescue and the neo-Catholics were eventually stabilized. It was not till 1735–51 that foreigners, Serbs mostly, stirred up the schism which reduced the Catholics by a half, and from which are descended the dissident Orthodox in Transylvania today. Some of the evil effects of this were modified and the Catholics greatly strengthened and encouraged by the activities of their fourth bishop, the holy Peter Paul Aron (1752–64).

In 1721 the Latin Bishop of the Ardeal invoked canon 9 of the Fourth Lateran Council against the successor of Athanasius, John Pataky, claiming that Pataky was simply his "ritual vicar." Pope Innocent XIII replied by a declaration that Pataky was the bishop-in-ordinary of the Catholics of his rite, but that he should reside at Fagaras instead of Alba Julia; future bishops would be appointed on the presentation of the Austrian emperor. Empress Maria-Teresa obtained the erection of a second episcopal see in 1777, and two more followed in 1853, when Fagaras became an archbishopric.

A curious abuse, shared with the Orthodox, persisted among the Catholic Rumanians until the middle of last century; namely, the granting of decrees of complete dissolution of marriage in cases of adultery.

On the establishment of the kingdom of Great Rumania in 1919 the Catholics found themselves for the first time under a sovereign of their own nationality.

---

[22] Note, also, that this reunion was therefore conditional. Theologically, its basis was the acceptance of the "four points" of Florence (see p. 14).

PRESENT STATE

Organization. The Catholic Rumanians of the Byzantine rite form an ecclesiastical province, consisting of the metropolitan see of Fagaras and Alba Julia (resident at Blaj), with the four suffragan sees of Gherla and Cluj, Oradea Mare, Lugoj, and Maramures; there is a vicariate of the last-named for the Ruthenian colony (62,000 souls) in that eparchy. The Archbishop of Fagaras has jurisdiction over the small minority of Catholics of his rite who live in the "Old Kingdom," including Bessarabia and the Bukovina. All five bishops are *ex officio* senators of the realm; by the concordat of 1929 they are nominated by the Holy See, the civil government approving the nominees. Representatives of all the clergy have an advisory voice in the selection of the metropolitan who has almost patriarchal powers. The cathedrals have chapters of canons.

Parochial clergy. These number over 1,500, of whom 90 per cent are married. There are "great" seminaries for their training at Blaj, Oradea Mare, and Gherla, and a Pontifical Rumanian College was erected at Rome in 1930. A faculty of Catholic theology was granted in the national University of Bukarest in 1932 but has not yet been set up. The parishes are arranged in 116 deaneries, of which the deans are called "protopopes." The protopope has considerable powers, and constitutes an ecclesiastical court of the first instance. The clergy wear the Western cassock and (like their Orthodox brethren) put on the *kalemaukion* only in church; the *rason* has been almost entirely given up, except by bishops and they wear it only on certain formal occasions. Clean-shaven clergy are now often seen in towns, even among the dissidents.

Religious institutes. A few years ago there were no monks or nuns left among the Catholic Rumanians.[23] There is now a small monastery of the *Basilians of St. Josaphat* (see p. 85) at Biksad, which has started a daughter-house at Moiseu. The *Conventual friars minor* have opened a college at Oradea Mare

---

[23] Thanks to the Emperor Joseph II. He would allow only Hungarian monasteries in Transylvania, so Rumanian aspirants had either to turn Latin or Orthodox!

for Byzantine candidates for their order; four of the friars have passed to the rite. Since 1923 the *Assumptionists* have a vice-province of the Byzantine rite in Rumania (12 priests). They have opened a special house for the spiritual formation of the clergy at Blaj (the *Casa Domnului*, "Lord's House"), and been entrusted with the direction of the old-established *Pavelian* school at Beius, and other works.[24] The *Jesuits* are now providing for Byzantine candidates in their provisional novitiate at Satu Mare (15 priests of the rite), and the *Brothers of the Christian Schools* at Oradea.

The Assumptionists have opened two Eastern convents of their Oblate Sisters, and a teaching and nursing congregation the *Sisters of the Most Holy Mother of God*, founded by Mgr. Suciu, the late metropolitan, in 1921, has already 38 professed religious in five houses.

The concordat between Rumania and the Holy See stipulates that all members of religious orders shall be Rumanian subjects.

The Faithful form the second largest body of Catholic Orientals, nearly 1½ million (the Latin Catholics are rather less,[25] and the dissidents not far off 15 millions), whose prestige and influence is out of all proportion to their numbers, especially in Transylvania where the Orthodox have only a bare majority. The Rumanians are a pious people; burial without religious rites is unknown and public opinion is so strong that the Protestants of Valachia are obliged to put *eikons* of our Lady in their chapels. In spite of the secular submission to foreign powers, the Rumanian professional classes in Transylvania are the *élite* of the country, and relations between Catholics and Orthodox are on the whole good. It is often difficult

---

[24] Things have changed a lot since the days (1875–88) when a seminary had to be taken from the charge of a certain Western congregation because all the best subjects were being enticed to become Latins and join it! But similar things still happen in some parts of the world.

[25] Since the eleventh century these have been looked on by the Rumanians at large as "foreigners" and "oppressors," as to a large extent they were, being Hungarians, Poles, and Germans. By the concordat the Latins have rather to "take a back seat"; e.g., only *one* of their five bishops is a senator, while *all* the Byzantine Catholic bishops are.

to see what divides them, and the Catholic bishop of Oradea Mare, Mgr. Valerius Frentiu, believes that their reunion is an administrative and personal problem rather than a doctrinal and ideological one; extremely strong opinions in favour of reunion are expressed by Orthodox clergy from time to time, e.g., in Bessarabia in 1932.

OTHER JURISDICTIONS

United States. Many Catholic Rumanians have been lost to the Church through insufficiency of clergy; there are now some 8,000, subject to the Latin bishops, half of them around Cincinnati. Their first church was built at Cleveland in 1904.

PARTICULAR CUSTOMS

The Rumanians keep their Byzantine rite in a high degree of purity, some of the few small modifications being shared by the Orthodox. The Gregorian calendar was adopted by both in 1924 for the celebration of fixed feasts only; Easter is therefore still observed according to the Julian reckoning. The liturgical language is Rumanian, which began to take the place of Staroslav in the seventeenth century—the first example since the early centuries of a Catholic liturgy being authorized for celebration in a vernacular. In Transylvania there is a traditional church music, derived from the chant of Byzantium, but the national architecture has been almost ousted by the neo-classical in that province; *eikonostases* reach nearly to the roof. At the Catholic Rumanian church of San Salvatore alla Coppelle in Rome the congregation at the Easter ceremonies is made up almost entirely of Rumanian dissidents.

Certain extra-liturgical practices from the West have been introduced among the faithful.

BIBLIOGRAPHY

*Samuelson, *Rumania, Past and Present* (London, 1882).
*Jorga, *Histoire des Roumains* (Bukarest, 1922).

7. THE MELKITES

General Ecclesiastical History

After the Council of Chalcedon the Monophysites in the patriarchates of Alexandria, Antioch, and Jerusalem dubbed the orthodox Catholics "Melkites," from Syrian *malok*, "king," because they professed the orthodoxy of the Emperor. The name stuck and is often used without qualification to designate the Catholic Byzantines of Syria and Egypt, though the dissident Orthodox are equally Melkites.[26] After the Arab invasion in the seventh century the Melkites of all three patriarchates came for a time more and more under the ecclesiastical domination of Constantinople, and by the end of the thirteenth century they had abandoned their own liturgies to the Monophysites and adopted that of imperial Byzantium.

There was another important change after Chalcedon, in the *personnel* that made up these patriarchates. Alexandria was originally Greco-Egyptian, Antioch and Jerusalem Greco-Syrian. Today, the Orthodox of Alexandria are predominantly Greek (though the Syrian element has been recently enlarged by emigration), those of Jerusalem are Syrian ("Palestinian") under a Greek ecclesiastical caucus, those of Antioch are almost entirely Syro-Arab. The Catholic Melkites, both of Egypt and Syria, are fundamentally Syro-Arabs, racially more or less one with the Catholic (West) Syrians and Maronites, but with more Greek blood.

[26] In the popular speech of the Levant the word "Catholic" primarily means "Catholic Melkite." A Syrian divides the principal Christians into "*Rûm* (Roman = Orthodox) *wa Kathulik wa Lateen wa Maroniyeh.*" This shows a nice historical sense, for of the half dozen Catholic rites represented in Syria, Palestine, and Egypt, the Melkites are hierarchically the "authentic local Catholics": the present Syrian and Maronite bodies are due to heresies in the past, the Armenians are refugees mostly, and the Latin rite also is a foreign importation.

Though numerically insignificant the patriarchate of Antioch is of great historical interest and ecclesiastical importance because of the large number of its patriarchs and bishops who were in communion with Rome between the Byzantine schism of 1054[27] and the definite emergence of two hierarchies, Catholic and dissident Orthodox, in 1724: so much so that it has been claimed that throughout that period the Antiochene patriarchs (even while resident at Constantinople) considered themselves subject to the Pope as supreme pontiff.[28] But this is certainly an exaggeration.

When the Crusaders captured Antioch in 1098 they acknowledged the Catholicity and jurisdiction of its patriarch, John IV; but after the death of the papal legate Adhemar du Puy, their attitude altered and they treated John so badly that he fled to Constantinople.[29] It is not believable that his successors there were not in schism. But Theodosius V signed the act of union at Lyons in 1274 and resigned his see rather than repudiate it; others must have followed his example, for Saracen writers of the fourteenth and fifteenth centuries make a clear distinction between the Melkites who submit to the Pope of Rome and the other Christians (Jacobites, etc.) who do not.

---

[27] The contemporary patriarch, Peter III, implored Cerularius not to separate himself and his church from Rome and the West.

[28] There have been a number of Catholic patriarchs of Alexandria, too, since the eleventh century, and two are reported at Jerusalem in the seventeenth.

[29] Thereupon the Crusaders instituted that anomaly a Latin patriarch of Antioch. It was this playing fast and loose with Eastern sees and their holders (to say nothing of such things as their sacking of Constantinople in 1204) that made the name of Crusader—and consequently of Catholic—stink in the nostrils of pious orientals. What Pope Innocent III thought of the heroes of the Fourth Crusade can be read in his letter to Cardinal Peter of Capua: "The Latins have given an example only of perversity and works of darkness. It is natural that (the Greeks) should regard them as curs. These soldiers of Christ . . . are drenched in Christian blood." Unfortunately, the Pope adopted a policy that was the very reverse of pacifying. There are still Latin patriarchs of Constantinople, Alexandria, and Antioch, titular prelates of the papal court, and one in residence at Jerusalem; he is, of course, really only an archbishop, for the Pope is the only real Latin patriarch.

The patriarch of Antioch, Dorotheos I, accepted the union of Florence, and there is reason to think that the three Melkite patriarchs did not relapse into schism again until the Turks cut off Syria from the West in 1516 and the Greeks seized the patriarchal throne of Jerusalem from the Syrians in 1534. But again in 1560 Joachim V was a Catholic, and in 1585 the retired patriarch, Michael VII, and with the seventeenth century there began a strong movement toward definitive reunion. The patriarchs Athanasius III, Ignatius III, Euthymios II (who welcomed the Jesuits into his territory), Eutychius, Makarios III, and Cyril V, and the bishops Euthymios Saifi of Tyre, Gregory of Aleppo, Gerasimos of Saidnaia, Pathenios of Diarbekr, and others, all made formal profession of allegiance to the Holy See between 1600 and 1720; the Jesuit missionaries, indeed, seem to have recognized all Melkite bishops in Syria as the legitimate ordinaries of their rite.

When the patriarch, Athanasius III, a schismatic, died in 1724, a nephew of Euthymios of Tyre who had been educated in Rome, Seraphim Tanas, was elected in his place; he took the name of Cyril VI. Thereupon those who were not in favour of communion with Rome (and some who were) selected a candidate, Silvester, and sent him off to Constantinople, where he was consecrated and put forward as the true patriarch of Antioch.[30] Silvester had the support of only five bishops out of fifteen, but he obtained the favour of the Turkish government first and Cyril had to take refuge in a remote monastery in the Lebanon.

THE CATHOLIC MELKITES

For a time there was a violent persecution of the Catholics, and even when it died down the reign of Cyril continued to be troubled; he fell foul both of the Jesuits and of the Maronites, and Pope Benedict XIV had to send a severe instruction that

---

[30] From this time on there are two lines of patriarchs, one for Catholics, one for dissidents. The Catholic patriarch is the historical as well as the spiritual successor of St. Evodius, St. Ignatius the God-bearer, and the Flavians. The Orthodox have contested the validity of the election of Cyril VI, but the synod of Constantinople itself admitted it by claiming to depose him!

the Maronites were not to induce Melkites to join their rite and that Melkites were not to call Maronites heretics! Cyril VI Tanas resigned in 1759, but the state of the Catholic Melkites continued to be disturbed. For example, a synod at Karkafah in 1806 published a number of "acts" which later had to be condemned by the Holy See for their "conciliarism," there were quarrels between the patriarch Agapios III and the Metropolitan of Beirut, and from 1817 till 1832 there was a bloody persecution at the hands of the Turks— nine Melkites were murdered out of hatred of the Faith at Aleppo on April 16, 1818.[31]

The rule of the great Maximos III Mazlum (1833–55) was a period of reform and progress, culminating in his obtaining from the Turkish government complete civil autonomy for his people under their patriarch. In the time of his successor, Clement Bahath, there was for three years a small but very noisy schism caused by the imposition of the Gregorian calendar in place of the Julian. Gregory II Yusuf (1864–97) was another energetic and far-seeing patriarch. He suggested the formation of the seminary of St. Anne at Jerusalem, and at the epoch-making international eucharistic congress held in that city in 1893 Mgr. Gregory was the outstanding figure. He had assisted at the Vatican Council and was well known to the West.

The present patriarch is Mgr. Cyril IX Mogabgab. Under his rule and that of his predecessor, Mgr. Dimitrios Kadi, the losses of the Catholic Melkites during the Great War and by emigration have been compensated by a remarkable extension of his church in the regions of Tripoli, Galilee, and Transjordania.

PRESENT STATE

Patriarch. The supreme head under the Sovereign Pontiff of the Catholic Melkites is the "Patriarch of Antioch and of All the East"; since the days of Maximos III each holder has had the personal privilege of adding the titles of Alexandria

[31] Earlier martyrs were David the Greek (1660) and Ibrahim al-Dallal (1742).

and Jerusalem.[32] His jurisdiction extends to all the faithful of his church in what was in 1894 the Turkish empire and Egypt. He is elected by the bishops, residential and titular, of the jurisdiction united in synod. The Holy See confirms the election upon receiving notification and a profession of faith (although the elect is enthroned at once after the synod) and sends the *pallium*.[33] Until this confirmation is received, the patriarch may not exercise his functions, but this rule has been often disregarded. Among the patriarchal rights are the nomination of three persons from whom a bishop is chosen for a vacant see, the appointment of titular bishops (*synkelloi*) at will, the ordination of all bishops and their canonical deposition, the consecration of Chrism for his whole church, the convening of a plenary synod, as well as certain civil rights in respect of his flock. He confers the *omophorion* on his bishops as the Pope does the *pallium* on Western archbishops. His chief residence is at Damascus,[34] with others at Beirut and Cairo. Altogether, the Melkite patriarch's position, *vis-á-vis* both his own people and the Holy See, approximates more closely to that of a pre-schism patriarch than in the case of any other Catholic Eastern pontiff; it is therefore the more remarkable that he has no patriarchal *curia* beyond two councillors who are titular bishops: every bishop is the sole judge of causes in his own eparchy.

Bishops. The sees are Damascus (the patriarchal eparchy), Tyre, Aleppo, Bosra and the Hauran, Beirut, Homs, St. John of Akka (Ptolemais), Sidon, Paneas, Tripoli, Baalbek, Zahleh,

---

[32] On solemn occasions he is "The most blessed, holy, and venerable chief and head, Patriarch of the great cities of Antioch, Alexandria, and Jerusalem, of Cilicia, Syria, and Iberia, of Arabia, Mesopotamia, and the Pentapolis, of Ethiopia, Egypt, and all the East, the lord N., Father of Fathers, Shepherd of shepherds, High priest of high priests, and Thirteenth Apostle!" "The East" is the Roman prefecture *Oriens*.

[33] He sometimes wears it to be buried in. The *pallium* has no historical significance in the East; it is the Pope's recognition of communion with the new patriarch.

[34] None of the five governing patriarchs (Catholic Melkite, Syrian, Maronite, Orthodox Melkite, and Jacobite) who have the title of Antioch live there. "Antakiyeh" is now a Mohammedan town with about 30,000 inhabitants.

and Amman (Transjordania). The first six of these are metropolitan according to some old lists, but all the bishops are
called archbishops and are subject directly to the patriarch.
The authority of the Patriarch of Antioch was extended to the
Melkites in the patriarchates of Alexandria and Jerusalem in
1772; for those of Egypt he has vicars patriarchal (with the
title of archimandrite) at Alexandria, Cairo, and Khartum,
and at Jerusalem a vicar with a title of exarch.

The Holy See has neither voice nor part in the appointment
of Melkite bishops. When a see is vacant, the patriarch in
consultation with the bishops puts forward two or three
names and choice is made therefrom by the clergy of the
eparchy and, in practice, the leading laymen.[35]

The patriarch and bishops still act to a large extent as
judges in civil causes.

Parochial clergy. Before the days of Maximos III practically
all the parishes were served by monks, who still have charge
of many of them. A seminary was founded in 1811 at Ain
Traz in the Lebanon, a great Melkite centre where three
plenary synods have been held; its career was chequered and
not very successful, and it was finally closed in 1899. After
the Crimean War the Turkish government presented to
France, as a *baksheesh* for her part in the campaign, the
crusaders' church of St. Anne in Jerusalem. Here in 1882
Cardinal Lavigerie, at the suggestion of the patriarch Gregory
II, opened a Byzantine seminary under the direction of the
White Fathers. By 1931 this institution had produced eight
bishops, 126 priests, and three permanent deacons, of whom
Mgr. Lagier says, "Their modesty, unworldliness, cultured
wide-spiritedness and dignity of soul make up a priestly *ensemble* that is surpassed nowhere in the Catholic Church"
(but they are very French). All the St. Anne's priests have
voluntarily accepted celibacy, but there is also a number of
married priests among the Melkite clergy, who are hard-

---

[35] By a special privilege, approved by Pope Pius VII, the metropolitan
of Aleppo is elected by the clergy and twelve laymen (who, however,
have only an advisory part), without reference to the patriarch.

working and highly respected men. A few aspirants are sent to the Greek College at Rome, and there are several diocesan "little" seminaries.

The names of *exarch* and *archimandrite*[36] are conferred as titles of honour, the holders of which affect certain distinctions of dress. The clergy wear the traditional Byzantine *rason* and *kalemaukion* and some retain the custom of long hair.

Religious institutes. For two hundred years the monks were the mainstay of the Catholic Melkite church. In 1708 Mgr. Euthymios Saifi of Tyre built a monastery at Masmuseh, near Sidon. He put its members under the "rule of St. Basil," but his object was to form a congregation more on the lines of the clerks regular of the West; nevertheless they are canonically reckoned as monks. His foundation prospered and grew, receiving the name of *Salvatorian* Basilians from its mother-house "of the Saviour," Dair al-Mukhallis. The *Shuwairite* Basilian monks were founded about the same time at Shuwair by two hieromonks from the Orthodox monastery of Balamand ("Belmont"), near Tripoli. Their organization was more strictly monastic than that of the Salvatorians, but they also were soon engaged in parochial and mission work. Almost from the beginning there was friction between the Shuwairite monasteries in the Lebanon mountains and those of Aleppo, which was ended in 1832 by the formation of a separate congregation of *Aleppine* Basilians (the others are sometimes called Baladites, i.e., rustics). These three congregations all developed under direct Western influence, principally of the Jesuits and Capuchins, and their earlier constitutions were modeled on those of the Maronite Antonians, which were to a considerable degree "made in Italy." On account of the shortage of secular priests the Melkite Basilians have throughout their history been principally engaged in serving parishes, and the value of the service they have done to the Catholics of

---

[36] Any bishop may confer this title on any priest he pleases. The White Father Père Abel Couturier, that "ghost from the *lauras* of Pharan," was named archimandrite by the patriarch and by the bishops of Ptolemais and Sidon as well.

their rite is incalculable. To a monk of Shuwair, Abdullah Zahir, was due the establishment of the first Arabic printing press in the Ottoman Empire, early in the eighteenth century.

The Salvatorians have seven monasteries and seven "cells" (*metokhia*) with 190 monks, nearly all priests; the Shuwairites, five monasteries and five cells, with 110 monks; and the Aleppines, two monasteries, six cells, 50 hieromonks and 25 monks. Of the total of 330 hieromonks nearly two thirds live in and serve parishes. They wear the traditional Byzantine dress. Recently the Melkite Basilians have been undergoing an apostolic visitation, which resulted in 1934 in a complete reorganization. The visitors appointed were Dom Benedict Gariador, abbot general of the Cassinese Benedictines of the Primitive Observance, Dom de Lajudie, monk of the same congregation, and Dom Menez, monk of Solesmes, under the presidency of the Patriarch, Mgr. Mogabgab. The new constitutions, while organizing each congregation on the lines of the later Western orders, with an effective superior general (protoarchimandrite) at the head of each, provide for a greater degree of monastic regularity in the monasteries. But local superiors are appointed by the superior general, who can also transfer monks from one house to another at will.

After he retired from the see of Baalbek in 1894 Mgr. Germanos Muakkad[37] founded the society of *Missionaries of St. Paul*, at Harisa in the Lebanon. Its numbers are still very small, but they do a great work in giving missions and retreats and running a polyglot printing establishment. All three Basilian congregations have convents of nuns affiliated, totaling probably over 150 members, whose life is strictly contemplative and the most traditionally Eastern of any nuns in the Catholic Church, being entirely free from foreign influence. There is a number of Melkites among the Mariamettes, an inter-ritual congregation of teaching sisters.

The Faithful. There are nominally 150,000, but certainly more Catholic Melkites in the patriarchal territory, 19,500 of

---

[37] Dr. Adrian Fortescue said of him, "I have rarely met any man who gave the impression of being a saint as did Germanos Muakkad."

whom are in Egypt and many[88] in Palestine (the dissident Orthodox Melkites of the three patriarchates total only 275,000). In Syria many and in Egypt all of them live in the towns, and form prosperous communities whose social and religious prestige is high; in the rural districts of Syria and Transjordania increasing numbers of peasants become Melkite Catholics. By blood these claim to be pure Arabs of the Hauran, especially of the Banu Ghassan, originally from the Yemen in southern Arabia, and descended from Solomon and the Queen of Sheba—a common oriental boast! In some of the more remote parts religious education is insufficient, and in the towns the influence of Freemasonry (imported by returned immigrants) has been most harmful.

In extensive districts of Syria the Melkites are recognized as the principal authentic local and indigenous expression of Catholicism (see footnote on p. 106), but in Palestine their position is not so satisfactory. Here the course of history has brought about a predominance of Latin influence, and lately the formation of a native clergy and laity of the Roman rite, in spite of canon 98 and other legislation. But in Galilee and Transjordania there is a movement of Palestinian Catholics and Orthodox back to their proper Melkite Catholic church. The resulting atmosphere of rivalry between Latins and Byzantines is very regrettable, and indeed there is not always among the Catholic bodies of Syria in general that accord, good feeling, and mixing with one another that one would wish to find. Their rivalries are of old standing, and are kept alive particularly by some of the laity and lower clergy. The Latin minority is often ignorant about orientals, patronizing and superior; the Melkites, as heirs of Constantinople, Alexandria, Antioch, and Jerusalem, have a touch of Byzantine aggressiveness about them—they have not forgotten that the Latin church is not native to Palestine, Syria, and Egypt; the Maronites have more than a touch of that self-satisfiedness which sometimes characterizes a body of people who have for centuries maintained their orthodoxy under oppression in the

---

[88] *Statistica* gives 21,800; but 30,000 would be nearer the mark.

face of those whose orthodoxy is a more recent acquisition; the little group of the "pure" Syrian rite is less involved in these unhappy squabbles.

OTHER JURISDICTIONS

United States. There has been emigration of Melkites to America for nearly fifty years, with the inevitable loss of many to religion.[39] There are now 13,600 in U. S. A., with a dozen priests, subject to the American ordinaries. Their chief churches are at New York, Lawrence, Cleveland, Dubois, and La Crosse. Here they seem to call themselves Syrian Greek Catholics.

Elsewhere. There are two or three thousand Melkites in other parts of the world. They have churches at Marseilles (founded 1821), Paris (St. Julien-le-Pauvre), Montreal, Sydney, and Brisbane.

PARTICULAR CUSTOMS

The Melkites are more jealous for the exact observance of their rite than any other Eastern Catholics in the Levant. The Byzantine liturgy and other rites are celebrated normally entirely in Arabic, and have been modified only in small points, chiefly of externals. Their chant is in substance that of Constantinople. "And from the Son" is sung in the Creed, and Baptism is administered by seating the child in the font and pouring water over it. The segregation of women during divine service is insisted on with all the rigour of the ancient canons. A number of the smaller churches are too poor to have an *eikonostasis*.

The use of the traditional spoon for giving holy Communion is being more and more superseded by the practice of dipping the holy Body in the sacred Blood and administering them by hand; this reform led to a notable increase in communions even before the decree of Pope Pius X in 1905. The Melkites have a strong devotion toward the Blessed Sacrament and accorded it a degree of external *cultus* before any other

---

[39] The demoralizing effect of emigration is insufficiently appreciated: e.g., of the 1¼ million Irish in Canada, less than one third are Catholics.

Catholics of Eastern rite. So early as the end of the seventeenth century an old Arabic *Pentecostarion* was found at Damascus containing an office for Corpus Christi, and since the plague was stayed at Aleppo in 1732 the feast has been observed with increased solemnity. Benediction of the Blessed Sacrament, with a completely different ceremonial from that of the West, has been introduced into some eparchies, as has the entirely unnecessary innovation of giving absolution by the Western indicative formula (in Arabic).

One or two Western devotions are practised among the Melkites, e.g., the rosary, but there are no statues in the churches, only pictures. Their calendar is, except for the Gregorian reckoning and Corpus Christi, that of Constantinople. In addition to Sundays there are now 32 holydays, but hardly regarded as of obligation. The ancient customs of fasting and abstinence have been modified (see p. 65).

BIBLIOGRAPHY

Charon, *Histoire des Patriarcats melkites.* 2 vols. (Paris, 1911).

Fortescue, *The Uniate Eastern Churches* (Italo-Greeks and Melkites), (London, 1923).

Couturier, *Cours de Liturgie Grecque-Melkite.* 3 vols. (Paris, 1912).

Couturier, *Syllitourgikon* (the music in Eastern and Western notation), (Paris, 1926).

A MARONITE BISHOP
(The late Mgr. Hoyek)

A GREEK BISHOP
(Mgr. George Kalavassy)

8. THE GREEKS

GENERAL ECCLESIASTICAL HISTORY

Before the rise of Constantinople to civil and ecclesiastical power the country now called the Republic of the Hellenes was, as part of the Roman prefecture of Illyricum, within the patriarchal jurisdiction of the Roman pontiff. But eastern Illyricum was part of the Eastern Empire, and from the fifth century the Patriarch of Constantinople claimed to have jurisdiction over it. The question was a source of never-ending dispute between Old Rome and New Rome until the schism of 1054, when what is now Greece was definitively involved on the side of Constantinople and became part of its schismatic patriarchate, sharing its political and religious history until the establishment of the modern Greek state in the early part of the nineteenth century; then, in 1833, the Greek assembly declared the national church autocephalous and it was so recognized by Constantinople seventeen years later.

After the Greek-speaking lands fell into the hands of the Turks, Pope Gregory XIII, in 1576, founded the Greek College at Rome, primarily for refugees from Greece who wanted to study for the priesthood; but, although there were many individual Greek bishops, priests, and others who returned to unity during the seventeenth and eighteenth centuries,[40] it was not found possible to form a Catholic community of Byzantine rite among the Greek people, so the college was utilized for others of that rite.

---

[40] Cyril Kontaris, Oecumenical Patriarch of Constantinople, saved his church from Protestantism and in 1638 entered into communion with the Supreme Pontiff. He was dethroned, imprisoned at Tunis, and there murdered by the Turks in 1640. The cause of his beatification as a martyr was introduced at Rome, but has never been finished.

THE CATHOLIC GREEKS

In 1829 the sultan Mohammed II emancipated his non-Latin Catholic subjects from the civil authority of the dissident patriarchs, and a body of Greek Catholics of the Byzantine rite came into existence. The leading spirit in its formation was a Latin priest from Sira, Father John Hyacinth Marango, who in 1856 started work at Constantinople with the object of persuading the Orthodox to return to unity. The results were hardly commensurate with his enthusiasm and energy,[41] but by 1861 he had a small nucleus at Pera, in whose direction he was succeeded in 1878 by Father Polycarp Anastasiadis, a former student of the Orthodox seminary at Halki. In 1895 Pope Leo XIII invited the French Assumptionists to go to Constantinople, where they organized a seminary and two parishes of the Greek rite, and began those learned studies of oriental religious matters whose fruits are so valuable to scholars.

Pope Pius X gave these Greeks a titular bishop as ordinary (exarch) in 1911, in the distinguished person of Mgr. Isaias Papadopoulos, who had led a Catholic movement in the Thracian village of Malgara and suffered much for the Faith. He was called to Rome in 1917 and his place was taken three years later by Mgr. George Kalavassy, who in the face of great hardship and difficulties established himself and part of his flock at Athens. In 1932 those at Constantinople were made a separate ordinariate, with Mgr. Dionisios Varoukhas as bishop. The Catholics of Malgara and Dandeli imigrated to near Salonika.

PRESENT STATE

Organization. The two ordinariates of Greece and Turkey are subject to the Sacred Eastern Congregation at Rome, which appoints the bishops.

Parochial clergy. These are fifteen in number, all voluntarily celibate, with one permanent deacon. There is a clerical

---

[41] Nevertheless, it was due to him that two contemporary Orthodox bishops, Meletios of Drama and Benjamin of Neapolis, died Catholics.

school at Athens, preparatory for the Greek College at Rome; the Assumptionist oriental seminary at Kadi-Keuy (Chalcedon) has been closed since the war. The clergy conduct a boy's orphanage and a printing press.

Religious institutes. The secular priests are united in a society ("of the Most Holy Trinity"), but it is not a religious congregation. Several of the Assumptionist priests are of the Greek rite, but their Institute of Byzantine Studies at Kadi-Keuy is directed by Latins. The *Sisters of the Theotokos Pammakaristos,* founded by Mgr. Kalavassy, have eleven members, and conduct a school at Athens.

The Faithful. They number less than 2,500. Those who emigrated to Athens in 1923 have had to suffer a good deal of harsh treatment at the hands of their dissident brethren, for Catholics of Eastern rite were not known in Greece (there are 43,000 Latins, mostly of foreign origin but now completely hellenized) and they were accordingly accused of dishonest propaganda. These Catholics, whether Latins or Byzantines, are the only people who can properly be called "Greek Catholics."[42] There is now a Byzantine church on the island of Sira. (The dissident Orthodox of Greece and Turkey number over six millions.)

In 1929 some of the Greek community in *Lyons,* dissatisfied with the ministration of their bishop for Western Europe, asked to be received into the communion of the Catholic Church. A priest was sent to them from Athens by Mgr. Kalavassy.

OTHER JURISDICTIONS

There are three tiny groups of Greek Catholics separate from the above, which should be mentioned here rather than with the Italo-Greeks as is usually done.

Corsica. When the Turks conquered Greece seven hundred people fled from Boitylos in the Morea in 1675 and the Genoese Republic gave them a home in Corsica. They accepted the

---

[42] The name is nevertheless often used in popular speech of and by the Catholic Melkites, Ruthenians, and others, especially in North America. The Hellenes are sometimes distinguished as "Pure Greeks."

jurisdiction of the Holy See, and settled down first at Paomia and then at Ajaccio. In 1770 the first French governor, the Count de Marboeuf, built for them the township of Cargèse, which their descendants now occupy. They number 500 souls and, though they have nearly lost their Greek language, they still keep their Greek rites, modified by Western practices, e.g., Confirmation is separated from Baptism and administered according to the Roman rite by the Bishop of Ajaccio. They have a fine church and one priest.

Algeria. A colony from Cargèse went to Algeria in 1875 and founded the village of Sidi-Meruan. They now number some 250, with one priest.

Malta. When the Knights of St. John of Jerusalem occupied Malta upon being driven from Rhodes by the Turks in 1522, a church of Byzantine rite was built at Valletta for those Greeks who accompanied them. It is still in use, served by one priest, but his flock numbers less than 20 souls.

PARTICULAR CUSTOMS

The Catholic Greeks of Greece, Turkey, and Lyons use the Byzantine rite and customs, in ecclesiastical Greek, according to pure Constantinopolitan usages, without any admixture or addition of specifically Western observances.

BIBLIOGRAPHY

Fortescue, *The Orthodox Eastern Church* (London, 1911).
Chappet, *Eucologe . . . de la Paroisse de Cargèse* (Marseilles, 1932).

9. THE BULGARS

GENERAL ECCLESIASTICAL HISTORY

The Bulgars are a Finno-Turkish people, who established an independent kingdom in their present country and its borders during the seventh century. About the year 865 their Tsar Boris, largely for political motives, accepted Christianity from Constantinople and imposed it on his people. But Boris wanted his church to be independent, and turned to Pope St. Nicholas I, asking him to give Bulgaria a patriarch. Nicholas sent an archbishop. This precipitated a long contest for jurisdiction over the Bulgars, both Rome and Constantinople claiming that they were in their patriarchate. The Slavs, too, had a hand in the conversion of the Bulgars. When the Germans made things impossible for the followers of St. Methodius in Moravia and Pannonia, a number of them fled into Bulgaria about the year 885 and evangelized the heathen there. Their leader St. Clement and four of his clergy, together with SS. Cyril and Methodius are venerated as the Seven Apostles of the Bulgars.

The Emperor Basil II ("the Bulgar-slayer") conquered Bulgaria in 1018, and the ecclesiastical province of Okhrida was eventually involved in the Byzantine schism. But it continued to be an autonomous church till 1767, when it was reduced to complete dependence on the Greek Patriarch of Constantinople. Eastern Bulgaria recovered independence in 1185, and from 1204 to 1234 was in unambiguous communion with Rome, its primatial see being at Tirnovo. Then the politics of the Tsar John Assen II dragged the church of Tirnovo into schism, and when Bulgaria was conquered by the Ottoman Turks in 1393 its territory was united to that of Okhrida, but it managed to maintain a semi-independence till 1767.

When in that year all the Bulgarian eparchies were brought

121

under the direct control of Constantinople they were subjected to a ruthless process of hellenizing: Greek became the compulsory liturgical language and only Greeks were appointed to episcopal sees. National consciousness awoke in Bulgaria and when, in 1856, the Turkish government decreed the freedom and equality of its Christian subjects, Bulgarian representatives demanded for their church a number of far-reaching reforms. (Political freedom was their ultimate object; it was gained in 1879.) The Patriarch of Constantinople made certain concessions, including the appointment of some bishops of Bulgarian nationality. But it was too late; Bulgaria was now demanding an autonomous national church, and in 1870 it was granted by an imperial *firman* from the Ottoman *Porte:* the Bulgarian Church was to be autocephalous under an exarch (primate) and synod. Whereupon in 1872, a council of the Church of Constantinople declared the Bulgars excommunicated.[43]

THE CATHOLIC BULGARS

At the beginning of their struggle with Constantinople there was an influential minority of Bulgars who sought ecclesiastical independence of the Greeks by means of reunion with Rome. Assured by the Catholic Armenian archbishop of Constantinople, Mgr. Hassun, that their rites and customs would be respected, they sent a deputation to Rome in 1861, where Pope Pius IX himself consecrated their leader, the archimandrite Joseph Sokolsky, as prelate of the Catholic Bulgars of the Byzantine rite.

But the movement was spoiled in an unforeseen way. The growth of Catholicism in the Balkans was obnoxious to the political aims of Russia and, diplomacy having failed, a month after his return to Constantinople Mgr. Sokolsky was kidnapped, taken to Odessa, and interned for the remaining eighteen years of his life in the monastery of the Caves at Kiev.[44] Then the Russian diplomats set themselves to encour-

---

[43] The Greek Orthodox churches are still not in communion with the Bulgarian exarchate; the other Orthodox churches are.

[44] That Mgr. Sokolsky connived at his removal and reverted to Orthodoxy has been asserted, but not proved.

age the Turks to favour an independent Orthodox Bulgarian church, whose establishment killed the Romeward movement.

At this time there were over 60,000 Bulgars reunited with Rome,[45] they were given another prelate and Augustinians of the Assumption and other Western congregations were sent to help them. But by 1872 three quarters of them had returned to Orthodoxy, and most of the remainder lived, not in Bulgaria, but in Macedonia and Thrace. Accordingly, in 1883 Pope Leo XIII appointed them a vicar apostolic in each of these districts. After the Balkan war of 1912–13 the Orthodox Bulgars of Macedonia again contemplated reunion with Rome, and again were frustrated by political forces. This war brought ruin to both vicariates, and after the European war of 1914–18 what remained of the Catholic Bulgars sought refuge in their own country.

PRESENT STATE

Organization. The Catholic Bulgars are now in charge of an administrator apostolic of their rite (Mgr. Cyril Kurtev, consecrated in 1926), who resides at Sofia and depends on the Sacred Eastern Congregation through the delegate apostolic to Bulgaria.

Parochial clergy. These number 41, about half of whom are married. The Assumptionists (who have a few priests of the Byzantine rite serving parishes) conduct "little" seminaries at Yambol and Plovdiv (Phillippopolis), studies being completed at oriental seminaries elsewhere; the fine seminary at Karagatch, near Adrianople, was destroyed during the war.

Religious institutes. The *Resurrectionists*, a congregation of Polish origin having both Latin and Eastern members, have two houses of Byzantine rite in Bulgaria, with four priests. There is a convent of *Eucharistines*, engaged in charitable works at Sofia, having fifteen Sisters.

---

[45] One of the most remarkable among them was the aged monk Panteleimon, who tried to introduce frequent communion among the monks of Mount Athos. He became a Catholic in 1863 and founded two monasteries, one for men and one for women. They failed after his death in 1868. He was ordained only in 1865, at the expressed wish of Pius IX.

The Faithful now number only 5,500 all told, mostly engaged in agriculture but with good communities at Sofia and Varna. The Augustinians do admirable educational work among them. There is a number of Catholics of the Latin rite, but the overwhelming majority of the Bulgars are dissident Orthodox (four million).

PARTICULAR CUSTOMS

The Bulgarian liturgy is the Byzantine according to Slavonic usages, in the Staroslav language, and innovations are avoided; even the Julian calendar is in use. Church music is either an adaptation of the Greek chant or Russian polyphony. The Bulgars are not in origin Slavs, but the use of Church Slavonic as a "national custom" seems to have begun soon after their conversion, when the followers of St. Methodius from Moravia introduced the practice at the court of the Tsar Boris, who adopted it as a sign of independence of Constantinople.

BIBLIOGRAPHY

*Brailsford, *Macedonia* (London, 1906).
Songeon, *Histoire de la Bulgarie* (Paris, 1913).
Canisius, *Aux Avant-Postes du Monde Slave* (Louvain, 1931).
Kristov, *Pantéléimon* (Paris, n. d.).

10. THE RUSSIANS

General Ecclesiastical History

The Russians date their conversion to Christ from the year 989, when St. Vladimir, Grand Prince of Kiev, gave the new religion to his people.[46] Russia received its faith, rites, and early bishops from Constantinople and at the time midway between the two epoch-making schisms of Photius and Cerularius. It is true that Russians played no part (on either side) in the events that led to the tragedy of 1054, but in the circumstances it is impossible that the fact and significance of communion with the Holy See of Rome can have had much importance in their religious consciousness. Greek influence was predominant in their church and, in the words of Father Pierling, S.J., "One looks in vain for an exact date or outstanding event that can be registered as the point of departure for the separation between Russia and Rome. It came about by implication, without shock or apparent reason, simply because of Russia's hierarchical submission to the Patriarch of Constantinople."

There were, however, diplomatic relations between the Russian princes and the popes during the Middle Ages and a certain amount of intermittent activity on the part of missionaries from the West, as well as such incidents as the request of Prince Basil (Vasilko) of Vladimir in Volhynia and his brother Daniel of Galicz (Galicia), who was subsequently crowned king of that principality, to be admitted to communion with Pope Innocent IV in 1247. At the Council of Florence Russia was represented by a Greek, Isidore, Metropolitan of Kiev (Moscow), who was in favour of reunion.

---

[46] There were Christians in Russia before Vladimir, *e.g.*, his grandmother, St. Olga.

Pope Eugenius IV created him cardinal (and the great Bessarion of Nicaea as well) and sent him home as legate to confirm the union, but the grand prince of Muscovy, Basil II, and his other bishops would have none of it and Isidore had to escape to Rome.

In 1589 the patriarch of Constantinople, Jeremias II, acknowledged Russia as a separate patriarchate of the Orthodox Church, with its patriarchal see at Moscow ("the Third Rome"). Six years later took place the union with Rome of the Metropolitan of Kiev and other bishops in southwest Russia, under the rule of Poland, whose people included those whom we now call Ruthenians (see p. 77). Peter the Great abolished the patriarchal office in 1700, and set up a "Holy Governing Synod" to rule the Russian Church in concert with the civil power (1721). This lasted till the revolution of 1917, when a patriarch of Moscow was again elected. At that time the number of dissident Russian Orthodox Christians was about 110 millions (including sects).

THE RUSSIAN CATHOLICS

During the centuries after the Council of Florence there were very few Catholics indeed under Russian rule until the partition of Poland in 1773–1795.[47] Toward the end of the nineteenth century, largely under the influence of the great philosopher and theologian Vladimir Soloviev, began a movement in favour of Russians who became Catholics keeping their own rite. Such a thing was legally impossible—a Byzantine *had* to be Orthodox—even after 1905, when Nicholas II issued an edict of religious toleration.[48] But from that time groups

---

[47] Before the revolution there were some three million Latin Catholics in Russia (excluding Poland), a small minority of them Russians. It is curious to note that, in spite of her anti-papal activities, the Empress Catherine II invited the Jesuits to White Russia and refused to allow the promulgation of Clement XIV's brief of suppression in 1773. She was thus the means of maintaining the unbroken continuity of the order.

[48] There were in fact Catholics of Eastern rite before 1905. Soloviev himself made his profession of faith before Father Nicholas Tolstoy, a Byzantine priest, in 1896 at Moscow; and there was Father Alexis Zertchaninov, who was exiled to a monastery—the Bolshevists sent him to Tobolsk.

of Russian Catholics of Byzantine rite were formed here and there (a few of converts from the sect of *Starovery*, "Old Believers"). In 1917 the Ruthenian archbishop of Lwów, Mgr. Andrew Szepticky, in whom Pope Pius X had recognized plenary powers over the Catholic Byzantines in Russia, appointed Mgr. Leonidas Fedorov to be their exarch. The provisional government of that year gave official recognition to them, with Mgr. Leonidas at their head, but after the outbreak of the bolshevist revolution he was imprisoned at Solovky and his small flock scattered.[49] Among them were twenty-five nuns (following the rule of the Third Order of St. Dominic, adapted to their rite), who had done much good work in Moscow and deeply impressed their Orthodox neighbours; most of them were sentenced to varying periods of detention in Solovky, Siberia, and elsewhere, a religious congregation being looked on as a "counter-revolutionary activity." It is gratifying to note that three of these young nuns were Poles, who had given up their Latin rite to work for reunion and therefore were specially obnoxious to the Soviet authorities.

Present State

Western Europe. The Catholic Russian *émigrés* in Paris, Lyons, Lille, Berlin, Prague, etc., number about 1,200 and are in charge of a bishop of their rite (Mgr. Peter Bucys, appointed in 1930), who resides at Kaunas in Lithuania. A Catholic church of the Slav-Byzantine rite has been established at Narva in Estonia, in charge of two priests. Missionary Sisters of the Sacred Heart from Vilna have opened a school, which is very popular.

Far East. The centre for some thousands of Catholic Russians of China and Manchuria (e.g., 200 at Shanghai, with priest, church, and school) is at Kharbin, where their ordinary, Mgr. Fabian Abrantovich, has his headquarters. They

---

[49] Mgr. Leonidas died, still in prison at Vjatka on March 7, 1935. He had spent fourteen of his twenty-two years of priestly life in jail: first under the tzars as a Byzantine Catholic; then under the bolshevists as a Christian.

have there a "little seminary," an orphanage, and two schools, the one for girls conducted by Ursuline nuns (under an English superioress) who have adopted the Eastern rite.

Most of the clergy serving these two scattered groups are former dissident Orthodox priests. The clergy of the future are being formed at the *Russicum* college in Rome, founded for that purpose in 1929. The college is in the Via Carlo Cattaneo, adjoining the church of St. Anthony the Abbot, which is now the public church for Russian Catholics in the city. In 1925 Pius XI confided all Russian affairs to a special commission, whose first president, Mgr. Michael d'Herbigny, S.J., titular Bishop of Ilium, resigned at the end of 1933. There is a Dominican centre for Russian studies at Lille, where the friars are of the Slav-Byzantine rite.

Poland. Most of the three million Orthodox in what was formerly Russian Poland are descendants of the oriental Catholics who were forcibly "reconverted" to Orthodoxy by the Russian emperors (see pp. 78, 79). Many of them (some 18,000 in 50 parishes) have returned to unity,[50] and it was the desire of Pope Pius XI to unite them under a diocesan bishop immediately subject to the Holy See; the chauvinistic attitude of the government of Poland (a Catholic state!) made this impossible, so a semi-permanent visitor apostolic, Mgr. Nicholas Czarnecky, was given them in 1931.

The work of reaggregating these people to the Catholic Church obviously belongs to their Ruthenian neighbours in Galicia, but again political considerations are in the way, so it has been especially entrusted to two Western congregations who have members qualified and willing to adopt the Eastern rite. The *Jesuits* have their headquarters at Albertyn near Vilna, on which depend 15 priests, all of the Slav-Byzantine rite. It is a completely oriental establishment, and over forty scholastics are being trained there for work among all or any Slavonic peoples. The same order conducts a sem-

---

[50] On the other hand, over 20,000 Galician Ruthenians have "turned Orthodox" in recent years, to say nothing of the Podcarpathians.

RUSSIAN CHAPEL AT LYONS

(*Byzantine Rite*)

RUSSIAN CLERGY ASSEMBLED IN ROME

In the centre Mgr. Peter Bucys, Titular Bishop of Olympus

inary at Dubno, founded by the Holy See at the instance of Mgr. Czarnecky.[51] The *Redemptorist* house is at Kovel, where there is a number of priests of that institute, all of Eastern rite. The *Missionary Sisters of the Sacred Heart*, founded at Warsaw specifically for reunion work in 1927, have 30 sisters in 6 houses.

In 1935 all Russians of Eastern rite were withdrawn from the jurisdiction of the pontifical commission for Russian affairs and came under the Sacred Eastern Congregation.

PARTICULAR CUSTOMS

These Catholics have the Byzantine liturgy and sacraments, in Church Slavonic (Staroslav), in strict accordance with the so-called synodal books, and their formal religious practices and outlook are completely oriental. Russians attach great importance to liturgical purity and "hybridization" is carefully avoided. Married men are entitled to be ordained deacon and priest, but voluntary celibacy is encouraged.

BIBLIOGRAPHY

d'Herbigny, *Vladimir Soloviev* (London, 1918); and an article by the same writer, *La formation d'un clergé russe* in *Etudes* of June 5, 1920.

Pierling, *La Russie et le Saint Siege*, 5 vols. (Paris, 1896–1912), continued by Father Boudon.

Pierling, *Rome et Moscou* (Paris, 1883).

*Palmer, *Notes of a Visit to the Russian Church* (London, 1895).

Roma e l'Oriente, Vol. XIV, pp. 55–64 and 78–79. (Grottaferrata, 1917).

---

[51] Father Vladimir Ledokhovsky began to prepare an oriental branch of the Society of Jesus in 1920, at the wish of Pope Benedict XV. There are now 35 priests of the Society who are Byzantines, and chapels of the rite have been provided in Rome at the *Casa generalizia* (St. Vladimir's) and at the *Gregorianum* (Our Lady of Kazan's).

11. OTHER BYZANTINE ELEMENTS

Albania. Two thirds of the Albanians are Mohammedan; the rest are dissident Orthodox and Latin Catholics in the proportion of about two to one.[52] From 1628 there was a body of Catholics of the Byzantine rite in the coastal region of Simarra, served for a time by Basilian monks from Sicily, but the mission collapsed in 1765. They had a vicar apostolic from 1692 till 1737.

Since the Patriarch of Constantinople refused to recognize the Orthodox Albanians as self-governing in 1924, there has been some talk of reunion with Rome. About 1920 this step was taken by the archimandrite Germanos at Elbassan, and he ministers to the small group of lay people who followed him.

Georgia, or Iberia, lies between Armenia and Russia, south of the Caucasus, and was evangelized during the fourth century, probably from Armenia and Syria.[53] Later, it came under the influence of Constantinople and drifted into schism in the earlier years of the thirteenth century. From then on Latin missionaries worked in Georgia, and at least one king and one katholikos were formally Catholic. In 1801 the Emperor Alexander I annexed Georgia to his dominions, and its Orthodox church became an exarchate of the Church of Russia; it was released from this thraldom at the revolution, only to fall into the hands of a soviet socialist republic.

In 1917 there were 2½ million Orthodox Georgians and

---

[52] The mountainous district of the south is pretty solidly Catholic. There our priests are most picturesque people, with huge moustaches but no beard.

[53] The national apostle is a rather mysterious female saint, Nino. She is commemorated in the Roman Martyrology on December 15, under the style of *Sancta Christiana, ancilla.*

about 40,000 Catholics, of whom 32,000 were of the Latin rite and the rest of the Armenian (no Byzantine Catholics were allowed in imperial Russia). Today there are a few hundred Georgians of the Byzantine rite, whose liturgical language is Georgian. They are ministered to by priests of a congregation founded at Constantinople by Father Peter Karischiaranti in 1861 to minister to his countrymen of whatever rite. He also founded an auxiliary sisterhood. There is an administrator apostolic at Tiflis for all the Georgians in U. S. S. R.

BIBLIOGRAPHY

*Peacock, *Albania* (London, 1914).
Tamarati, *L'Eglise Géorgienne* (Rome, 1910).
Karst, *Litterature Géorgienne chrétienne* (Paris, 1934).
*Wardrop, *The Kingdom of Georgia* (London, 1888).

Chapter VI

THE ALEXANDRIAN RITE

1. THE COPTS (EGYPT)
2. THE ETHIOPIANS (ABYSSINIA)

THE ALEXANDRIAN RITE

1. THE COPTS

I. HISTORY AND PRESENT STATE

GENERAL ECCLESIASTICAL HISTORY

From its beginnings the heresy of Monophysism (see p. 6) had its stronghold in Egypt, where the patriarch of Alexandria, Dioscoros, was its spokesman and leader. After six years of controversy and violence he was deposed and his teaching condemned by the Council of Chalcedon in 451. Practically all the clergy and people of Egypt (and many in Syria) refused to accept the decisions of the council, not altogether on account of religious enthusiasm but also because national passions were involved: it was bad enough to be subject to a foreign emperor without having "Byzantine theology" as well. The century that followed was an outrageous period of ecclesiastical quarreling, minor schisms, persecution, political chicanery, and physical violence. The see of Alexandria was bandied between hierarchs who were sometimes orthodox but more often monophysite, till in 567 two lines of patriarchs were definitely established: one for the mostly foreign minority of orthodox Catholics, the other for the solid mass of Egyptian Monophysites, today called the Coptic Church.[1] With the modification that the orthodox line is now in schism from Rome, that is still the position.

The Monophysite Egyptians continued to be troubled by domestic quarrels, by the Catholics, and in 616–628, by Persian

---

[1] A Copt is simply an Egyptian (Arabic *Kibti* = Gk. [Aἰ] *gúpt* [ιos]), in actual use a Christian Egyptian.

invaders who bitterly persecuted them. Eleven years later the Arab conquest was begun, and the anti-imperialist Copts are said to have given aid to the Khalifah against the Byzantines. They had their reward, and for century after century were oppressed by Arabs, Mameluks, and Turks; massacres were frequent and apostasies so numerous that today 90 per cent of the Egyptians are Mohammedan. But there were also many martyrs. The Copts did not get on well with the Crusaders, and though two legates of the Coptic patriarch John II signed an act of union at the Council of Florence it never became effective. An attempt at reunion by the patriarch Gabriel VIII in 1594 was no more successful.

Early in the seventeenth century Capuchin missions were established in the Levant by Father Joseph of Paris (Joseph Leclerc du Tremblay, "the Grey Cardinal"), and a foundation was made at Cairo in 1630. For a time it prospered, under the direction of Father Agathangelo of Vendôme. The patriarch opened all his churches to the friars, and Father Agathangelo gave spiritual conferences in the schismatical monasteries of the Lower Thebaid.[2] Unhappily, and not for the only time in history, the great obstacle to Coptic reunion was the Latin Catholics resident in the country. Father Agathangelo referred to the household of the French consul as a "synagogue of Satan," and the general behaviour of the Europeans was such than when the Coptic patriarch complained bitterly that "the Roman Church in this country is a brothel" Father Agathangelo could not deny his reasons for saying so. He appealed to the cardinal prefect of Propaganda to have the worst offenders excommunicated. But nothing was done and Father Agathangelo went off in despair to Ethiopia and to martyrdom.

THE CATHOLIC COPTS

In 1675 the Friars Minor of the Observance were given charge of a prefecture apostolic in Upper Egypt and the Jesuits came to Cairo, but the Coptic mission languished until

[2] One of the two books he used for this purpose was *On the Holy Will of God*, by Father Benedict of Canfield (William Fitch), the first Capuchin missionary in England in penal times. Fr. Agathangelo and his companion, Fr. Cassian, were beatified in 1905.

1741, when the dissident bishop living at Jerusalem, Amba Athanasius, became a Catholic and was put in charge of those of his rite. At this time the learned Raphael Tukhi was editing and publishing the Coptic liturgical books in Rome and was made ordaining bishop for Coptic seminarists in the City. The first two successors of Amba Athanasius as vicars apostolic, John Faragi (1781) and Matthew Righet (1788), could not receive episcopal consecration, apparently because there was no Catholic bishop in Egypt and a voyage to Europe was too difficult. The third, Maximos Joed, was nominated in 1824 and consecrated by a Byzantine, Ignatius V. Kattan, Melkite patriarch of Antioch. Meanwhile, the Catholic Copts had no churches of their rite and had to use those of the Franciscans; this and the overlapping of jurisdictions caused numerous difficulties. It was believed that the khedive Mohammed Ali wished the Catholics to have a patriarchate of their own, and accordingly it was erected by Pope Leo XII in 1824. But it was not made operative, and there was a further succession of three vicars apostolic, of whom the learned Amba Aghapios Bishai represented his church at the Vatican Council.

In 1893 the Franciscans made over ten churches to the sole use of the Copts, and two years later Pope Leo XIII divided them into three dioceses and appointed Amba Cyril Makarios as administrator; in 1899 he was advanced to the rank of patriarch. From this time onward the Catholics of the Coptic rite have continued to increase in numbers and effectiveness, progress in which the Franciscan and Jesuit fathers have played a large part. Mgr. Makarios held a synod of his church at Cairo in 1898, and continued to govern it for ten years, when certain difficulties made it necessary for him to resign. He went into schism for a time. The patriarchal throne has since remained vacant, being administered first by Amba Maximos Sedfaui and then by Amba Mark Khuzam, the present bishop of Thebes and administrator apostolic.

PRESENT STATE

Patriarch. His title is "Patriarch of Alexandria of the Copts," and he is appointed directly by the Holy See. His powers are little more than those of a metropolitan. The civil power recognizes him (and during a vacancy the administrator) as the competent judge in the matrimonial and testamentary causes of his people.

Bishops. The Coptic sees are Alexandria (comprising the whole of Lower Egypt, with residence at Cairo), Hermopolis Major (residence at Minieh), and Thebes (residence at Tahta). The bishops are appointed by the Holy See.

Parochial clergy. The "great" seminary founded by Pope Leo XIII at Tahta in 1899 was reorganized in 1920, and the "little" seminary, conducted by the Jesuits at Cairo from 1879 till 1907, was reopened in 1927. Both are now directed by the Coptic secular clergy, the junior seminarians studying under Jesuit professors at a neighbouring college. Other aspirants go to the oriental seminary at Beirut. The clergy have been bound to celibacy since the synod of 1898, but dispensations are sometimes accorded by the Holy See (the patriarch has not this power), especially in the case of married priests converted from Monophysism. About four fifths of the 70 Coptic priests are celibate.

Religious institutes. The *African Missionaries of Lyons* administer three districts in Lower Egypt, under the jurisdiction of the vicar apostolic of the Latins in the Nile delta. Two of their priests have adopted the Coptic rite. The Friars Minor have also begun to form subjects of that rite in their college at Assiut. The *Coptic Sisters of the Sacred Heart* have three convents (31 religious) and schools in Cairo, Tahta, and Sohag.

The Faithful. In 1894 there were 5,000 Catholics of the Coptic rite; in 1934 there were 39,000.[8] With a few individual exceptions they are of the poorest class of Egyptian *fellahin*. The Jesuits have done much educational and spiritual work for them since 1879, and the Friars Minor minister to many in their Egyptian vicariate.

---

[8] There are still 900,000 dissidents. The better among the laity and lower clergy tend to be dissatisfied with their own church and to turn toward Catholicism. But as we lack means to build churches and schools and train priests, Protestant missions reap much of this harvest. For some years abjurations of heresy have averaged over 1,100 a year.

II. LITURGY AND CUSTOMS

Church buildings. A church of the Coptic rite has a distinctive arrangement. It is divided for the whole of its width into sanctuary, choir, and nave, and further subdivided for men and women, by screens of carved and inlaid wood, often open lattice work, and as the central door is not closed the altar is never entirely hidden. Within the triple-domed sanctuary (*haikal*) are three altars in a line, each in an apse, standing clear of the wall; they are of brick or stone with a wooden top, without gradines, wholly covered by linen or silk cloths; on each are a crucifix and two candles and a sort of box (*al-kursi*) in which the chalice stands during the Liturgy. On the *haikal*-screen are a few pictures and others, with mosaics and wall-paintings, around the church. Actually most Catholic Coptic churches at the present day are tiny tumble-down buildings with no screens and having a "Western" altar with gradines and flowerpots, but preserving the wooden *mensa* (tablet); the Blessed Sacrament is reserved in a tabernacle. Such innovations as seats and statues are sometimes seen. The cathedral of the Bishop of Thebes at Tahta is planned in the traditional way; the same applies to Minieh, but it has been long unfinished for lack of funds.[4]

Vestments. These are in some respects peculiar to the Copts but except for a sort of amice (*kidaris*) they correspond to those of the Byzantine rite. The *burnus* (chasuble) is open all down the front, rather like a cope. Deacons wear a *stikharion* (or alb) and stole just as a Greek deacon does. Bishops wear the Latin mitre, but for crozier have the Eastern twined serpents; they also wear the *omophorion* but not the *sakkos*. Servers are seen in surprising costumes—cottas, albs, stoles, and lace collars! Out of church the clerical hat (the dissidents

---

[4] The average superficial area of the three Catholic Coptic pro-cathedrals was less than 16 square metres! There is a curious bit of folk-lore to account for the lavish use of ostrich-eggs as an ornament in Coptic and other Levantine churches. They may have really been used originally to prevent mice climbing down the cords and getting at the oil in the many hanging lamps.

wear a turban) is a black cylinder about six inches high, growing wider to the top—a thoroughly European-looking headdress (bishops cover it with a veil). All wear the wide-sleeved *rason* over the cassock.

Liturgical books. These were arranged and printed in Rome by Raphael Tukhi between 1736 and 1764. Mgr. Makarios published the missal, ritual, and office-book at Cairo (1898–1906), and some of them have been reprinted there since, the Divine Office in 1930, revised by Mgr. Khuzam.

Altar-vessels and bread. The vessels are very similar to those of the Latin rite, with three small and two large veils to cover the offerings, but the paten is larger and deeper. The bread (*korban*) is leavened, round and thick, marked with twelve crosses. *Ripidia* are carried in processions, and a hand-cross is used to give some blessings.

Music. The Coptic lay people have a remarkable knowledge of the text of their liturgy and they take an active part in a solemn celebration, singing the traditional chant by heart, with copious variations. Some of this music was first written down by the Jesuit fathers Blin and Badet at the end of the last century. Cymbals, triangles, and occasionally the flute (*mizmar*) are the only instruments.

Liturgical language. This is Coptic (i.e., the last stage of Egyptian, a tongue otherwise dead since the fifteenth century), with many Greek words and some phrases. Arabic is the vernacular of Egypt and more and more tends unofficially to displace Coptic in the Liturgy: it is used officially for the Divine Office and certain occasional rites. The Bohaïric dialect of Lower Egypt is used throughout the country.

The Eucharistic Liturgy

The Coptic Liturgy is a form of the original Greek Liturgy of Alexandria with three alternative *anaphoras:* an adaptation of the Byzantine "St. Basil" (as below) for use on ordinary days and Sundays; "of St. Mark," or "St. Cyril," used on his and St. Cyril's feasts and when a bishop is consecrated; and "of St. Gregory Nazianzen," for great feasts (this last is addressed throughout to our Lord). The Catholics have a

CLERGY OF THE COPTIC RITE

In the centre, the Bishop of Thebes

COPTIC BISHOP, PRIESTS AND DEACON

CHURCH OF THE COPTIC RITE

form of "low Mass," which is celebrated in a low voice. The Coptic Liturgy (*Prosfora*) may be concelebrated with any number of celebrants; there is no Liturgy of the Presanctified.

After the Offices of the Third and Sixth Hours have been said or sung the priest goes to the altar, blesses the people and says the Our Father with them, and begins the preparation, the prayers of which are said in a low voice. He washes his hands, chooses a host from several offered by the deacon, and recollects the intention for which he is offering the Liturgy. Then he takes the bread in a veil and, followed by the deacon with wine and other ministers with candles, walks once round the altar while the people sing a variable psalm-verse. At the front of the altar again he blesses the bread and wine, of which he pours some into the chalice, adding a little water. Then he says aloud the prayer of thanksgiving "of St. Mark":

> "Let us give thanks to the beneficent and merciful God . . . let us pray that the Almighty, the Lord our God, will keep us in all peace this holy day and all the days of our life."

Deacon: "Pray ye" (Greek).

People: "*Kyrie eleison.*"

Priest: "O Master, Lord, God Almighty . . ." and continues his prayer. This litany form continues throughout the Liturgy.

Then follows an offertory prayer, addressed to Christ, and afterwards he covers the offering and leaves the sanctuary. Standing before the people who bow their heads, he pronounces the long prayer of absolution, "of the Son," in the second part of which he invokes (among others) the Apostles, "the seer of God, blessed Mark, apostle, evangelist and martyr," the 318 Fathers of the Council of Nicaea, the 150 of Constantinople, the 200 of Ephesus, and the 630 of Chalcedon.[5] If an ecclesiastic higher in rank than the celebrant is present, this absolution is given by him.

The celebrant now re-enters the sanctuary for the liturgy

---

[5] Needless to say the non-Catholic Copts do not mention Chalcedon.

of the catechumens. He puts incense into the thurible and says "the prayer of incense of the Pauline epistle," for the acceptance of the sacrifice, walking with the deacon three times round the altar as he censes it. Then he leaves the sanctuary and, with appropriate prayers, censes the *haikal*-door, the picture of our Lady, the other images, and the people, then returns to the altar and offers incense on their behalf, praying for them inaudibly as he goes once round the altar. Meanwhile a lesson is being read outside the *haikal*-screen facing the people; on Sundays and many other days there are three, from St. Paul, from the Catholic Epistles, and from the Acts. These should be read by a reader, subdeacon, and deacon respectively, but usually the deacon or server does them all, with much incense and ceremony. Each lesson is said in Coptic and repeated in Arabic; during the Arabic of the first epistle the celebrant says inaudibly the "prayer of the Pauline epistle," and during the second epistle in Arabic he says in like manner the "prayer of the Catholic Epistle." While the Acts lesson is being read in Coptic the celebrant says a short "prayer of the Offerings," and during the third lesson goes three times round the altar, censing it and praying litanywise with the deacon for peace, etc. After circumambulating the altar he censes the images, etc., as before, and reads a notice of the saint of the day. Then the *Trisagion* is sung three times, and the celebrant censes the altar and the gospel-book. A procession is formed led by the priest, followed by the deacon carrying the book, which goes round the altar (the Byzantine "little entrance") and out at the *haikal*-gates, while the choir sings psalm verses. The deacon exclaims, "Stand in the fear of God and hear the holy Gospel," and the priest, after two prayers, proceeds to chant it, the thurible being swung all the time; afterwards it is repeated in Arabic by the deacon.[6] At the end is said, "Glory be to our God for everlasting ages, Amen," and the people reply, "Glory to thee, O Lord."

After an inaudible litany and prayer the liturgy of the

---

[6] The Gospel in Coptic is very commonly sung by the celebrant, even though he be a bishop.

faithful begins by the priest blessing the people: "Peace ✠ be to all."[7] Then there are three chanted prayers, for the Church, hierarchy, and for the people and their needs, and the altar, gifts, and people are again censed and the Creed is said by all in Arabic; it is in the plural (*We* believe, etc.), and the *Filioque*[8] is added; the last clause only is chanted (in Coptic). The priest washes his hands, wringing and drying them before the people, whom he blesses, and says the "prayer of the Kiss" with the deacon; but the kiss of peace is no longer given except among the clergy; the people touch hands. The bread and wine are uncovered, the priest and deacon waving the largest veil (which is sewn with little bells) over them while the deacon commands: "Offer, offer, offer in order. Stand ye with fear. Look to the east. Let us attend to the mercy of peace and the sacrifice of praise." There is the usual dialogue leading to the preface, which is said in a high voice. The deacon exhorts the people, "Ye that are seated, stand up!" and "Look to the east!"; they sing a short verse, and all join in the *Sanctus* (*Benedictus* is not added), which the celebrant then expands into a eucharistic prayer in which the redemption is set forth and leads up to:

> "And he hath instituted for us this great mystery of good-
> ness (*he puts his hands for a moment into the smoke of
> the thurible and then stretches them over the offerings*).
> For when he was determined to give himself to death for
> the life of the world. . . ."

People: "We believe, we believe that it is indeed so. Amen."

Priest: "He took bread into his holy, spotless, pure, blessed and life-giving hands" (*he takes it*).

People: "We believe that it is indeed so. Amen."

Priest: "He looked up to Heaven, to thee, O God, who art his Father and Lord of all (*he looks up*). He gave ✠ thanks. (*People:* "Amen.") He blessed ✠ it. ("Amen.") He sanctified ✠ it."

---

[7] Εἰρήνη Πᾶσι. This and all similar salutations are in Greek.

[8] *Filioque* appears in many Monophysite MSS; it has apparently been dropped merely out of imitation of the Orthodox, a form of flattery toward them of which the dissident Copts have given several examples.

People: "Amen. Amen. Amen. Amen. We believe and we confess and praise him" (*in Greek*).

Priest: "He broke it (*he breaks a little at the edge*). He gave it to his blessed disciples and holy apostles saying: Take, eat ye all of this, *for this is my Body* which shall be broken for you for many to be given for the remission of sins. Do this in memory of me" (*he prostrates, but does not elevate the Host*).

The precious Blood is in a like manner consecrated[9] and the people make an act of faith aloud while the commemoration of the Passion is said. Then, lifting up his hands, the celebrant in a low voice makes the *epiklesis*, which is addressed to our Lord but otherwise similar to that in the Byzantine rite. Then he begins the intercession for the living:

". . . Remember, O Lord, the peace of thy One Only Holy Catholic and Apostolic Church."

Deacon: "Pray for the peace of the One Holy Catholic and Apostolic Orthodox Church of God."

People: "*Kyrie eleison.*"

Priest: "Which thou hast purchased unto thyself with the glorious blood of thy Christ. Keep her in peace together with all her orthodox bishops. And first, remember, O Lord, the supreme Pontiff, the Pope Pius, and our reverend and blessed father, the patriarch Amba N., archbishop of the great city of Alexandria, and likewise their fellow-servant, the bishop Amba M."

Deacon: "Pray for the pontiff," etc.

People: "*Kyrie eleison.*"

And so on for the clergy, religious, and all folk, all sacred places, the fruitfulness of the earth (with a special petition for the rising of the Nile, from June 19 to October 21), and those who offer the sacrifice. The saints are commemorated,

---

[9] The Coptic words of institution say of the chalice that our Lord tasted it. Cf. the 82nd homily of St. John Chrysostom and certain Syriac *anaphoras.* The chalice is slightly tilted in the form of a cross at the words "Take and drink."

naming the holy Mother of God, John the Forerunner, Stephen, Mark, Athanasius, Cyril, and others, and intercession made inaudibly for the dead. The priest blesses the people, invoking the prayers of our Lady, the archangels, prophets, martyrs, and the Four Incorporeal Living Creatures (Ezech. i. 5–14) and the Four and Twenty Elders (Apoc. iv. 4), to whom the Copts have great devotion, celebrating liturgical feasts in their honour.

The fraction is preceded by an elevation of both species together. Here follows a variable "prayer of the Fraction," during which the Host is broken into three parts; then the Our Father is said in Arabic, ending ". . . evil, through Jesus Christ our Lord." After further prayers the priest takes up a particle of the Host, raises it above his head, and says in Greek, "Holy things to the holy ones." He dips the particle into the precious Blood, touches with it the other two particles, saying in Greek, "The holy body and the precious and true blood of Jesus Christ, the Son of our God. Amen," signs the Chalice with it, saying similar words, and drops it in, saying in Coptic, "This is in truth the body and blood of Emmanuel our God. Amen." (*People:* "Amen. I believe.")

The priest makes a further act of faith in the Real Presence (in a prayer which even among the non-Catholics attests the teaching of Chalcedon), and then lifts up the Host on the paten so that it can be seen by the people, who then sing Psalm 150 with alleluia after each verse, followed by a hymn. The celebrant then receives the holy Body and Blood. He kisses the Host before consuming it. The Catholic lay people now generally receive communion in one kind only, kneeling, the words of administration being: "This is in truth the body of Emmanuel our God." *Communicant:* "Amen"; but sometimes standing, in both kinds separately or by intinction. Afterwards the celebrant blesses the people, cleanses the vessels, saying prayers of thanksgiving, and standing before the people prays for the help of Almighty God and the saints, naming the titular of the church and him whose feast it is. He gives a final blessing, sprinkling the people with water blessed before the offertory. The deacon makes the dismissal: "The grace of our Lord and God and Saviour Jesus Christ be with you all. Go in peace."

People: "Amen. An hundred years" (i.e., for an infinity of time). Blessed bread is distributed.

THE DIVINE OFFICE

There are seven "hours," collectively called *al-Agbieh,* namely Prayer of Sunset (*al-Ghurub*), of Repose (*an-Naum*), of Midnight (*Nusf al-Lail*), of the Dawn (*al-Baker*), and of the Third, Sixth, and Ninth Hours; bishops and religious have an extra evening office, "of the Veil" (*as-Satar*). The night-office has three nocturns of twelve psalms and a gospel each, with *troparia,* and prayers, and the Creed after each nocturn; the other hours each consists of twelve psalms (some "at choice") a gospel and *troparia* (*al-Baker* has nineteen psalms); all the hours have several short prayers, the *Trisagion,* Our Father, and *Kyrie eleison* (41 times). Nearly all the Office is in Arabic since 1906.

THE SACRAMENTS

Baptism is a long ceremony. After prayers and blessing of the oil of catechumens the priest anoints the forehead, breast, hands, and back of the child. Then there are exorcisms, renunciations and profession of faith by the godparent, and the anointings of the breast and hands are repeated. The water is blessed at great length: there are three lessons and a gospel, prayers for the sick, dead, and others not immediately concerned, a little oil of catechumens is poured into the water three times and it is breathed upon crosswise thrice; there is a marvellous panegyrical exorcism and benediction of the water, modeled on the prayer of the eucharistic *anaphora,* and a little Chrism is added. Then the deacon brings the child "from the west to the east over against Jordan" (the font), and the priest immerses it three times saying, "N., I baptize thee in the name of the Father . . . ," etc. Baptism is administered by pouring water in cases of necessity, of adults, and of conditional baptism.[10] The rite ends with a characteristic "prayer at the pouring away of the water."

Confirmation follows immediately. The child is anointed with Chrism on the forehead, mouth, hands, breast, back, and soles of the feet, in such a way as to make 21 anointings, with varying formulas; then the priest imposes his right hand and breathes on the child, saying, "Receive the Holy Ghost and be a cleansed vessel. . . . " The child is dressed in a white robe, with a girdle and fillet ("crown") and final prayers are said, followed by a procession and Liturgy.

Penance. Absolution is given in a long deprecatory formula: ". . . Do thou, O God, grant him forgiveness of his sins, and may he be absolved by the All-holy Trinity, Father, Son, and Holy Ghost, through my unworthy mouth. . . ."

Eucharist. See page 145.

Extreme Unction. Again a very long rite, in which seven priests one by one light seven lamps or candles, with an epistle, psalm, gospel, and prayer at each lighting. Finally the gospel-book is laid on his head and the sick man is anointed once on the forehead and wrists, with a prayer that he may be healed in body and soul, and further prayers (including *Gloria in excelsis Deo*) said. In practice one priest only is present and he lights all seven lamps, with the prayers appropriate thereto; an abridged version of this rite was published for Catholic use in 1933.

Holy Orders. Singers are ordained by a prayer and a blessing, readers and subdeacons by imposition of hands on the temples; deacons and priests receive two impositions of the right hand on the head, and are invested with the girdle and stole respectively. The formula for ordaining a bishop names the powers which he is to exercise, and all bishops present lay their hands twice on his shoulders and forearms and breathe on his face. The formula for a priest is: "Fill him with the Holy Spirit and the grace and wisdom . . . ," etc. "We call you N., to be a priest for the ministry of the altar which

[10] This is often necessary for converts from the dissidents, owing to the careless and fanciful ways in which many of their priests administer the sacrament.

was first given to right-believers, in the name of the Father.
. . . Amen."

Marriage. The wedding service consists of two parts, the
betrothal (epistle and gospel, three long prayers, the Creed,
a thanksgiving, and a blessing of the wedding garments) and
the crowning. After an epistle (Ephes. v. 22– vi. 3), gospel
(Matt. xix. 1–6), litany, and prayers, the priest blesses oil and
anoints both parties on the head and wrists; then he crowns
them while "Worthy the bridegroom and his bride" is sung
thrice. The rite is concluded by exhortations, broken up by
antiphons sung by the choir.

Calendar. The Copts date their years according to the "era
of the Martyrs," i.e., beginning from August 29 or September
13, 284, the date of the accession of Diocletian. Their year
has twelve months of thirty days each, and a "little month,"
ordinarily of five days (these lines are written on Pharemuthi
2, 1650, i.e., April 2, 1934, according to them), but the Catholics of Lower Egypt fix Easter by the Gregorian computation
and those of Upper Egypt by the computation of the patriarch
Demetrios (d. 231).

Feasts are divided into three classes, and there are numerous
saints' days, most of them Egyptian. A number of festivals are
common to the Coptic and Roman calendars, but most of them
fall on different dates; they commemorate the Primacy of St.
Peter the Apostle on Misri 7 (Aug. 1). Of more recent Western
feasts, Corpus Christi and the Sacred Heart are the principal
ones adopted. Sundays and nine other days are holydays of
obligation.

Penitential seasons. During Lent (47 days) fasting from food,
drink, and tobacco lasts till noon and abstinence is observed
even on Sundays. Abstinence is further observed on every
Wednesday and Friday (except in paschal-time), for 16 days
before Christmas, 3 before SS. Peter and Paul, and 15 before
the Assumption. A fortnight before Lent begins there are
three days of penitence called the "fast of Nineveh." This
observance is known in all Eastern churches except the Byzantine: it commemorates the penance of the Ninevites at the
preaching of Jonas.

General observations. Copts make the sign of the cross from left to right, and the Catholic lay people show respect by genuflecting instead of the customary prostration on both knees, which is confined to the Liturgy. Water is solemnly blessed at the Epiphany (a common Eastern custom, referring to our Lord's baptism), at the Supper of the New Covenant, i.e., Maundy Thursday, and on SS. Peter and Paul's day; on the last two days there is a washing of feet in every church. The usual Western devotions, Benediction of the Blessed Sacrament, rosary, stations of the cross, etc., are practised, but the effects of Western influence are far less noticeable in Upper than in Lower Egypt.

BIBLIOGRAPHY

Fortescue, *The Lesser Eastern Churches* (London, 1913).

Khuzam, *The Catholic Coptic Mission* (Cairo, 1929).

Bute, *The Coptic Morning Service* (London, 1908).

*Woolley, *Coptic Offices* (London, 1930).

Blin, *Chants liturgiques des Coptes* (Cairo, 1889).

*Malan, *Original Documents of the Coptic Church* (London, 1872–8).

2. THE ETHIOPIANS

I. HISTORY AND PRESENT STATE

General Ecclesiastical History

The Ethiopians[11] are believed to be partly of Semitic stock, and their ancestors before the Christian era probably emigrated to Africa from southern Arabia. They now occupy the mountainous country between the Sudan, Kenya, and the sea, though their seaboard is in the hands of the British, French, and Italians.

The first authentic evangelization of the Ethiopians of which there is record was toward the middle of the fourth century, when two youths from Tyre, Frumentius and Aedesius, spared from a massacre of their fellow-voyagers, attained influence at the Ethiopian court at Aksum and preached the gospel there. St. Frumentius was eventually consecrated bishop for his converts by the then archbishop of Alexandria, the great St. Athanasius himself. A more extensive evangelization was carried on some hundred and fifty years later by the "Nine Saints," who were monks and probably Monophysites from Syria. In the time of Justinian there was lively competition between the Catholics and Monophysites of Egypt for control of the Ethiopic mission; the last-named won, and the Ethiopian Church has ever since remained hierarchically dependent on the Coptic patriarch of Alexandria, and accordingly monophysite. Until the sixteenth century little is known of the history of Christianity in Ethiopia: especially after the Arab conquest of Egypt communication even with the oppressed mother-church was difficult and often interrupted. There was a religious and intellectual revival in the thirteenth century, followed by the arrival of Dominican missionaries, who had no success. A further revival in the fifteenth century

---

[11] I prefer "Ethiopia" and "Ethiopians" because those are their own names for their country and themselves, and there is nothing against them. The more usual "Abyssinia" and "Abyssinians" originated as an offensive nickname, "the mongrels."

led to the sending of an embassy to the Council of Florence and another to Rome, of which the only result was the establishment by Pope Sixtus IV of a church, monastery, and hospice for Ethiopian pilgrims behind St. Peter's, San Stefano dei Mori, "of the Moors."[12]

The Ethiopian King (*negus*) David III, who reigned from 1505 to 1540, entered into frequent correspondence both with John of Portugal and with the Roman See. The Portugese physician, Bermudez, who was selected as ecclesiastical superior and later as patriarch of Ethiopia, was forced to withdraw because of the ill-will of David's successor Claudius.[13] In 1555 Pope Julius III, in conjunction with the Portugese, appointed Nuñez Barreto, S.J., as patriarch of Ethiopia. The latter never reached his destination but sent his two fellow Jesuits, Orviedo and Carneyro, as bishops. Some converts were made, but the work was carried on under extreme difficulties.

A new development took place with the arrival of Peter Paez, S.J., known as the Second Apostle of Ethiopia. Disguised as an Armenian he set out in 1589 from Ormuz, but was captured and dragged away into slavery before reaching Ethiopia. Ransomed after seven years, he labored in India until 1603, when he finally succeeded in making his desired entrance into Ethiopia. He here converted the *negus* himself, Za Denghel, who because of this was murdered in 1604. His successor Seghed, however, known as Socinius or Socinianus, was in turn converted by the intrepid missionary. An insurrection which occurred in 1624 was put down by this *negus* and he decided on officially adopting the Catholic Faith as the state religion.

To second the strivings after church unity Pope Gregory

---

[12] A monk who lived here, Tasfa Sion, published in 1548–49 a translation of the New Testament into Geéz, which included the "common parts" and one *anaphora* of the Ethiopian Liturgy with a Latin version—the first published text of it. The monastery was unoccupied by 1700 and came for a time into the hands of the Copts, when it sheltered their great liturgical scholar, Raphael Tukhi (d. 1787).

[13] Cf. Schmidlin, *Catholic Mission History*, translated by Matthias Braun, S.V.D. (pp. 287–88), which gives a brief but well-documented account of the Ethiopian mission.

XV had appointed Alfons Mendez, S.J., patriarch of Ethiopia, and this was later confirmed by Urban VIII. On February 7, 1626, the new patriarch was solemnly received by Socinius and four days later took place the public ceremonies of the union of the Ethiopian Church with Rome, the clergy as well as the nobles and King taking the oath of allegiance. Unfortunately the reform decrees which followed were often carried out with great cruelty by overzealous royal officials, while the missionaries themselves acted unwisely and too impetuously in seeking to enforce the new customs, language, and liturgy. The popular dissatisfaction which thus developed was utilized by political conspirators to spread their revolutionary propaganda. The favor of the *negus* himself declined and with his death an attitude of positive hostility toward the Church was assumed by his successor Basilides. The missionaries were exiled and a bloody persecution ensued. The Jesuits who remained in hiding among the persecuted faithful did so at the peril of their lives. The Franciscans and Capuchins sent by the Propaganda could not retrieve the situation. The successor of Mendez, Appolinario de Almeida, who for eight years faced every suffering and danger, finally endured martyrdom with two companions in 1638. The Capuchin Fathers, Agathangelo of Vendôme and Cassian of Nantes were beatified by Pius X as martyrs of the Ethiopian Mission. We may add that we possess an unusual wealth of original documents concerning the Ethiopian mission.[14]

The Catholic Ethiopians

Ethiopia was closed to Catholic missionaries for two hundred years: a native bishop sent there from Rome at the end of the eighteenth century was simply murdered, and several Franciscans had suffered before him. An attempt to establish relations, in accordance with tradition, between the Ethiopians and the Catholic Copts through Amba Theodore abu-Karim,

---

[14] Beccari, S.J., has gathered these into numerous volumes in the Edition of *Notizia e Saggi di opere e documenti inediti riguardanti la storia di Etiopia durante i secoli XVI, XVII e XVIII*, Rome, 1903, and in *Rerum Aethiopicarum Scriptores occidentales inediti a saeculo XVI ad XIX* (14 volumes).

vicar apostolic in Egypt, came to nothing. But in 1839 the famous Irish-French traveler Arnauld d'Abbadie d'Arrast used his influence to get a prefecture apostolic erected at Adowa; it was confided to the Lazarists, with the venerable Father Justin de Jacobis at their head. Seven years later the Capuchins established a vicariate in the Galla country under Mgr. (afterwards Cardinal) Massaia, and another vicariate, "of Abyssinia," was organized from Alitiena by the Lazarists. Mgr. de Jacobis opened a seminary which he put in charge of a distinguished ex-monophysite monk, Aba Michael Ghebra, who eventually reconciled the reigning *negus* with Rome. But in 1854 this *negus* was deposed by the vigorous soldier Kassa (Theodore II), and abandoned his faith in the face of persecution. The dissident primate, Salama,[15] was recalled, and he seized and tortured Aba Michael in a vain attempt to make him apostatize. Having been reprieved from death upon the intervention of the British consul Walter Chichele Plowden (who had supported Theodore's usurpation), he was sentenced to perpetual imprisonment and died from hardship and exposure three months later. Michael Ghebra was beatified as a martyr in 1926. In such ways did the Catholic Church in Ethiopia begin slowly to recover the souls who were thrown away by European aggressiveness in the seventeenth century. The accession of Menelik II in 1889 brought peace to the missionaries and their flocks.

Present State

Organization. The Catholics of the Harrar and Kaffa districts are all of the Latin rite and therefore are no concern of ours here; so for the most part are those of the Lazarist vicariate in the northern part of the country: it was some time before there were any facilities for enabling Catholic Ethiopians to continue in the usages to which they were accustomed. But this was remedied in the north by the time the Capuchins were

---

[15] *Abuna*, "our father," is the title of the metropolitan of Ethiopia since the days of St. Frumentius himself, who was called *Abuna* or *Aba Salama*, "father of peace." But Salama seems to have been really the name of Aba Michael's persecutor.

given a separate prefecture in Eritrea in 1894, and in 1930 an ordinariate of Eastern rite was formed in that Italian colony, Aba Khidaneh-Mariam Kassa being appointed its first bishop, with the title of the old African see of Thibaris. His residence is at Asmara.

Parochial clergy. In 1919 Pope Benedict XV restored the church behind St. Peter's, the old St. Stephen's of the Abyssinians, to serve as the chapel for a college of their rite which he founded close by. This seminary is under the charge of the Italian Capuchins, with an Ethiopian priest as spiritual director. There is an oriental seminary for them in Eritrea, and the Lazarist seminaries in the neighbouring vicariate are available for aspirants of the Eastern rite. These are bound to celibacy but married priests converted from schism are given a dispensation.

Religious institutes. Monasticism (often of a very loose kind) has always been widespread in Ethiopia, and there are today hundreds of monks among the dissidents. To provide for Catholics, twenty-three young Ethiopians and two priests were in 1931 accepted at the Cistercian abbey of Casamiri, in Italy, where they are being trained to form a nucleus of Catholic monks in their own country. Sixteen of these young men were "professed" in September, 1933. There are already nuns there, of a kind now surviving nowhere else in the Church: they take a private vow of perfect chastity, but are not bound to the common life; there are about a hundred of these sisters, living in their homes and engaged in works of mercy.

The Faithful number 27,415 in Eritrea, and 2,422 under the care of the Lazarist vicar apostolic elsewhere, having ninety priests (there is about the same number of Latin Ethiopians and probably nearly three million dissidents, as well as many Mohammedans and heathens). They are an intelligent people, devoted to their religion, but for the most part ignorant and poor. There is a tiny colony of Catholic Ethiopians at Jerusalem.

II. LITURGY AND CUSTOMS

The Ethiopic liturgical rite is substantially that of the Copts, translated into Geéz, but owing to need of revision of the books the Catholics for some time used the Roman rite in that tongue, as they still do for most purposes except the Eucharistic Liturgy. Pope Pius XI ordered that this revision should be carried out in strict accordance with the best Ethiopic liturgical tradition and this has been done so far as the text is concerned, but European influence has led to some regrettable modifications in accessories: a glaring example is the church of the Ethiopian College itself at Rome, which is completely Western, even to the Latin text upon the altar cloth.[16]

Church buildings. The normal plan of an Ethiopian church is now circular, divided into three concentric circles with the altar in the middle, but there are many old churches of basilican shape in Ethiopia and those of the Catholics are generally rectangular. The dissidents treat with great reverence the *tabot*, a box on the altar that contains the wooden altar-board (there are national legends about the Queen of Sheba and the Ark of the Covenant concerning this piece of furniture); Catholics replace it by a tabernacle containing the Blessed Sacrament.

Vestments. These are of the usual eastern type, with a very full chasuble having a sort of embroidered shoulder-cape attached, from which depend four short "orphreys"; bishops and other dignitaries wear a "crown" of a very exotic pattern. But Catholics often wear almost purely Byzantine vestments (with the inevitably lacy alb instead of the *stikharion*), and the bishop has the Roman mitre and crozier. Clerical dress consists of a round black cap (or else a *kalemaukion*) with a wide-sleeved gown over a cassock.

Liturgical books. The book of the Liturgy was published at Asmara in 1913 and the "breviary," containing the psalter,

---

[16] This is the sort of thing that provokes non-Catholic orientals to maintain that, whatever the Holy See may say, the Roman policy is to "hybridize" Eastern Christians with the ultimate object, or result, of making them Latins.

lessons, and office of our Lady, in 1926. The Geéz edition of the Roman *Rituale* was last printed at Asmara in 1924 and the *Pontificale* at Rome in 1931.

Altar-vessels and bread. The altar-vessels are as in the Latin rite. The bread is an extraordinary example of hybridization: in Eritrea, unleavened is practically universally used by Catholics; elsewhere, unleavened at a "low Mass" but leavened at a solemn celebration! Blessings are given with a hand-cross.

Music. The Ethiopian chant, enharmonic, of course, has received little study. To western ears it is wild and barbaric, and is accompanied *ad libitum* by drums, cymbals, and rattles of bells. Organs are unknown.

Liturgical language. This is Geéz, the classical Ethiopian tongue, a Semitic language closely allied to Arabic; since before the thirteenth century it has been transformed into the present vernacular dialects, principally Amharic and Tigreh.

THE EUCHARISTIC LITURGY

As has been said above, the Liturgy (*Keddase*) is "according to the order of our fathers the Egyptians," translated into Geéz and modified by time. There are fourteen *anaphoras*, that "of the Apostles" being most commonly used, and this one is, in fact, independent of the Coptic rite, though derived from Egypt through the ancient *Ethiopic Church Order*. The "common" parts of the Liturgy are a form of the Alexandrian "St. Mark." There is no concelebration or Liturgy of the Presanctified; the Catholics have a form of "low" celebration for ordinary days.

When the priest has vested, and prepared the gifts with appropriate prayers and ceremonies, the deacon commands "Stand up for prayer!" and the people reply "*Kyrie eleison*" (one of the few Greek phrases surviving in this Liturgy). Certain prayers and responses lead to the "prayer of the Anaphora," a sort of *epiklesis*, addressed to our Lord, then, after a long absolution, a diaconal litany for all the various classes of mankind and their needs, e.g.,

"For our archpope Aba N . . . , and the blessed father Aba M . . . , we beseech the Lord to spare them to us for a long time, that with clean and understanding heart they may rightly speak the word of faith as guardians of the Church."

People: "*Kyrie eleison.*"

"For the weak among Christians, we beseech the Lord to grant them their part in the cleansing from sin and seal them with the seal of holiness." "*Kyrie eleison.*"

Then the priest blesses incense and censes the altar, the sanctuary, and the church, after a lovely prayer beginning "I will offer to thee incense and rams; all thy garments smell of myrrh, aloes, and cassia; let my prayer be as incense in thy sight." Before the lessons is said a form of the Hail Mary, otherwise unknown in the East (unless introduced from the West) and occurring in no other Liturgy:

"Hail, Mary, full of grace (three times), the Lord is with thee. Blessed art thou amongst women and blessed is the fruit of thy womb. Pray to and intercede with thy beloved Son that he forgive us our sins."

There are three lessons, from St. Paul, the Catholic epistles, and the Acts, and then the *Trisagion* is sung thrice in a special way, commemorating the birth, baptism, death, resurrection, ascension, and second coming of our divine Lord. The Hail Mary is repeated, and the gospel-book carried processionally to the place. Then, after a prayer for all sorts and conditions of men, the gospel is sung by the celebrant or deacon, with a scriptural conclusion that varies according to the evangelist read, e.g., for St. Mark, "he that hath ears to hear, let him hear."

The liturgy of the faithful begins with a short litany between priest, deacon, and people for the Church and her hierarchy and the sovereign and people; the deacon says "Stand up for prayer."

People: "*Kyrie eleison.*"
Priest: "Peace be to you all."
People: "And with thy spirit."

The priest asks God for peace in the Church.

Deacon: "Pray for the peace of the one holy apostolic Church, orthodox in the Lord."

And the people pray silently (this litany form is common throughout the Liturgy). The priest uncovers the gifts and washes his hands, sprinkling the people with the water, and the kiss of peace is given. Then the Nicene creed is said in its fifth-century Egyptian form (Catholics add "and from the Son") and the *anaphora* of the Twelve Apostles, "whose prayers and praise are with us for ever and ever," begins with the usual dialogue ("Lift up your hearts," etc.).

The preface is preceded by an intercessory prayer for the living and dead, during which the deacon commemorates aloud our Lady, the evangelists, apostles, and other saints; during the inaudible preface he exclaims "Ye who sit,[17] stand up! . . . Look to the East! . . . Let us pay attention!" The *Sanctus* runs "Holy, holy, holy Lord of Sabaoth, the heavens and the earth are wholly full of the holiness of Thy glory," and *Benedictus* is not sung. The celebrant incenses the gifts and goes straight to the consecration aloud: "In the same night that he was betrayed he took bread into his sacred and unblemished hands."

People: "We believe that this is true: we believe."
Priest: "He looked up to Heaven towards thee, his father; he gave thanks; he ✠ blessed and brake (he breaks but does not divide the bread) and gave it to his disciples, saying to them: *Take, eat, this bread is my body,* which is broken for you for the forgiveness of sins."
People: "Amen, amen, amen. We believe and confess, we praise thee, our Lord and our God. We believe."

And in like manner the chalice is consecrated, and the invocation of the Holy Ghost follows immediately.

---

[17] On the floor, generally.

In the prayers which follow the celebrant uses a curious form of words of the Blessed Sacrament: "Truly the body and blood, even to his hands and feet"; and in a prayer for forgiveness of sin he refers to "our father Peter" and quotes our Lord's commission to him. The great intercession for living and dead is short (part of it is really interpolated before the preface). Then the priest lifts up the Holy Things, singing "Holiness to the holy ones," and the breaking of the Bread and putting of one piece into the Chalice follows. After further acts of faith in the real presence, the passion, and the divinity of our Lord ("his godhead was not divided from his manhood for an hour, not for the twinkling of an eye"), the celebrant receives communion and gives it to the people.

Among Catholics there is diversity and a good deal of freedom in the manner of receiving it. At a solemn Liturgy it is always received in both kinds; at a "low Mass," generally in one only, but sometimes in both. The Body and Blood are administered *separately* (the Blood in a spoon), and the words used are, respectively, "The bread of life which came down from Heaven, the body of Christ," and "The cup of life which came down from Heaven, the precious blood of Christ."

A hymn of thanksgiving is sung, and not till now do celebrant and people say the Lord's Prayer. After the cleansing of the vessels blessing is invoked upon the people, and our Lady and the four archangels, Isaac, Jacob, St. Mark, the Holy Innocents, the Fathers of the early oecumenical councils, and several Egyptian and Ethiopian saints called upon. The priest pronounces a long final blessing, and the deacon says "Go in peace!"

THE DIVINE OFFICE

The Ethiopic office consists almost entirely of psalms, with lessons from the prophets and short poetical compositions interspersed.

THE SACRAMENTS

With the exception of the Eucharist (see above) these are all administered according to the Roman forms, pending the revision of the Ethiopian books. Until recently the priest administered *Confirmation* after Baptism, but now it is deferred and given by the bishop or his delegate. The seven holy *Orders* of the West are conferred.

Calendar. According to Ethiopian chronology we are now (1934) in the year A.D. 1926, but their annual calendar is similar to that of the Copts. Their new year's day is August 29 according to the Julian reckoning, September 11 according to the Gregorian which the Catholics follow (at the cost of much complication).

Feasts. The calendar of feasts is that of the Copts, with local saints added or substituted. It has had to undergo a good deal of modification for Catholic use, for the dissidents celebrate, e.g., Pontius Pilate—because he said he was innocent! But no later Western feasts have yet been adopted.

Penitential seasons. There are forty fasting days in Lent, which includes Sundays (a unique observance); 15 days before the Assumption; 3 days "of Niniveh" before Lent; the eves of Christmas and the Epiphany; and in a modified form every Wednesday and Friday. Strict fasting includes abstinence from eggs and milk as well as meat, but there is no fasting at all during the fifty days of paschal-time.

BIBLIOGRAPHY

Beccari, Camillo, S.J., *Notizia e Saggi di opere e documenti inediti riguardanti la storia di Ethiopia durante i secoli XVI, XVII e XVIII* (Rome, 1903).

——— *Rerum Aethiopicarum Scriptores occidentales inediti a saeculo XVI ad XIX* (Rome, 1903–1914) 14 vols.

Fortescue, *The Lesser Eastern Churches* (London, 1913).

*Hyatt, *The Church of Abyssinia* (London, 1928).

*Mercer, *The Ethiopic Liturgy* (London, 1915).

Chapter VII

THE ANTIOCHENE RITE

THE ANTIOCHENE RITE

1. THE SYRIANS

I. HISTORY AND PRESENT STATE

GENERAL ECCLESIASTICAL HISTORY

The position in the patriarchate of Antioch after the Council of Chalcedon was much the same as in that of Alexandria, except that even western Syria was never solidly monophysite like Egypt. Those that refused to accept the Council's decrees were to a considerable extent moved by political, anti-imperial passions, and were egged on by dissident Egyptian monks. The patriarchal throne of Antioch, like that of Egypt, was bandied between orthodox Catholic and monophysite occupants until the Emperor Justinian I imprisoned all bishops professing or suspect of Monophysism. The sect would then probably have died out in Syria had it not been for the action of the Empress Theodora, who favoured the heretics. At the request of the chief of the Ghassanid Arabs, Haret ibn-Jabal, she procured the clandestine consecration of two monks in the year 543, one of whom, Jacob Baradai, spent the rest of his life secretly organizing the Monophysites in Syria. He gave them a patriarch (called "of Antioch" but residing in eastern Syria) and is said to have ordained 27 bishops and over two thousand priests. From this time on there are two churches in Syria, that of the orthodox Catholics (Melkites) and that of the Monophysites, commonly called the Jacobite Church, after its tireless organizer.

The Jacobites welcomed the Arab invasion in 636, and were alternately patronized and persecuted by their conquerors; large numbers of them turned Mohammedan. They had fairly amiable relations with the Crusaders, and in the twelfth and thirteenth centuries, as in the West and in Ethiopia, there was a revival of religious and intellectual life. Its great ornament was Barhebraeus (John Abdul-Faraj), who was as good as he was learned. At the instance of Dominican and Franciscan missionaries there were several movements for union with Rome, notably in 1237 and 1247, but this promising phase was followed by a long period of internal disorder. After the Council of Florence there was a further prospect of union, but it came to nothing.

In consequence of the encouraging attitude of the then Jacobite patriarch, Naamat-Allah, Pope Gregory XIII sent a legate to Aleppo in 1583, who paved the way for the establishment of the Capuchins and Jesuits there in 1626. Jacobites at once began to come into communion with the Holy See and in such numbers that by 1656 they were strong enough to elect a Catholic, Andrew Akhidjan, to the vacant Jacobite see of Aleppo. He was consecrated by a Maronite bishop, and five years later became patriarch. The dissident Jacobites resorted to violence, and the persecution went on for a hundred years. Andrew's successor was Peter, ex-Jacobite bishop of Jerusalem, to whom the Jacobites opposed a patriarch of their own. In spite of a guarantee of protection obtained by the German emperor from the Turks at the instance of the Pope, Peter was thrown into prison at Adana in 1701, together with a Catholic archbishop and ten priests. The two prelates died in chains five years later, leaving the Catholic Syrians without a leader, and during the succeeding 77 years they were all but destroyed by the severity of the repressive measures taken against them.

His Beatitude Mar GABRIEL TAPPUNI,
Syrian Patriarch of Antioch

Reader

Priest

SYRIAN CLERGY

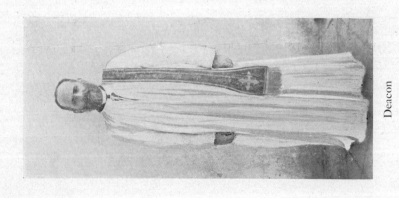

Deacon

THE CATHOLIC SYRIANS[1]

Before he died in 1783 the then Jacobite patriarch of Antioch nominated as his successor the archbishop of Aleppo, Mar[2] Michael Jarweh. He had recently become a Catholic and, hastening to take possession of the patriarchal residence at Mardin, he gained the support of four bishops and sent to Rome for confirmation of what he had done. The anti-Catholic party meantime elected another patriarch, who succeeded in getting a *berat* of recognition from the Turkish government before Jarweh, whom he put in prison. Jarweh escaped, first to Bagdad and then to the Lebanon, that secular refuge of persecuted Catholics. He established himself in a monastery formed in the building of a village school at Sharfeh, and governed his followers from there till his death in 1801. Michael Jarweh is accounted the first patriarch of Antioch of the Catholic Syrians.

In 1830 the patriarchal residence was moved to Aleppo and the Turks recognized the Catholics as a separate body from the Jacobites, their patriarch becoming civil head of the "nation" (*milleh*) in 1843. Between 1820 and 1850 five Jacobite bishops submitted to Rome, and in the latter year the patriarch Gregory Jarweh moved his residence to the centre of Jacobite influence, Mardin, persecution both by dissidents and Mohammedans having made Aleppo untenable. This led to more submissions, again including several bishops,[3] but the

---

[1] Sometimes called, with their schismatical counterpart the Jacobites, *West* Syrians, or *Pure* Syrians, to distinguish them clearly from the Chaldeans and Nestorians, though a good half of them in fact live in Irak and the eastern parts of Syria.

[2] *Mar* (Syriac, "lord"; fem., *mart*) is used in all Syriac rites as a title for saints and bishops.

[3] And an ex-patriarch, Mar Abdal-Massih, in 1913, but he returned to schism soon after. The only other noteworthy case of schism in recent years was that of Mar Gregory Sattuf, Bishop of Homs, who went back to the Jacobites in 1905 and later became patriarch. Their original abjurations of Jacobitism were chiefly due to quarrels and grievances— that is, alas! so often the case in these "submissions"; the reconciliation of Mar Ivanios in India is a most happy example of better things.

progress of the Catholic Syrians was abruptly checked by the Great War.[4] In 1915 Mar Flavian Michael Malkeh, Bishop of Gezirah, was murdered in prison by the Turks, with four of his clergy. The patriarch, Mar Ephrem II Rahmani (1898–1929) left Mardin for personal reasons and went to live at Beirut, where the patriarchal resident will now remain fixed. The late Mgr. Rahmani worthily maintained the reputation of the Syrian Church for learning, and his reputation as a scholar extended to the West.[5]

PRESENT STATE

Patriarch. The Syrian Patriarch of Antioch is elected by the bishops of his church, and the choice has to be confirmed by the Holy See, which sends him the *pallium*, but enthronization takes place the Sunday after election.[6] He always takes the name of Ignatius (in memory of the great bishop of his see martyred at Rome *c.* 107) in addition to another name. He has jurisdiction over the faithful of his rite in the old Turkish empire and Egypt; he receives appeals from lower courts, appoints titular bishops at will, summons plenary synods, and consecrates the bishops and Chrism for his whole church. He lives at Beirut and deals directly with the Sacred Eastern Congregation. The present patriarch is Mar Ignatius Gabriel Tappuni, elected in 1929 (he was condemned to death by the Turks, but ransomed, at Mardin during the war).

Bishops. The Syrian sees are that of Mardin and Amida, the patriarchal diocese, administered by a titular archbishop as vicar; Bagdad, Mosul, Aleppo, Damascus, which are archiepiscopal; Homs, Beirut, and Cairo, which are episcopal; but all the bishops are subject directly to the patriarch. Palestine is a vicariate patriarchal. A vacant see is filled by the synod of

---

[4] The patriarch Mar Philip Ankus assisted at the Vatican Council.

[5] He published the first full text, with Latin translation and introduction, of the Syriac *Testamentum Domini Nostri* (Mainz, 1899).

[6] What is the significance of this conferring of the *pallium?* Undoubtedly it was originally a token of recognition and communion, but latterly Rome has considered it as conferring jurisdiction. Nevertheless, the Melkite, Syrian, and Maronite patriarchs certainly exercise jurisdiction *de facto* before they receive papal confirmation.

bishops, who choose one from a number of candidates recommended by the clergy and people of the diocese.

Parochial clergy. Since the second synod of Sharfeh in 1888 priests have been bound to celibacy, but dispensations are accorded, especially in the case of converts from the Jacobites. There is a considerable prejudice against celibate pastoral clergy among some of the people. In 1930 the patriarchal seminary at Sharfeh (erected 1801) was put under the direction of the Subiaco Benedictines of the French province, who since 1901 had conducted a seminary of the Syrian rite at Jerusalem; this is still maintained by them but now as a "little" seminary. The education and formation given by the Benedictines is entirely conditioned by the Syrian liturgy, and they bid fair to turn out priests as worthy as those of St. Anne's for the Melkites. Other aspirants to the priesthood go to the Dominicans' Syro-Chaldean college at Mosul and the Propaganda college in Rome.

The vicar general of each diocese is called *chorepiskopos,* and this title is sometimes accorded to priests occupying responsible posts outside the dioceses. It is conferred by the bishop with an imposition of hands; its insignia are a violet cassock and small hood (*masnaphta*), and sometimes the pectoral cross. Bishops-elect always receive the chorepiscopal blessing eight days before their consecration, if they have not already received it. The *periodeut* ("visitor") is a diocesan prelate who has charge of the discipline of the clergy. There is no permanent office of archdeacon among the Catholic Syrians.

Religious institutes. The few monks and nuns of this rite were dispersed during the Great War, and there are now none; but there is in process of formation at Sharfeh a house of Syro-Benedictines whose first members will be European monks who have adopted the Syrian rite. There existed at Sharfeh from 1785 a congregation of "clerks regular" whose existence was very precarious; an attempt was made to revive them at Mardin in 1882 as the *Missionaries of St. Ephrem,* but they still number only half a dozen priests. There is a wealthy monastery at Mar Behmam, near Mosul, with a few brethren in charge of a secular priest.

The Faithful of the Syrian rite number 50,000 with 164 priests in the patriarchal territory, chiefly in Syria and Irak. Many of them are refugees from the Turks. The Jacobites, who have suffered from the same massacres and deportations, are only about 80,000 and show a certain tendency toward the Catholic Church. Mgr. Rahmani reported 800 converts at Aleppo, 1,000 at Homs, and 1,500 among the refugees at Beirut in 1925; more recently an episcopal vicar patriarchal has had to be appointed for the converts in the Jezirah district. The Syrians are all very poor and simple, and have insufficient good schools of their own, though over a score have been opened for refugees since 1918; they are helped so far as possible by Western congregations working in Syria, particularly the Jesuits and the Mariamette Sisters.

OTHER JURISDICTIONS

United States. There are 6,800 Catholic Syrians (not to be confused with the Catholic Melkites or the Maronites, also Syrians) in U. S. A., chiefly in New York, Boston, and Cincinnati. Even now they have no priests of their rite.

Elsewhere. There are another 7,734 in various other parts of the world, almost entirely without clergy. There are two priests in the Argentine, and one each in Chili and Paris,[7] for the colonies in those places. Brisbane apparently has a church for its 700 faithful, but no priest. This defect is due to lack of clergy, and is a matter of great anxiety to the patriarch and bishops. Lacking one of their own, Syrians are encouraged to attend Catholic Melkite churches, which are more familiar to them than Latin ones.

II. LITURGY AND CUSTOMS

Church buildings. There is nothing very distinctive about a Syrian Catholic church. There are generally three altars in a row, the middle one, under a *ciborium*, having a tabernacle, crucifix, and an indeterminate number of candles. The *mensa* is

---

[7] Their church of St. Ephrem in the rue des Carmes was formerly the chapel of the Irish College.

of wood or stone, and always portable, covered by a "corporal" with a silk or linen cloth beneath. On the north side is a shrine of our Lady with its image and on the south one of the saints, with relics. *Ripidia* stand behind the altar for use in processions. In front of the sanctuary and separated from it by wooden railings is the choir, raised one step above the nave. Normally there are no seats, and men are accommodated in front, women behind. Round statues now take the place of pictures in some town churches, and confessional boxes have been adopted. The Catholics have some ancient churches around Mosul and the cathedral at Aleppo; others, e.g., the cathedral at Beirut, look like bad Latin churches.

Vestments. The eucharistic dress consists of a white alb, stole rather of the Byzantine pattern (*uhroro*), embroidered belt (*zunaro*), cuffs (*zende*), and a chasuble (*phanio*) like a cope without hood or orphreys. The deacon wears an ungirdled alblike garment (*kuthino*), of any colour, with his stole falling back and front over the left shoulder.

A bishop adds to the sacerdotal garments an embroidered hood (*masnaphta*), rather like a Dominican amice, the *epigonation*, and the *omophorion*, which is like a large scapular embroidered with crosses falling back and front over the *phanio*. Catholic bishops affect the Roman mitre (the Jacobites have none) and crozier, but the patriarch carries a pastoral staff of the Byzantine pattern. The ordinary dress of the clergy is a black gown or cassock (violet for prelates), with a wide-sleeved open gown (*jubba*) and *kalemaukion* (sometimes with a polygonal brim) for outdoors and in church. Catholic bishops have adopted that head-dress (over a small black hood) in place of their traditional turban; they carry a hand-cross, wrapped in a silk veil, to bless with, and wear a ring and pectoral cross. Out of doors they carry an ebony staff (the Byzantine *khazranion*), and sometimes wear a peculiar open cloak with a shoulder cape.

Altar-vessels and bread. Both chalice and paten are either fitted with metal lids or covered with linen cloths; there is also a larger veil to go over both vessels. The purificator is now in use, but it is still called a "sponge." A spoon is needed for the priest's communion. The altar-bread is round, thick, and leavened, with a little salt added, and mixed with dough from the previous baking; it is stamped with twelve crosses. Syrian prescriptions about altar-bread are very exacting; e.g., it is supposed to be baked fresh for each Liturgy, and it must not be used if made by an infidel or non-Catholic, or if it has fallen to the ground. The reserved host, on which a few drops of the consecrated Wine are sprinkled, must be renewed every day.

Liturgical books. These are numerous and have been printed from time to time at Rome, Beirut, Mosul, and elsewhere. The 1922 "missal" of Sharfeh was a reformed and improved edition. There are 64 known Syrian *anaphoras* (see p. 173, note), but only seven are printed in the Catholic books, of which the principal, "of St. James," is sketched below. The Liturgy is celebrated in the evening on the vigils of Easter and Christmas, and then entirely in Syriac (as on the feast of St. Ephrem).

Music. The Syrian chant has lately been the subject of a good deal of study, encouraged by Mgr. Rahmani. The Benedictines at the Jerusalem seminary have set down over 8,000 pieces in Western notation. As the native singers know it by tradition alone, not having been able to read its "notation" for many generations, its variations are endless. It is strictly rhythmical and rather monotonous.

Liturgical language. This is the "Edessene" dialect of Syriac (Aramaic, the language of Jesus Christ),[8] with the "western" pronunciation and characters. All the people speak Arabic (except a few in Irak and elsewhere, who still have a corrupt Syriac), and the scriptural lessons and certain pre-anaphoral prayers of the Liturgy are sung or read in that tongue. The rubrics in the older books are Arabic printed in Syrian characters (i.e., "Karshuni"). Syrians call the Liturgy *Kurobo*, "sacrifice."

---

[8] Such phrases of the Holy Scriptures as *Ephata* (Mark vii. 34), *Eli, eli, lama sabaktani* (Matt. xxvii. 46), *Telitha kumi* (Mark v. 41), and *Maran-atha* (I Cor. xvi. 22), and the words *korban, mammona, rabuni,* etc., are in this tongue.

THE EUCHARISTIC LITURGY

This represents the original rite of Antioch, which was modified for use in Jerusalem; this modified form then supplanted its parent at Antioch and throughout the patriarchate, and is known as the Liturgy of St. James. It was originally in Greek, but was soon translated into Syriac in various places, and after the Monophysite schism the orthodox Catholics maintained its use in the first language, the Jacobites in the second; it was the source of the Byzantine, the Armenian, and perhaps the Chaldean Liturgies, and the Maronite is simply a romanized form of it.[9] There are now considerable discrepancies between the Greek and Syriac versions.

The Syrians use their Liturgy of the Presanctified only on Good Friday. They never concelebrate, but on Maundy Thursday several separate Liturgies are celebrated at the same time on one improvised altar, the senior alone celebrating aloud and facing the people, the others on either side of him facing one another. There is, of course, now an approximation to "low Mass."

Normally a curtain should be drawn across the sanctuary while the preparatory part of the Liturgy takes place. The priest goes within it *in his ordinary clothes* and prepares the offerings at the altar with suitable prayers (the wine and water are occasionally mixed in a separate vessel and poured into the chalice together). He then goes to the sacristy to vest and the curtain is withdrawn.

The celebrant goes to the foot of the altar and says *secreto*, a prayer for forgiveness of sins and preservation against temptation. He then goes up to the altar, kisses it, uncovers the offerings, takes the paten in his right hand and the chalice in his left, crosses his arms and offers them up, saying inaudibly

---

[9] The local Orthodox, after they went into schism, entirely abandoned the Antiochene rite for its Byzantine daughter as we have seen above (p. 106). The Catholics of the Syrian rite therefore represent the native church of our Lord's land in a rather special way. The dissident Orthodox have revived the use of the Greek St. James twice a year, at Zakynthos and Jerusalem.

a prayer commemorating the economy of our salvation, the saints, the living and dead, and naming the priest's special intention. He then makes a special memento of the day, prays for his ancestors, parents and relations, and covers up the offerings, saying: "The heavens have been covered by his mighty splendour and the earth filled with his glory."

He blesses incense and censes the altar three times, the offerings, the clergy, and the people, saying a long prayer the while; the offerings are incensed toward the four points of the compass, in honour of our Lady (east), prophets, apostles, and martyrs (west), doctors, clergy, the righteous (north), the Church and her children (south); these commemorations are repeated by the people. He says the Our Father before censing the people, and then a procession is formed, the celebrant carrying the gospel-book and the deacon incensing it (the above prayers are said aloud only in pontifical Liturgies). They go around the altar from right to left, while the choir sings a hymn, a version of the Greek Μονογενής. Returned to whence they started, the *Trisagion* is sung three times, thus: (*Priest*) "Holy God, holy Strong One, holy Deathless One"— (*Choir*) "Have mercy on us." The third time they add *Kyrie eleison* thrice and go on to the antiphon of the epistle, consisting chiefly of Gal. i. 8. Then the deacon (or server) comes to the altar-rails and chants the epistle in Arabic facing the people. After a chant the priest takes the gospel-book and goes to the altar-rails, singing: "Peace to you all." (This is the common social greeting as well. When the priest uses it liturgically he extends his right arm in the manner of the old Roman—and modern fascist—salute).

People: "And with thy spirit."

Priest: "The holy gospel of our Lord Jesus Christ, the message of life, according to N., the apostle (or evangelist), who announces life and salvation to the world."

People: "Blessed be he who is come and who is to come; our worship to him who sent him and may his mercies be with us always."

Priest: "During the dispensation of our Lord, our God, and

THE SYRIAN LITURGY

The Celebrant Blesses the People with the Holy Things

BISHOPS OF THE SYRO-MALANKARA AND (CENTRE) SYRO-MALABARESE RITES

Mar Ivanios of Trivandrum   Mar Augustine of Ernakulam   Mar Theophilos of Tiruvella

our Saviour, Jesus Christ, life-giving Word, God incarnate of the blessed virgin Mary, these things took place." *People:* "We believe and we confess it."

The priest, surrounded by lights and the deacon swinging the thurible, chants the gospel in Arabic from a lectern facing the people. A variable hymn is sung, e.g., the following, referring to past discipline: "Let him who has not received the seal go out—so orders the Church. But you, children of baptism, approach the altar. Woe to the man whose spirit goes wandering in the bazaars during the celebration of the holy Mysteries," etc.

The liturgy of the faithful begins with a hymn, followed by a prayer in which the celebrant prays aloud for the divine mercy to pardon his and his flock's delinquencies, etc. He blesses incense, and while he prays appropriately the deacon incenses the altar, celebrant, etc. Then the priest intones the creed, "*We* believe in one holy God" (*Filioque* is added). It is continued by the deacon or people in the plural while the priest incenses the altar, clergy, and people; he washes his hands, says, "My brethren and my friends, pray for me," accuses himself of sin *secreto*, and returns to the altar to begin the *anaphora*.[10] He says the "prayer of peace" and kisses the altar; the deacon kisses the altar, embraces the priest and kisses his hand, and takes the salute to the ministers, saying: "Let us give peace to one another, each to his neighbour by a holy embrace and with love of our God. And after this holy peace has been given to us, let us bow down before the God of Mercy." The ministers and people convey the kiss of peace by touching hands, kissing them, and drawing them down the face. Meanwhile the celebrant says aloud two prayers for the mercy of God on the congregation and uncovers the offerings over which he flutters the veil while the deacon calls on the people to be attentive.

---

[10] The *anaphora* "of St. James Brother of the Lord." Other *anaphoras* used by the Catholic Syrians are "of St. John the Evangelist," "of the twelve Apostles," "of St. Mark the Evangelist," "of St. Eustace of Antioch," "of St. Basil of Caesarea," and "of St. Cyril of Jerusalem." There is also a Liturgy of the Presanctified.

Priest: "✠ May the love of God the Father, ✠ the grace of the one Son, ✠ the communion of the Holy Ghost, be with you all."

People: "And with thy spirit."

Priest: "Let us lift up our minds, our thoughts, and our hearts."

People: "They are, to the Lord."

Priest: "Let us give thanks to the Lord with fear."

People: "It is just and right."

The priest begins the invariable preface in a low voice, gradually raising it to full, and the choir adds the *Sanctus* and *Benedictus* ("Blessed is he that came and is to come . . ."), which the celebrant amplifies inaudibly into a prayer leading directly to the consecration:

"When he was about to suffer a willing death for us sinners, he, who knew not sin, on this night when he was to be given up for the life and salvation of the world, took bread (*he takes the host in his right hand and chants aloud*) into his holy, spotless and unblemished hands, lifted his eyes to heaven and showed it to God the Father, and ✠ gave thanks, ✠ blessed it, ✠ sanctified it, broke it, and gave it to his disciples, saying: Take, eat of it. *This is my Body*, which will be broken and given up for you and for a great number for the forgiveness of sins and everlasting life. (*People:* "Amen.") In like manner after supper he took the cup, mingled wine and water, and ✠ gave thanks, ✠ blessed it, ✠ sanctified it, and gave it to the same disciples and apostles, saying: Take, drink ye all of it. *This is my Blood* of the new covenant which for you and for a great number will be poured out and given for the forgiveness of sins and everlasting life. (*People:* "Amen.") Do this in remembrance of me. So often as you," etc.

There are no elevations but after each consecration a bell is rung, the Holy Things censed by the deacon, and the priest makes a profound bow. The invocation of the Holy Ghost immediately follows the *anamnesis* (commemoration), which is addressed to God the Son; the deacon calls the people to attention and prayer, they say *Kyrie eleison* three times in reply to the priest's "Hear me, O Lord (three times): have mercy and spare us, O thou holy One," and answer "Amen" to the invocations upon the Bread and upon the Wine, over which the celebrant flutters his hands as if they were the wings of a dove. The *epiklesis* has not been mutilated.

The great intercession is very long and of an imposing form. The deacon prays, in the form of a litany, for the living Fathers (i.e., the Pope, patriarch, and hierarchy), for all the people, for sovereigns and rulers, for the intercession of the saints, for the fathers of the Church now dead, for all the faithful departed;[11] during each litany the priest says inaudibly a prayer to the same effect, continued and concluded aloud after the deacon has finished each division, the people singing Amen. Thus he begins: "We offer this great and bloodless sacrifice for thy holy Church who puts her confidence therein, particularly for Sion,[12] the mother of all orthodox churches. Grant her, O Lord, the precious gifts of thy Spirit. Remember, O Lord, our holy bishops who deliver to us the words of life, above all our blessed fathers, Mar Pius, the pope of Rome, Mar N., our patriarch, Mar M., our bishop, and all orthodox bishops . . ." and ends the intercession with a blessing over the people.

The breaking and mingling of the Host is a peculiar and rather complicated rite. It is first divided into two equal parts; each part alternately is then partially dipped into the precious Blood and with this the other half is, so to say, "anointed." Next, the pieces of the Host that were immersed are detached; one of them is dropped into the Chalice and the other is dipped several times into the precious Blood and with it all the other consecrated particles are severally anointed, as with a brush. The Our Father is then recited in Arabic by the people, prefaced by the celebrant, ending "For thine is the Kingdom," etc., and followed by the priest's embolism.

---

[11] On the altar is a tablet bearing the names of the dead for whom prayers are asked. At this point the celebrant touches the Host with his right hand and makes a triple sign of the cross over the names.

[12] An indication of the origins of this Liturgy.

Then, after several verses and responses and a blessing the priest lifts the Host on the paten to the level of his eyes, chanting, "Holy things to the holy and pure," and in like manner the Chalice but without chanting, the deacon replying, "The Father alone is holy, the Son alone is holy, the Holy Ghost alone is holy. Glory be," etc. The priest kisses the paten and chalice, making the sign of the cross therewith as he elevates them. While the choir sings a hymn he goes to the foot of the altar-steps and says inaudibly prayers before communion, then receives the sacred Host from the chalice with a golden spoon and drinks of the precious Blood.

Afterwards he takes the chalice and paten in either hand, turns to the people, and recites three prayers (in a pontifical Liturgy the bishop descends one step at each prayer and so arrives at the altar-rails, where he hands the holy vessels to the deacon). The communicants stand and he puts a particle into the mouth of each one (as each particle has been anointed with the species of wine, they thus receive under both kinds). The words of administration are: "The propitiatory coal[13] of the Body and Blood of Christ our Lord is given to the loyal and faithful one for the forgiveness of sins and pardon of faults for ever and ever." The communicant replies "Amen."

The celebrant then retakes the chalice and paten and blesses the people with the Holy Things. After reciting a prayer of thanksgiving he salutes the people: "Peace be with you all."

People: "And with thy spirit." Then he says the "postcommunion" and dismisses them: "✠ Go in peace, brethren, and pray for me."

He then consumes what remains of the Holy Things, cleanses his hands and the vessels, and makes his thanksgiving. This should end with a prayer before the altar: "Remain in peace, O holy altar of the Lord, I know not if I shall again return to thee or no (kissing it thrice). Remain in peace, table of life, to be a witness for me before our Lord Jesus

---

[13] "Glowing coal," a common name for the Blessed Sacrament in the East; also called "the pearl" (cf., Isa. vi. 6). It may be noted that the dissident Jacobites receive Holy Communion in just the same way.

Christ of whom I will not cease to think, henceforth and for ever. Amen."

DIVINE OFFICE

The Syrian canonical prayers have seven "hours," which are recited in two parts: office of the Ninth hour, Vespers (*Ramsho*), and prayer of Protection (*Setoro*) in the evening; Night Office (*Lilyo*) with three nocturns, Lauds (*Teshebho-tho*), Morning Prayer (*Saphro*), and offices of the Third and Sixth hours before the Liturgy. The office is peculiarly rich in hymns and poetical compositions[14] but there are few psalms, in some hours none at all. Each hour begins with the *Trisagion* and Our Father and always includes prayer for the dead; the *Te Deum* is sung at Lauds. What psalms there are, are mostly invariable, according to whether it is a week day or Sunday or great feast. The version of the holy Scriptures used for liturgical purposes in all the Syrian rites is the Peshitto. Daily recitation of the office was made obligatory on the clergy by the synod of Sharfeh in 1888. Wherever there are four or more priests together they sing at least part of it in church.

THE SACRAMENTS

Baptism. The water is blessed for the occasion before each baptism. After certain prayers the priest pronounces the exorcisms and anoints the child with oil three times on the forehead. Then he seats it in the font and pours water on its head three times, saying, "N., is baptized in the name of the Father," etc. He at once proceeds to

Confirmation, which consists essentially of anointing with Chrism the forehead, eyelids, nostrils, lips, ears, hands, chest, back, and feet, with the words: "N., is sealed unto everlasting life in the name of the Father, etc., with the holy Chrism, the sweet perfume of the divine Christ, sign and seal of the true faith and of the accomplishment of the gifts of the Holy Ghost."

---

[14] Many by and still more attributed to St. Ephrem the Deacon, doctor of the Church, whose feast both Latins and Syrians observe on June 18.

Penance is administered with the Latin formulas translated into Syriac or Arabic.

Eucharist. The manner of receiving Holy Communion has been described on page 176. Deacons and subdeacons are communicated with the spoon from the chalice.

Extreme Unction is now administered according to the *Rituale Romanum* in Syriac, as the proper rite requires the assistance of seven priests, as is usual in the East. The oil is consecrated as required by the priest.

Orders. The orders of the Syrian rite are singer, reader and acolyte, subdeacon; deacon, priest, bishop. All orders are conferred during the Liturgy by laying on of hands and delivery of instruments of office, without anointing. The formula resembles that of the eucharistic invocation of the Holy Ghost. The subdeacon is given a lighted candle, as his particular business is to care for the lights. Before ordination to the diaconate and upwards a profession of faith must be signed. There is no concelebration at the ordaining of bishops and priests.

Marriage. The wedding ceremony consists of two parts, the blessing of the rings and the crowning. A ring is given to each party and each is crowned with a wreath. The priest commits them to the care of one another, but there is no explicit contract, which is, however, implicit in the assurance that they have to give, that they are freely entering into matrimony.

Calendar. The Gregorian reckoning is in use and the ecclesiastical year begins on the Sunday nearest to November 1. The calendar is substantially the ancient one of the Church of Antioch; many of the feasts that we have in common are observed on different days. The seasons are Advent, Christmas, preparation for Lent, Lent, paschal-time, time after Pentecost, time after Holy Cross.

Feasts. Corpus Christi is adopted from the West, and the Immaculate Conception, All Saints, and St. Joseph transferred to our dates. In addition to Sundays there are twenty general holydays (not all of obligation) as well as local ones; they include the Praises of Our Lady (Dec. 26), St. Ephrem (June

18), the Praises of St. John the Forerunner (Jan. 7), and St. George (April 23).

Penitential season. During Lent (seven weeks) a complete fast from food and drink lasts till noon, with abstinence from certain foods for the rest of the day, except on Saturdays and Sundays. Nearly all Wednesdays and Fridays are days of abstinence, as well as three days three weeks before Lent (fast of Niniveh), four days before SS. Peter and Paul, seven days before the Assumption, and nine days before Christmas.

General observations. Catholic Syrians make the sign of the cross as in the West. All the Western devotions are in use, including Benediction of the Blessed Sacrament. Holy Cross day (Sept. 14) is a great occasion, marked by the lighting of bonfires, and on the Assumption the Aleppines eat blessed grapes in memory of their dead.

BIBLIOGRAPHY

Fortescue, *The Lesser Eastern Churches* (London, 1913).

Lammens, *La Syrie; précis historique* (Beirut, 1921).

Petit Manuel de la Messe Syrienne (Paris, 1923).

Khayatte, *Manuel de Prières . . . selon le Rite Syrien* (Paris, 1926).

Jeannin, *Mélodies liturgiques Syriennes et Chaldéenes*, 2 vols. (Beirut, 1925-8).

2. THE MARONITES

I. HISTORY AND PRESENT STATE

GENERAL ECCLESIASTICAL HISTORY

The Maronites are Syrians, living chiefly in the Lebanon, and of the same race as the Catholic Syrians (described previously), Jacobites, and Melkites of both obediences (see pp. 106 ff.). Their existence as a separate "nation" is apparently entirely due to their ecclesiastical origins. There are no non-Catholic Maronites,[15] but the tradition (not found in writings previous to the sixteenth century) of their "perpetual orthodoxy" has now been abandoned by all except a few of the die-hards.[16]

The origins and early history of the Maronite Church have aroused controversy, not always conducted with urbanity. It would seem that after the Council of Chalcedon the monks of Beit-Marun, a monastery built around the shrine of St. Maro,[17] a fifth-century hermit, on the right bank of the river Orontes between Emesa (Homs) and Apamea, distinguished themselves by their strong opposition to the Monophysites. This conduct was naturally approved by the emperors, who greatly favoured

---

[15] Yet if you ask a Maronite if he is a Catholic he says, "No. I am a Maronite." To him "Catholic" means Catholic Melkite. Nevertheless, he does not object to frequenting Latin churches: some Catholic orientals do, very much, as much as the average Latin would dislike having to frequent an Eastern church.

[16] Catholics are sometimes accused by their opponents of insinuating that the Catholics of Eastern rites have been in uninterrupted communion with Rome. Yet it is "Roman" scholars who have maintained in the teeth of the Maronites that the Maronites were at one time in schism!

[17] He must not be confused with the seventh-century "St. John Maro, Patriarch of Antioch," who is known only from Maronite tradition. Grave doubts have been thrown on his existence.

the monastery in consequence, so that its influence spread throughout Syria Secunda.

But in the first half of the seventh century the Emperor Heraclius, seeking to unite his Syrian subjects against the invading Arabs, concocted with the Patriarchs of Constantinople and Antioch a theological formula which they hoped would conciliate the Monophysites. Unfortunately it was heretical, and was promptly condemned by three successive Popes and the Patriarch of Jerusalem.[18] But Heraclius and his successor stuck to it, and the monks of Beit-Marun faithfully followed their patrons the emperors. After the Arab conquest and the third general council of Constantinople they and the people under their influence did not, for some unknown reason, return to orthodoxy, and they continued to profess Monothelism long after it had died out everywhere else.[19] It is surmised that, while the patriarchs of Antioch were in exile at Constantinople during the first half of the eighth century, the monks decided to elect a primate for themselves and so began the separate line of Maronite patriarchs of Antioch; they certainly had a bishop in their monastery in the middle of the eighth century. After the destruction of Beit-Marun at the end of the ninth century the monks and their followers withdrew themselves entirely into the Lebanon mountains.

In the year 1182 almost the whole nation of the Maronites, 40,000 in number, moved, as the chronicler William of Tyre says, "by an inspiration from Heaven," submitted to the Holy See through Amaury, the third of the Latin patriarchs whom the Crusaders had set up at Antioch. The Maronite patriarch Jeremias II al-Amshiti was present at the Lateran Council in 1215, and Rome had no doubt of their previous Monothelism then, for when Jeremias went home with a papal legate Pope

---

[18] And finally by the Sixth Oecumenical Council (III Constantinople) in 680. The heresy was Monothelism, i.e., the denial that our Lord had a human as well as a divine will; it struck at His real humanity.

[19] The traditional Maronite explanation is that they denied the two wills (if they did) in error and in ignorance of the decisions of the oecumenical council. When they first heard of its teaching—from the Crusaders!—they at once embraced it.

Innocent III wrote insisting that he should make a solemn profession of faith in the two wills in Jesus Christ.

The Maronites who had emigrated to Cyprus were apparently heretical till after the Council of Florence, for they made an abjuration and submission in 1445, with their bishop at their head, and there seem to have been others disaffected here and there even during the late Middle Ages. But by the beginning of the sixteenth century the Maronites were stabilized, and since the fifth Lateran Council (1512–17) they have been in close and uninterrupted contact with the Holy See. In 1584 Pope Gregory XIII founded the Maronite College in Rome. An outstanding figure was Germanos Farhat, Archbishop of Aleppo (1670–1732), founder at Ehden of the Aleppine Antonian monks. He was a great scholar, widely traveled in Europe, and of surpassing holiness of life.

By the eighteenth century ecclesiastical discipline had become very lax among the Maronites and the existence of abusive customs made reform difficult. The Holy See accordingly insisted on a plenary synod, which was eventually convened in 1736 at the monastery of Saidat al-Luaizeh, "our Lady of the Almond Trees." Joseph Assemani was the papal delegate and decrees were enacted aiming at the abolition of an excessive number of bishops, the sale of dispensations, the failure to reserve the Blessed Sacrament in rural churches, the neglect of the poor and of church buildings, the remarriage of widowed priests, and other abuses. To these were added certain liturgical prescriptions, some of which were necessary and some were not: e.g., *azyme* bread was imposed and communion in both kinds taken away from the laity. The acts of this synod were formally approved by Pope Benedict XIV but it took a century for them to be generally accepted and enforced. Their troubles were further aggravated by disputed patriarchal elections and by the activities of a nun of Aleppo named Anna Aggemi. In spite of the errors into which she fell (which culminated in her claiming to be hypostatically united to the Second Person of the Holy Trinity!) her reputation for holiness gained her the support of the patriarch, Joseph Stephani, and of a Lazarist father, Godez. The Holy See had to interfere in 1779, con-

demning her, censuring her partizans, and dissolving the sisterhood she had founded. But there were those who maintained
her sanctity fifty years afterwards. The great Maronite figure
of the nineteenth century was the patriarch Paul Massad, who
ruled for 35 difficult years. Four of his bishops assisted at the
Vatican Council, but Massad himself did not attend—it is said,
because he feared that pressure would be brought to bear on
him to abate some of his privileges.

After the Turkish conquest the people of the Lebanon,
Maronites and Druzes,[20] were never governed directly by the
Turks but came under the control of native emirs. The resulting semi-independence caused the Lebanon to be the refuge
of oppressed Catholics of Eastern rites, Melkites, Syrians,
Armenians, until they were emancipated from the civil control
of the dissident patriarchs after 1829. But by the beginning of
the nineteenth century the feudal organization of the Lebanon
was cracking; after the abdication of the vigorous old emir
Bashir II Shabab and the evacuation of Syria by Mohammed
Ali (1840), the political policies of the great powers precipitated a deadly struggle between Maronites and Druzes, aggravated by the internal reforms imposed on Turkey by the
Congress of Paris after the Crimean war. The situation went
out of control on May 30, 1860, the occasion being a quarrel
between a Druze and a Maronite at Beit-Mari. The Druzes
were armed and ready, but the Christians allowed themselves
to be disarmed by the Turkish authorities on the pretence of
maintaining order. In three weeks every Maronite village of
the main and southern Lebanon was pillaged and burned, and
six thousand Maronites were murdered, maimed, or outraged;
the abbot of Deir al-Kamar was flayed alive and his twenty
monks pole-axed. Khursud Pasha marched into the district
with a battalion of soldiers, fired a single gun, and then left
his troops to join in the massacre. On July 9 it broke out at
Damascus, where in three days the adult males alone numbered
three thousand victims. Of these, eight Friars Minor and three
Maronite laymen were shown by the circumstances of their

---

[20] A sect of Islam, regarded as infidel by the orthodox. The secular
rivals of the Maronites.

death to have been martyrs for the Faith, and were beatified by Pope Pius XI in 1926. The Maronites were brothers, Blessed Francis, Abdulmooti, and Raphael Masabki. In all, 16,000 Maronites were slain and 100,000 rendered homeless.

France sent a military expedition to restore order, and the Lebanon was given a constitution drawn up by a commission of the European powers; it became an autonomous province of the Turkish empire with a governor general, who was a Christian not belonging to any of the chief local communions. This lasted till the Great War; in 1926 the country was reorganized as the Republic of the Lebanon, under French mandate: the district of Kasrawan, northeast of Beirut, is almost exclusively Maronite. The Maronites are properly proud of their devotion to the Holy See; but they are an independent people and tenacious of their rights and privileges: the more so that in the past Western influence has sometimes tended to be coercive.

PRESENT STATE

Patriarch. The Maronite Patriarch of Antioch[21] is elected by the bishops gathered in synod; the office is at once conferred by the laying-on of hands of all the bishops present and the clergy and people do homage. Notice is sent to Rome with a profession of faith and obedience through the delegate apostolic in Syria, and the Holy See confirms the election by sending the *pallium*. His jurisdiction is over all the faithful of his rite in the old Turkish empire in Asia and Egypt. Among his rights and privileges are the ordination of all bishops, the nomination of titular bishops, *chorepiskopoi*, and *bardûts*, the convening of plenary synods, the exclusive consecration of Chrism, the receiving of appeals from lower courts, the absolution of certain reserved sins, the control of the publication of catechisms and liturgical books and of translations from Syriac into the vernacular. He is assisted by a curia of five

---

[21] The concession of this title can only be looked on as an act of grace on the part of the Holy See. It was first acknowledged by Pope Alexander IV in 1254.

titular bishops, and is bound to send an account of his charge to Rome every ten years.

The patriarchal residence has been fixed in many places; for a long time now it has been at Bekerkeh in the winter and Gedaidat-Kannubin in the summer. The present patriarch is Mar Antony Arida, elected in 1932.[22]

Bishops. The Maronite dioceses have been clearly delimitated and their bishops permanently resident only since the synods of 1736 and 1818. The sees are all episcopal and dependent directly on the patriarch (but each holder is called archbishop); they are Gibail and Batrun (the patriarchal dioceses, each administered by a titular archbishop of the curia), Aleppo, Baalbec, Beirut, Cyprus (practically all its subjects and their bishop live in the Lebanon), Damascus, Sidon, Tyre, and Tripoli. There are vicariates patriarchal for Egypt and Palestine. Vacant sees are filled by the patriarch and bishops in synod, the lower clergy and laity having an advisory voice. Among the bishops' means of support is a poll-tax on every adult in his diocese.

Parochial clergy. Parish priests are for the most part chosen by the faithful concerned (the bishop has a right of veto). Those in the rural parts are nearly all married and have often to support their families by working in the fields or plying a trade, as do the country clergy of several other rites. This class among the clergy is but poorly instructed, for though there were several diocesan seminaries only two were of any size. However, a general central seminary for the whole patriarchate was established in the autumn of 1934. It is situated at Ghazir and is directed by Jesuit fathers, the rector being of Maronite nationality. The Maronite College at Rome was re-founded in 1891, and is now under the direction of the Jesuits,[23] but it can accommodate only 24 students. A considerable number of

---

[22] While archbishop of Tripoli during the war Mgr. Arida sold everything of value he had, down to his pectoral cross, to feed his starving flock.

[23] Its most famous alumnus is the Syriac scholar Joseph Assemani (1687–1768).

Maronite priests are trained in the oriental seminary of the Society of Jesus at Beirut; some aspirants are sent to Latin seminaries. There are a thousand secular priests, but the number is insufficient, and so are vocations.

The offices of *chorepiskopos* and *bardut* (περιοδευτής, visitor), carry with them variable duties, e.g., to confirm and to confer minor orders for the bishop; archpriests and archdeacons are practically titular only.

Religious institutes. As is appropriate to a church that had its origins in a monastery, monasticism has always had many followers among the Maronites. Their monks of the Middle Ages led a rather go-as-you-please and unorganized life, and in 1700 the learned patriarch Stephen ad-Duwahi started a congregation modeled on Western lines, under the so-called Rule of St. Antony, the traditional patriarch of the solitary life. The enterprise prospered and spread, absorbing existing monasteries but, as in the case of the Melkite Basilians, the particularism of Aleppo caused trouble and in 1768 two distinct congregations were formed, the *Baladite* ("rural") *Antonians* and the *Aleppine Antonians*. During the same time a bishop, afterwards patriarch, Gabriel Blauzawi, united other monasteries into a congregation, which received the name of *Antonians of St. Isaias*, from its mother house.

The life and constitutions of all three congregations of Maronite Antonians closely resemble one another. They are primarily contemplative but about a third of the hieromonks serve parishes;[24] they are bound to perpetual abstinence from flesh-meat and tobacco. A few of them are definitely hermits, living alone in the neighbourhood of their monasteries. The habit is a black gown with a small round hood, leather belt, and sandals. All together there are 741 of these monks, 520 of whom are priests. Each congregation has an abbot general at the head and is divided into provinces. There are 72 monasteries and 46 residences, many of which have only one or two monks, who are dispensed from much of their rule and are engaged in looking after vast landed estates. It is said

---

[24] The Baladites also do missionary work among the half-Moslem, half-pagan Nuzayris around Biadieh in the Alauite country.

that a third of the Lebanon belongs to the Antonians, and this excessive territorial wealth is still the cause of certain irregularities among them;[25] these have been much worse in the past, and the synod of 1818 and others had to take strong measures against monastic abuses.

The Aleppine congregation has a small college for its students in Rome. The causes of beatification of three nineteenth-century Antonians, two monks and a nun, are before the Congregation of Sacred Rites.[26]

The *Missionaries of Kraim* form an active congregation on Western lines, preaching, giving retreats, and running a printing press. They were founded by Father John Habib in 1865, and have 27 priest members.

The *Antonian nuns* are strictly enclosed and contemplative, with solemn office in choir. There are 160 of them, in 13 convents. Other Maronite nuns are *Visitandines* and *Sisters of the Holy Family*, who are engaged in education. The Sisters of the Sacred Hearts of Jesus and Mary (*Mariamettes*), an inter-ritual congregation originated by two Jesuit fathers in 1853 which does splendid educational work in Syria, has a large proportion of Maronite members.

The Faithful. The Maronites of the patriarchate, though reduced by emigration and by famine during the Great War, still number 322,700 (10,000 in Egypt, 1,000 in Cyprus, 2,500 in Palestine, the rest in the Lebanon). By far the greater part of them are peasants and mountaineers, faithful to their religion and anxious to improve themselves; many a village has its catechism class and the Mariamettes' schools are eagerly sought. Unfortunately the influence of returned emigrants is corrupting: they have often lost the Faith entirely, but their objection to the monks' large estates seems not without reason.

---

[25] There are, for example, recognized "irregular monasteries" wherein the observance is relaxed and where the superior (*reis*) is sometimes to be found surrounded by his relatives or other lay people, who are supposed to assist him in the administration of the property of the monks.

[26] For an interesting account of a Maronite monastery, see Doughty's *Arabia Deserta*, Vol. II, cap. xiii, criticized in the *Dublin Review*, Jan., 1934.

Also "the influence of the Western press," says l'abbé Labourt, "is outrageously bad." The Maronites owe an incalculable debt to the Jesuits, who have worked in Syria from 1625 till 1773 and from 1831 on; their university and its oriental seminary at Beirut have been the door to intellectual and professional activities for many Maronites and others.

OTHER JURISDICTIONS

United States. There are 38,800 Maronites in the United States (many in the states of New York, Massachusetts, and Ohio). They are subject to *chorepiskopoi*, who depend on the American bishops but are empowered to confirm, consecrate churches and altars, etc. They have a score of churches and priests, and display considerable literary activity.

Uruguay. There is a colony of 16,000 here, presided over by a monk at Montevideo, who is a titular abbot.

Elsewhere there are 5,000 or so, with churches at Leghorn, Paris, Sydney, in Brazil, the Argentine, and other places.

II. LITURGY AND CUSTOMS

The Antiochene usages of the Maronites have been very seriously modified, even before the synod of 1736, and their fundamental orientalism is obscured by a mass of externals borrowed from the West. The appointments of their *churches*, and their *altar-vessels*, etc., are entirely Latin, though blessings are given with a hand-cross and *ripidia* are carried in processions. Altar-breads are unleavened and just the same as ours. Their *music* is in origin that of the Syrians, with cymbals to mark the rhythm but very different in detail.

Vestments. The eucharistic dress of a priest is purely Roman,[27] except that he generally wears embroidered cuffs instead of a maniple. The lower clergy wears Syrian vestments

---

[27] When they borrow from the West, orientals always choose the worst patterns. The first Maronite priest I ever saw, in a church at Cairo, had a chasuble of staring green, stiff as a board, with pink roses sprawling all over it. A very curious observance of some bishops is to change their *phanio* for a chasuble before the consecration!

(all with stoles worn in varying ways), and generally the bishops do too (with Roman mitre and crozier). Servers have cassocks and cotta.

The ordinary dress of the clergy is a black cassock (violet for prelates, red for the patriarch) with a round flat cap; a wide-sleeved gown and low turban (*tabieh*) for formal occasions. Bishops wear their turban over the Syrian *masnaphta* (hood).

Liturgical books. These were printed in Rome from 1594 and a complete edition definitively drawn up and issued after the 1736 synod, reprinted at Rome, Kosaya, and Beirut. They include a "missal" arranged in the Roman way. Of the 25 alternative *anaphoras* only eight are printed and used; the most recent and common is "of the Holy Roman Church."

The *liturgical language* is Syriac, but the lessons and some other prayers are in Arabic, and the use of this vernacular tends to increase. Rubrics are in Karshuni.

THE EUCHARISTIC LITURGY

This is simply the "common parts" of the Syrian Liturgy of St. James (into which one or other of the *anaphoras* is inserted), subjected to "adaptation, often useless and servile, to Roman usages" (Labourt). There is a uniform way of celebrating "low Mass," which I describe here (anaphora of the Roman Church), though in principle every Liturgy is sung. The people kneel throughout, women normally separate from men. Concelebration often takes place in monasteries and big churches and sometimes in smaller ones. The Liturgy of the Presanctified is confined to Good Friday.

The priest vests and goes to the foot of the altar, moves his head in the form of a cross saying, "I will go up to the altar of God . . . ," mounts the steps, genuflects and proceeds to the preparation of the offerings, all the prayers of which are said in a low voice. He covers up the gifts with three silk veils, draws back a little from the altar, says aloud, "In the name . . ." signing himself (the sign of the cross is made as with us), followed by a long prayer of self-reproach in Arabic analogous to the *Confiteor*. He turns to right and left saying, "Pray to our Lord for me" and proceeds to incense[28] the offerings, the altar and the people. He says *Kyrie eleison* three times and the *Trisagion*, and the Liturgy properly speaking begins with the Our Father in Arabic.

The server invites the people to pray for peace:

> "For the peace and salvation of the whole world, for the faithful people of Christ from one end thereof to the other, for those in sickness and trouble and for the souls which are in sorrow, and for our fathers and brethren and teachers, and because of our sins and faults and the wickednesses of us all, and for the faithful departed who have gone before us, we pray to the Lord."

The priest prays for courage and purity, the people answer "Amen" and he blesses them: "✠Peace be to the Church and to her children." The first clause of *Gloria in excelsis* is said followed by psalm-verses and a variable prayer of praise. The server then says:

> "Let there be remembrance of Mary the Mother of God, of the prophets and the apostles and the martyrs and the just, of the clergy and all the children of the Church from generation to generation and for ever and ever. Amen."

And, while the celebrant prays inaudibly, he proceeds to make these commemorations. Then *Kyrie eleison* is said three times and the priest, with his hands crossed over the gifts, commemorates our Lord, Adam and Eve, our Lady and the saints, including the titular of the church by name, and prays silently for those whom he wishes to name.

He strikes his breast three times, saying the offertory:

> "O holy Trinity, have mercy on me. O holy Trinity, forgive my sins. O holy and glorious Trinity, accept this offering from my sinful hands,"

commemorates the dead, and asks for protection from sin.

---

[28] Incense is always used at "low Mass." The "missal" remains on the northern side of the altar.

Priest: "Pray to the Lord for me."

Server: "May God receive thy offering and may he have mercy on us through thy prayers."

The server repeats the prayer "For the peace . . . we pray to the Lord," the priest prays aloud for worthiness and then incenses the altar, offerings, and people, who say with him the *Miserere* in Arabic. Then comes a prayer and the hymn of the day or feast and, while saying the *Trisagion* three times, the priest again incenses the offerings and altar; then he says to the server: "Sing! and glorify thy Creator."

The server says (or subdeacon sings) a variable psalm-verse and then the epistle in Arabic. A psalm-verse, alleluia, and *Kyrie eleison* (three times) are said or sung and then:

Priest: "Let us hear for the good of our souls the glad tidings of life and salvation, the holy gospel of our Lord Jesus Christ. The preaching of St. N. the Apostle (or Disciple) who hath preached life to the world. Jesus Christ, our Lord, our God and our Saviour, said during his life to the disciples and to the multitude."

People: "Father, bless us."

He pronounces a long blessing to which all answer "Amen," then, "Behold that which happened in the life of Jesus Christ, our Lord, our God, and our Saviour, the word of God who was made man for us."

People: "Lord, have mercy on us."

Priest: "May our Lord have mercy on us, on you, and on all the children of holy Church by the baptism which cleanses."

After these, so to say, ritual false starts, the gospel is read by the priest in Arabic[29] before the middle of the altar and facing the people.

The liturgy of the faithful begins with:

"The Lord reigneth, he is clothed with beauty. Alleluia. Our Lord said: I am the living bread which came down

---

[29] It is read in Syriac and other languages at Christmas.

from Heaven upon the earth that the world may have life in me. The Father sent me, his bodyless Word, and the womb of Mary received me as a rich seed of wheat in fertile ground. And behold, priests carry me in procession, in their hands, Alleluia. Accept our offering. . . ."

The gifts, altar, and people are incensed for the last time and the Creed (with *Filioque* added) is said by all in Arabic. The celebrant washes his fingers and returns to the middle of the altar where he begins the anaphora with the sign of the cross and prays aloud for peace, protection, and the power of the Holy Spirit. He touches the altar and vessels with his right hand saying:

"Peace be to thee, O altar of God; peace be to the holy mysteries that are upon thee. (*Giving his hand to the kneeling server or deacon who kisses it.*) Peace be to thee, servant of Jesus Christ; peace to the Church and to all her children."

The kiss of peace is conveyed among the people by a touching of hands. The celebrant removes the veils from the chalice and paten, blesses the people and offerings, and says: "Let us lift up our spirits, our minds and our hearts."

People: "They are lifted up to thee, O Lord."
Priest: "Let us praise God with fear and worship him with trembling."
People: "It is right and just."

The priest recites a very short preface, at the end of which all say the *Sanctus.*

Priest (with his hands over the offerings): "Holy art thou, O God the Father, who for our salvation hast sent thine only Son, our Lord Jesus Christ. Who, the day before he suffered" and so on, exactly as in the Roman canon, to "a commemoration of me."

All these words are said (or sung) aloud and the server says or the people sing "Amen" to each consecration; the celebrant genuflects and a bell is rung but there are no elevations.[30]

Two prayers of commemoration of the passion, resurrection, and ascension of our Lord are said, one by the server and one by the priest, several short prayers, and then a much modified *epiklesis* (suppressed entirely in some anaphoras), asking for the help of the Holy Spirit and the fruits of the sacrifice. There follows inaudibly the eucharistic intercession for the Church and faithful, living and dead; "for our holy Father, Pius, the Pope of Rome, for his Beatitude N., our patriarch, and Mar M., our bishop, and for all the children of the Orthodox, Catholic, and Apostolic Faith. . . . To them, O Lord, and to those who sleep in Christ give the repose of the dwellings of light and rest and grant to them and to us thy mercy"; and commemoration of the saints.

After the Our Father said by all in Arabic, preceded and followed by nearly the same clauses as in the Roman Mass, the bell is rung, the priest genuflects and raises the Host above his head, saying: "Holy things to the holy, with peace, purity, and holiness."

Likewise the Chalice, the priest saying:

> "In truth we have believed and do firmly believe, O Lord, in thee, as the holy Catholic Church hath believed in thee: that thou art one Father, the holy; praise be to him, Amen; one Son, the holy; glory be to him, Amen; one Spirit, the holy; praise and worship be to him for ever and ever. Amen."

At the fraction the Host is divided into three. One particle is dipped into the precious Blood and therewith three small signs of the cross made on the other parts of the Host; the dipped particle is then dropped into the Chalice: short prayers preparatory to communion are said the while. The bell is rung, the priest genuflects, strikes his breast three times with a sign of the cross before each, says "Pray for me," and receives the larger particle of the Host and a little of the precious Blood.

---

[30] In the anaphora "of St. Peter" the words of institution are expressed in the second person: "you took bread," "you lifted up your eyes," etc.

Then he says with the people "Lord I am not worthy . . ." followed by "Lamb of God . . ." three times, and Holy Communion is given to them under the species of bread only (since 1736), with the words: "The body of our Lord Jesus Christ is given to you for the pardon of offences, for the forgiveness of sins, and for life everlasting. Amen." When the Liturgy is sung the deacon also receives Communion and in both kinds.

After a sort of litany of thanksgiving and praise the celebrant takes up both chalice and paten, turns to the people, blesses them with the Holy Things, and then consumes what remains. He makes the ablutions, saying several prayers, and a long prayer of benediction ends with a pleasantly domestic form of dismissal:

> "My brethren and my friends . . . living or dead, go in peace. . . . We ask the help of your prayers, O our fathers and brethren, now and always. Amen."

Then with his hand-cross the priest gives the final blessing and, if the Liturgy has not been sung, the prayers for Russia are said in Arabic. The priest's private prayer before leaving the sanctuary is a manifestation of Eastern devotion to the altar of sacrifice, as in the pure Syrian rite.

THE DIVINE OFFICE

This has been obligatory on the clergy since 1736. It is a recasting of the Syrian office (see p. 177), with the same hours, except that it lacks Lauds.

THE SACRAMENTS

Baptism and *Penance* (in Arabic) are administered according to translations from the Roman ritual, and *Confirmation* and *Extreme Unction* very nearly so. The synod of 1736 separated Confirmation from Baptism and assigned its administration to the bishops. The *Eucharist* has been mentioned above. The *Holy Orders* are the same as those of the Syrians and conferred in similar fashion (p. 178); contrary both to common Eastern custom and to that of the Syrians, the subdeacon has the duty of singing the epistle. *Marriage* ceremonies also resemble those of the Syrians, carried out in Arabic and with added Latin elements.

Calendar and feasts. These closely resemble those of the Syrians, with the same Western importations, and others added, e.g., Rosary Sunday and the Holy Name of Mary. There are 23 holydays, of which St. Maro (Feb. 9) is naturally one of the most important. Feasts of Old Testament saints are numerous. The Gregorian reckoning was adopted in 1606 at Tripoli and elsewhere.

Penitential periods. Lent lasts seven weeks (no fasting on Saturdays and Sundays), and most Wednesdays and Fridays are days of abstinence, as well as four days before SS. Peter and Paul, eight before the Assumption, and twelve before Christmas. The "fast of the Ninevites" is represented by a period of special prayer.

General observations. In addition to all the principal Western "popular devotions" (especially those directed toward the Blessed Sacrament) the Maronites have adopted and adapted certain Roman liturgical observances, e.g., the blessing and imposition of ashes (first Monday in Lent), the covering of pictures and statues during passiontide, blessing of palms, and the washing of feet on Maundy Thursday, on which day, also, the patriarch must consecrate the Chrism. These are all carried out with considerable dramatic effect and popular excitement, which are further displayed in their own special customs, such as the "raising of Lazarus" (eve of Palm Sunday), and the "burial" and "resurrection of Christ." The Liturgy is celebrated at midnight on Christmas, the Epiphany, and Easter.

BIBLIOGRAPHY

Lammens, *La Syrie* (Beirut, 1921).

Phares, *Les Maronites du Liban* (Paris, 1908).

Sfeir, *The Language of Christ in America* (Buffalo, 1929).

Gorayeb, *The Maronite Liturgy* (Buffalo, 1915).

Phares, *La Semaine Sainte chez les Maronites* (Paris, 1908).

Charles, *Syrie Proche-Orient* (Paris, 1929).

3. THE MALANKARESE

General Ecclesiastical History

On pages 243–247 will be found a brief account of the Christians of Malabar in India and the events which led to their schism in 1653. Within ten years three quarters of them had returned to Catholic unity, but the rest remained obdurate under their leader the archdeacon Thomas Palakomatta (Parambil). He had received as commission only a sort of investiture by the imposition of hands of twelve priests, and he tried in vain to get episcopal orders from the Nestorians of Mesopotamia. Then he approached the Jacobite patriarch in the same country, who sent a bishop, Mar Gregory, to visit Malabar. He does not seem to have consecrated Thomas nor, in spite of Jacobite episcopal visitations from time to time, were any of his first four successors (all called Thomas) consecrated. However, the schismatics at last obtained a valid hierarchy in 1772, when the sixth Thomas was made bishop (as Dionysius I) by the episcopal delegates of the Jacobite patriarch. Dionysius presumably acknowledged some shadowy jurisdiction in that prelate, but the Malabar Jacobites claim that they never formally accepted Monophysite errors. The Malabar schismatics began to abandon their Chaldean or East Syrian liturgy for that of the Jacobites, the West Syrian or Antiochene, but this substitution was not complete for another hundred years.

Throughout the eighteenth and nineteenth centuries the story of the Malabar Jacobites is a wearisome succession of squabbles, lawsuits, and sub-schisms, complicated since 1816 by Protestant missionary efforts. Four attempts were made at reunion with Rome during the eighteenth century and they were all abortive; the last two, by Mar Dionysius I, had direct encouragement from the Holy See but were frustrated by the policy of the local Latin authorities.[31] So some of the Jacobites turned to the Anglicans (with more result) and, though there have been a number of individual reconciliations to the Chaldeo-Malabarese, there was no important reunion till our own day. In 1909 the Jacobite patriarch of Antioch, Abdullah Sattuf, came to Malabar, quarrelled with the metropolitan Dionysius V about church property, and excommunicated him. Since then the "orthodox" Jacobites have been split into two litigious parties, those who want to depend on the Patriarch of Antioch and those who want to be independent.

Nevertheless, side by side with this deplorable state of affairs there has been a certain quickening of religious consciousness among some of the Malabar Jacobites; this became noticeable about 1868, when it was confidently expected that the Metropolitan Dionysius IV would lead a large number of his people back to the Catholic Church, though this did not in fact happen. In 1919 Father Givergis (George) Panikkar, rector of the principal Jacobite seminary, founded at a place he called Bethany a religious brotherhood, "of the Imitation of Christ," for missionary and educational work, followed by a similar institute for nuns (for whom there was no provision among the Jacobites). In 1925 Father Givergis was consecrated bishop, taking the name of Ivanios (John).

At a synod of Jacobite bishops of the anti-patriarchal party held in the same year to consider measures for the spiritual regeneration of their church, Mar Ivanios was commissioned "to open correspondence with the Church of Rome with a view to explore the avenues for ending schisms so far as Malabar was concerned." In response to his overtures the Holy See replied that if the bishops abjured their errors and schism their Antiochene liturgy and customs would be maintained and, upon verification of the validity of their baptism

---

[31] One bishop concerned, a Portugese Carmelite, Jacob Soledad, is referred to by the Carmelite historian Friar Paulinus as a "naturally rough man, who was kind to nobody and caused endless disturbance on the Travancore coast" (*India Orientalis Christiana*, p. 124).

and ordination, the bishops would be confirmed in their offices and jurisdiction.

Of the five bishops concerned only two, Mar Ivanios and his suffragan Mar Theophilos, accepted the invitation. They were received into the visible communion of the Catholic Church on September 20, 1930, followed at once by two *rambans* (solitaries, who were also bishops designate) and other clergy, religious of the Imitation, and a thousand lay people (including the octogenarian parents of Mar Ivanios); there were many more later. To distinguish them from their fellows of the Chaldean and Latin rites in Malabar, they are called the Malankara Catholics.

Unlike so many reunions with Rome in the course of history this movement is distinguished as an entirely religious one, without any element of political, social, or other temporal consideration in it. On the contrary, the new Catholics have to suffer a good deal of petty persecution sometimes, and they lose all their ecclesiastical property, churches, cemeteries, etc., upon leaving the Jacobite body. The Brothers of the Imitation set the admirable example of not going to law in order to try and retain their possessions; they were literally penniless and homeless till a generous and sympathetic Hindu came to the rescue with a small piece of land. The reunion is calculated to have far-reaching effects among the Jacobites, who can now become Catholics without having to abandon their familiar rites and customs, and, in the case of married priests, without giving up either their wives or their sacerdotal functions, as is their case in joining the Chaldeo-Malabar or the Latin rites.

PRESENT STATE

The Malankara province of Malabar consists of the archdiocese of Trivandrum (Mar Ivanios, metropolitan) and the diocese of Tiruvalla (Mar Theophilos, bishop) in Travancore. The faithful number 18,000 (several hundreds being new converts from Hinduism), and there are fifty priests, most of them married. Priests who fill certain responsible offices (e.g., vicar general) rank as prelates and have the title *prodott*, "visitor."

Religious institutes. The members of the *Brotherhood of the*

Imitation of Christ are definitely missionaries to India, primarily by prayer and contemplation; they wear the yellow gown of the Hindu holy man (*sanyasin*), they avoid all flesh-meat, and their monastery is called an *ashram*. In drawing up their rule the founder Mar Ivanios sought a synthesis of the prescriptions of St. Basil, St. Benedict, and St. Francis of Assisi. There are six priests, ten brothers, and seven aspirants. Their superior is called the *reesh*, "governor." The Sisters, seventeen in number, conduct schools.

LITURGY AND CUSTOMS

These are simply those of the West Syrian rite (see pp. 176 ff.), without those modifications which the Catholics of that rite have introduced. Their *church appointments* are florid, and statues instead of pictures are sometimes to be seen. In the *Eucharistic Liturgy* the scriptural lessons and most of the prayers are read in the vernacular Malayalam; the priest's inaudible prayers are in Syriac. "And the Son" has not been added in the Creed. The *sacraments* are all administered according to the Syriac books. Concelebration is still in use.

The clergy wear the wide-sleeved gown, black or white, with a round flat cap, and bishops the turban over the small hood. They have on certain occasions the Western mitre and crozier, which the Malabar Jacobites use, and habitually carry the hand-cross.

Devotions in honour of the Blessed Sacrament have been introduced in the form of exposition and benediction. The last-named consists of an excerpt from the last part of the Liturgy, with a hymn and a blessing with the Holy Things added. Stations of the cross have been set up in some churches.

BIBLIOGRAPHY

*Rae, *The Syrian Church in India* (Edinburgh, 1892).

Ivanios, "The Malabar Reunion," in *Pax*, No. 114 (Prinknash Priory, 1931).

Vattathara, *Le Mouvement de Bethanie* (Louvain, 1931). See also the bibliography on p. 255.

Chapter VIII

THE ARMENIAN RITE

THE ARMENIAN RITE

I. HISTORY AND PRESENT STATE

General Ecclesiastical History

The scattered people whom we call Armenians were formerly localized in the country which is bounded, roughly, by the Caucasus and Taurus mountains, the Black Sea, and the Caspian Sea: Greater Armenia was to the east of the river Euphrates and Lesser Armenia to the west, later covering Cilicia to the Mediterranean. The Armenians are an Indo-European people, who call themselves Haikh and their country Hayastan, on account of a mythical descent from Haik, great-grandson of Noe. They have always been a compact people, with what we should now call a strong national sentiment, but their geographical situation was against their enjoying sovereignty for very long consecutive periods and they have been controlled and exploited in turn by the Medes, Romans, Persians, Byzantines, Arabs, Turks, and Russians.

The definitive conversion of the Armenians to Christianity was the work of St. Gregory the Illuminator,[1] a Parthian, who was made bishop by the Metropolitan of Caesarea in Cappadocia in 294. He baptized the king, Tiridates, and Armenia had the distinction of being the first nation to embrace Christianity officially and as a body. In 374 the new church repudiated its canonical dependence on the church of Caesarea, and became an isolated body under its own primate (the

---

[1] The non-Catholic Armenians are often distinguished as "Gregorians," they having evolved the theory that St. Gregory established a completely independent national church under his own rule.

katholikos); he was, and admitted that he was, subject to the universal pontifical authority of the Holy See—but that meant in practice much less then than it does now.

During the first half of the fifth century St. Isaac (Sahak) the Great reformed the Armenian Church on Byzantine lines and, with St. Mesrop, translated the Bible and the Liturgy into their vernacular. Owing to war with their Persian over- lords the Armenians took no part in the Monophysite troubles which culminated in the Council of Chalcedon (451); but some fifty years later, moved partly by political motives, a national synod repudiated that council. The Armenian Church thus cut itself off from the communion of the Catholic Church, and has ever since been reputed Monophysite, though it is not in communion with the churches professing that heresy.[2]

For the next seven hundred years the story of Armenian Christianity was one of bloody persecution by Persians and Arabs from without and quarrels within. The people naturally welcomed and helped the Crusaders against their Mohammedan oppressors, and at the end of the twelfth century those who had fled westward and formed the kingdom of Little Armenia in Cilicia were reunited to Rome. Outside Cilicia the union was weak or non-existent, but the Western ritual and disciplin- ary practices adopted from the Crusaders affected the whole Armenian Church and have persisted to this day. The union was maintained till the Saracens took Akka in 1291, and in a weak and decayed form till the end of the kingdom of Little Armenia in 1375. After that, though individual katholikoi were in communion with Rome, the church as a whole was in schism again.

During the following centuries Latin missionaries were very active among the Armenians and before 1356 there appeared that curious phenomenon, the Friars of Unity of St. Gregory the Illuminator. These were under the protection of the Do- minican Order on the one hand and of an Armenian abbot on

---

[2] It must be stated that many scholars, Armenian and other, Catholic and dissident, maintain that Chalcedon was repudiated under a mis- apprehension, and that the Armenians are not and never were Mo- nophysite heretics. But the dissidents are certainly in schism.

Mgr. PAUL PETER XIII TERZIAN,
Patriarch of Cilicia and Katholikos of the
Catholic Armenians

(d. 1931)

Bishop

Vartaped

Protodeacon

Subdeacon

CLERGY OF THE ARMENIAN RITE

the other, and they tried to combine oriental monasticism with the Rule of the Friars Preachers. As usually happens with such experiments the West crowded the East out, and it became to all intents and purposes a Western order with an Armenian exterior. But these friars did a tremendous amount of work and are said at one time to have numbered 600 members. The congregation survived till the eighteenth century, when the remnant was absorbed in the ordinary Dominican Order.

Armenia sent four representatives to the Council of Florence and a decree of reunion was published, but nothing of importance came of it—except the famous instruction *pro Armenis*, on the sacraments, in the bull *Exultate Deo*.

THE CATHOLIC ARMENIANS

Owing to the efforts of the Friars of Unity and others there were always groups of Catholics of the Armenian rite, and in the middle of the seventeenth century a Catholic was made patriarch of his nation in Constantinople. But an already troubled position was made worse by the shocking religio-political activity of the French ambassador, the Marquis Fériol, who abducted a subsequent dissident patriarch, Avedik of Tokat, and sent him to be tried by the Inquisition in France. During the ensuing persecution there suffered, in 1707, Der[3] Gomidas Keumurgian, who was beatified as a martyr at Rome in 1929.

The number of Armenian Catholics in the Near East continued to increase in spite of persecution,[4] and in 1742 Pope Benedict XIV approved the establishment of a Catholic patriarchal see in Asia Minor, at Bzommar in the Lebanon, with the title of Cilicia. In 1830 French influence obtained the recognition by Turkey of the Catholic Armenians as a separate "nation" (*millah*), with a civil head and an archbishop as religious head at Constantinople. This dual authority caused

---

[3] *Der*, short for *derder*, the title of a married Armenian priest.

[4] So numerous were they a hundred years ago in Constantinople that the word "Catholic" in that city popularly meant one of the Armenian rite and nothing else.

206 CATHOLIC EASTERN CHURCHES

grave difficulties till, in 1846, the two offices were united in the person of Mgr. Hassun, and in 1867 his elevation to the patriarchal throne also unified the two ecclesiastical primacies of Constantinople and Cilicia.

In the same year Pope Pius IX issued the bull *Reversurus*, which regulated the election and powers of the Armenian patriarch and bishops and restrained the participation of the laity in ecclesiastical affairs. Many took this bull as an infringement of secular rights, and the commotion lasted for ten years, entailing the schism of several bishops, all the so-called Antonian monks, and a number of lay people. When peace was restored, the great Mgr. Hassun resigned his office and died, a cardinal, in Rome four years later. He assisted at the Vatican Council.

But internal trouble continued, especially at Constantinople, a section of the lay people standing out for their old influence. The plenary synod of 1911 produced good results, but interested parties used the latent discontent for their own ends, and it became active again in 1927. A compromise was effected two years later.

During the massacres by Turks and Kurds in the war of 1914–18 the Catholic Armenians lost seven bishops, over 100 priests, 45 nuns, and thirty thousand lay folk; over 800 ecclesiastical buildings and schools were pillaged and destroyed, and a dozen dioceses laid waste. Moreover, the formation of a soviet socialist republic in Russian Armenia has cut off an indeterminate number of Catholics from their fellows.

A conference of Armenian bishops at Rome in 1928 reorganized their church in view of these events and of the conditions now obtaining.

Present State

Patriarch. The "Patriarch of the Catholic Armenians and Katholikos of Cilicia" is the supreme head under the Pope of all the faithful of his rite except those referred to below. His see is now again at Bzommar, near Beirut (it was at Constantinople from 1867 to 1928); a new residence has been built in the suburb of Ashrafieh as a gift from Pope Pius XI. He is elected by the bishops in synod and their choice must be confirmed by the Holy See, with the grant of the *pallium.* He has the right to consecrate the Chrism for his whole patriarchate and as delegate of the Supreme Pontiff to ordain its bishops, all of whom depend directly on him. He communicates with the Sacred Eastern Congregation through the delegate apostolic for Syria. All patriarchs take the name of Peter: the present one is Mgr. Avedis Peter XIV Arpiarian, elected in 1931.

Bishops are chosen by the clergy of the diocese with the approval of the patriarch. The present sees are the patriarchal diocese of Beirut; the archdioceses (without suffragans) of Aleppo, Constantinople, and Mardin (residence at Bagdad); and the dioceses of Alexandria and Ispahan; the other thirteen dioceses are in abeyance; the few Catholic Armenians of Palestine are in charge of a vicar patriarchal. The patriarch has a titular archbishop for vicar general, and there is an ordaining prelate attached to the Armenian College at Rome.

Parochial clergy. These are formed principally in the national college at Rome, founded 1883, and conducted by Armenian secular priests, in the patriarchal seminary at Bzommar, and in the oriental seminary of the Jesuits at Beirut; some at the Capuchin's seminary in Constantinople and others abroad, but the Armenian bishops are aiming at a more unified arrangement. Married men may be ordained to the diaconate and priesthood, but the custom of voluntary celibacy is practically universal. The patriarchal clergy form a sort of religious congregation.

The office of *vartaped* is a rank peculiar to the Armenian hierarchy, conferred by a sort of ordination ceremony. They are celibate secular priests of superior learning and ability who are put in charge of responsible posts; they are divided into senior and junior classes and, in theory, are the only authorized preachers under the bishops. The *archpriest* is a sort of rural dean.

Religious institutes. Since the defection of the "Antonians" under Father Malachy Ormanian in 1871, monasticism has been represented, and most worthily, only by the *Mekhitarists*. These monks were founded by the Venerable Mekhitar of Sivas in 1701, with the Rule of St. Benedict as the basis of their constitutions. War drove them to Venice, where they settled on the island of San Lazzaro in 1717; later, a separate branch was established at Vienna. The good they have done for their countrymen by missionary and educational work and the printing and diffusion of books is incalculable.[5] The Venice abbey has small houses and colleges at Padua, Rome, Constantinople, Budapest, and Sèvres, and the Vienna abbey others at Constantinople, Philippopolis, and Piraeus. The order has 104 monks, of whom 81 are priests. The two abbots are always titular archbishops.

The *Sisters of the Immaculate Conception*, founded by Mgr. Hassun in 1852, have some 145 members who conduct schools and orphanages in various places. Their mother house and novitiate is at Rome. The present superioress, Mother Elbis, is a woman of remarkable intellectual and literary attainments.

The Faithful. With the exception of the long-standing but now small disaffected party the Armenian laity are on the whole good, observant Christians. It is curious that, while a non-Catholic Armenian is generally an adherent of his national church or of nothing, the Catholics are often quite ready to abandon their own rite; there is accordingly an unknown number of them who belong to the Western church, sometimes by a tradition dating back several generations.

The Catholic Armenians of the patriarchate number 41,860, of whom 113 are pastoral clergy, most of them refugees scattered among the villages of Syria. Beirut has 7,000 and Aleppo 15,000. Of the number and state of those in Russian territory little certain information is available; they have been esti-

---

[5] The catalogue of their publications is amazing. It ranges from the Bible to the pagan classics and from Buffon's *Birds* to *Uncle Tom's Cabin!* And in other languages besides Armenian—over twenty books in English are listed. Byron was a frequent (and welcome) visitor at San Lazzaro.

mated at 50,000 or much less. An administrator apostolic with residence at Tiflis was appointed for them in 1921.[6]

Western religious institutes working among the Armenians include the Augustinians of the Assumption (Bulgaria, Constantinople), Capuchins (Constantinople, Syria), Jesuits (Constantinople, Syria), and Lazarists (Persia).

OTHER JURISDICTIONS

Greece. In 1925 an ordinary, immediately subject to the Holy See, was appointed for the 3,000 Catholic Armenian emigrants settled in Greece.

Poland. There were Armenians living in Galicia in the fourteenth century, and after great difficulties the majority of them, with their archbishop, submitted to Rome between 1630 and 1681. It is not surprising that, hemmed in by Latins and Ruthenians, they became very "hybridized" and many joined the Latin rite; this drift still goes on, and today only about 5,000 souls adhere to the local version of their proper rite. Their ecclesiastical superior is the Armenian Archbishop of Lwów (Leopol), immediately subject to and appointed by the Holy See, with the approval of the Polish government. There is a convent of Armenian Benedictine nuns (founded 1680) at Lwów, who have a school.

Rumania. Two thirds (some 36,000) of the old Armenian colony in what is now the kingdom of Rumania have been Catholics since the later part of the seventeenth century, and are latinized almost beyond recognition. In accordance with the Rumanian concordat the Holy See has now appointed for them an administrator apostolic, with residence at Gherla (Armenierstadt) subject to the Latin bishop of Alba Julia; in due course they will probably form a diocese.

Elsewhere. There are 8,675 Catholic Armenians in France and Belgium, with a few priests, subject to the French ordinaries, but at present in the immediate care of two bishops of their rite exiled from Turkey in Asia.

---

[6] The non-Catholic Armenians probably number round about two to three millions. Those in the soviet socialist republic of Armenia have recently been enabled to re-establish their hierarchy.

There are 2,739 in the United States (mostly in New York State), to whom priests have been sent from Constantinople; they are directly subject to the American bishops.

The 2,000 or so scattered elsewhere frequent Latin churches or, occasionally, those of their dissident brethren.

II. LITURGY AND CUSTOMS

Church buildings. An Armenian church is usually rectangular in plan, and its typical characteristic is a central dome which outside forms a low round tower with a cone-shaped roof. Inside it rather resembles a Latin church; sometimes they are almost indistinguishable. The sanctuary is open, considerably raised from the nave, and approached by two lateral flights of four or five steps; the altar may stand in the middle, beneath a *ciborium*, but is usually nearer the east wall in the midst of a sort of open screen. The altar table (of stone) is narrow and has at the back three, four, or even five gradines; on it is a crucifix, an indeterminate (but large) number of candlesticks, a small hand-cross with which blessings are given, and a tabernacle containing the reserved Sacrament. On the north side is a credence table or niche in the wall. Numerous lamps burn before this and other altars, of which there are generally two simpler ones, one on either side.

In front of the sanctuary is a raised and enclosed space for the choir. The singers stand here in a semi-circle, dressed in a long, wide-sleeved ungirdled garment with a short shoulder cape, varied in colour: I have seen them apple-green and heliotrope.

The nave now often has seats; properly, women are separated from men, sometimes in galleries, but this is passing out of use. There are a few pictures, e.g., behind the altars, and round statues and stations of the cross are now often found in Catholic churches.

Vestments. The vestments are the white *shapig* (equivalent to the alb, and sometimes replaced thereby), embroidered cuffs (*pazpan*), stole (*porurar*) in one piece hanging down in front with a loop for the head, over it an embroidered cincture (*koti*); then a tall, stiff, embroidered collar (*vagas*) which stands up around the neck—this is nothing but an adaptation of the mediaeval apparelled amice of the west, and a very handsome sort of ornament; and over all the *shurtshar* (chasuble) which is like a full cope, without hood or orphreys; finally the priest wears on his head the *saghavard*, which is simply the episcopal crown of the Byzantine rite, adopted by Armenian priests when their bishops took to wearing Latin mitres in 1181. Bishops add the *emiporon*, a big *pallium* worn over the shoulders, and the patriarch and archbishops have the *gonker* (the Byzantine *epigonation*), a lozenge-shaped ornament hanging at the right side. The deacon wears a coloured *shapig*, ungirdled, with wide sleeves, of silk or velvet and embroidered at wrists and shoulders, and a long stole (*urar*) over his left shoulder with the back end drawn round to come under his right arm and across his chest. When a bishop celebrates with six deacons, the protodeacon wears the sacerdotal crown. There are no liturgical colours; I have seen chasubles of golden brown silk with small black arabesques and another of plain saffron silk; black may be worn for funeral services.

Armenian bishops have used the Western mitre and crozier since the time of the Crusades. It is curious that the Latin ritual practices then borrowed (which non-Catholic Armenians claim to be customs of immemorial antiquity!) were retained when the schism reopened, and in a few trifling matters Western influence continued to make itself felt; for example, the mitre worn by even dissident Armenian bishops is not the soft low cap of the twelfth century, but a towering curved affair copied from the worst Roman models of the eighteenth,[7] and their crozier likewise is of the baroque pattern.

Bishops wear the pectoral cross and ring, and for choir

---

[7] At the Eucharistic Congress in Jerusalem in 1893 Mgr. Terzian, Bishop of Adana, said that, "I sometimes have to celebrate the holy Mysteries in the open air, for there is not always a room sufficiently high to hold me with a mitre on my head." He was, of course, referring to the poverty of his flock, but the statement provoked laughter.

dress put on a garment like a long very full cope, violet in colour, and a flat-topped cap covered with a veil. Vartapeds have the right to a staff-of-office (*gavazan*) resembling a Byzantine pastoral staff, as well as to a veil over their caps and sometimes a pectoral cross. In processions the patriarch and archbishops carry a staff surmounted by a sort of heraldic emblem of their diocese and are preceded by ministers carrying the archiepiscopal cross, the crozier, and the vartaped's staff.

The ordinary dress of the Catholic Armenian clergy (who wear the beard) is the cassock and cincture, to which a long full-sleeved black gown, open down the front, is added on formal occasions; priests have a black cloak for choir and a veil over the flat cap if celibates. The traditional conical cap (*pakegh*) is no longer in use by Catholics.

Liturgical books. The nine Armenian liturgical books are analogous to those of the Byzantine rite and are well and clearly arranged, the best of all Eastern church-books. Four of them are required for the celebration of a solemn Liturgy, namely the *Donatzuitz*, a sort of perpetual *Ordo;* the *Badarakamaduitz*, containing the celebrant's part; the *Jiashotz*, containing the epistles and gospels and other parts for the deacon and ministers; and the *Trebutiun*, which contains the hymns and chants of the choir. But "low Mass" is common among the Catholics and in 1879 Mgr. Hassun provided for this by publishing an edition of the *Badarakamaduitz* arranged on the lines of the Roman Missal.

The principal other book is the *Mashdotz*, equivalent to our *Rituale.* It gets its name from the surname of St. Mesrop, who is traditionally but erroneously regarded as its compiler; actually, its contents belong to different ages and are drawn from several sources. The books have been printed at Rome, Venice, and Vienna (by the Mekhitarists at the last two places).

Music. The very ancient Armenian ecclesiastical chant is of the usual Eastern enharmonic type: most beautiful really, but barbarous to those ears unable to listen with patience to anything outside the diatonic and chromatic scales. The singing is properly unaccompanied, except for the shaking of *ripidia* (*keshotz*) with little bells attached, cymbals being clashed to mark the rhythm; but organs are now sometimes found in the churches, and polyphony is occasionally heard.

THE EUCHARISTIC LITURGY

The Eucharistic Liturgy is essentially the Greek Liturgy of St. Basil, derived directly from Caesarea, translated into classical Armenian, but modified first by Syrian and Constantinopolitan and then by Latin influences till it has become *sui generis*.[8] The deacon's admonitions *"Orthi"* (ὀρθοί) and *"Proskhume"* (πρόσχωμεν) and *Amen* and *Alleluia* alone remain untranslated. It is remarkable among Eastern liturgies in that, like the Roman Mass, it has one fixed *anaphora*. The general "scheme" of the service is that the choir or people sing while the celebrant prays in a low voice, ending his prayers aloud, often at the invitation of the deacon ("Sir, bless!"). Solemn celebrations are carried out with very great magnificence. The Armenian Liturgy is never concelebrated by a number of celebrants nor is there a Liturgy of the Presanctified; according to the canons, the Liturgy should be celebrated only on Saturdays and Sundays during Lent.

The celebrant vests in the sacristy assisted by the deacon (and sometimes other ministers) and with appropriate prayers, while the choir sings a hymn. The Liturgy begins with preparatory prayers at the foot of the sanctuary, where the priest washes his hands, saying Psalm 25. Then, turning to the people, he says a *confiteor* in the Latin manner.

If there be another priest present he approaches from the choir and pronounces an absolution and the celebrant, raising his hand-cross, gives an absolution to the people. The choir sings Psalm 99 and then, after two short prayers, the priest says with the deacon the antiphon "I will go unto the altar of God" and Psalm 42 (*Iudica*); the deacon, who carries a

---

[8] The Armenians call it "The Liturgy of our Blessed Father the holy Gregory the Illuminator, revised and augmented by the holy patriarchs and teachers Isaac, Mesrop, Kud and John Mantaguni." This of course is not so. We of the west are not altogether free from a tendency to make patriotic flourishes of this sort.

candle, swings the thurible and at every two verses they ascend one step of the sanctuary; a most impressive entrance. The priest approaches the altar, the preparatory prayers are finished, and a large curtain is drawn, hiding the whole of the sanctuary.[9] All this was borrowed from the Roman Mass during the time of the mediaeval reunion.

While the choir sings a hymn according to the feast or season, the priest goes to the table or niche on the north side of the altar, and prepares the gifts. The bread is unleavened (even among the non-Catholics, who are the only oriental dissidents to use *azyme*) and resembles Latin altar-breads, but the discs are thicker and less crisp. A drop of water is added to the wine.[10] The priest offers up the gifts with a prayer, recites Psalm 92 as he covers them with a veil, and the curtain is withdrawn. Then the priest incenses the altar and, leaving the sanctuary, the other altars, the holy images, and the people.

During a prayer for mercy the choir sings the psalm and hymn for the day; the priest concludes his prayer with a blessing; then after a well-known prayer of St. John Chrysostom the deacon sings "*Proskhume*," "Let us attend," and the *Trisagion* is sung: "Holy God, holy Strong One, holy Deathless One, have mercy on us." During this the deacon, attended by other ministers, fetches the gospel-book, carrying it behind the altar from north to south to the edge of the sanctuary where it is offered to the senior priest in the choir, or to a distinguished layman, to kiss (the Byzantine "little entrance"). The deacon then chants a litany for all bishops, the ordinary, clergy, and faithful, living and dead, etc., the choir or people answering "Lord, have mercy on us (them)," while the celebrant prays for the acceptance of the petitions. A lector and subdeacon in the sanctuary, or a layman in the choir, then chant an Old Testament lesson and an epistle for the day (resting the book on a folding lectern facing the

---

[9] During Lent this curtain is drawn to cut off the sanctuary during the whole Liturgy.

[10] Alone of all Christians who have a valid Eucharist, the dissident Armenians do not add water to the chalice.

people), each preceded by a psalm and antiphon. Then the deacon sings "*Orthi*," "Stand up," the priest blesses the people, "Peace be with you all," and the deacon chants the gospel facing the people, holding the book in a veil, another minister incensing it after each verse. At "low Mass" it is read by the priest, with his back to the middle of the altar.

The deacon then goes to the altar and recites aloud, in the plural, a version of the creed of Nicaea-Constantinople (Catholics add the clause "and from the Son"), finishing it with the conciliar anathema and the celebrant adding the "profession of St. Gregory the Illuminator":

> "As for us, we glorify him who was before all ages, worshipping the Holy Trinity and the one Godhead of Father, Son and Holy Ghost, now and for ever, world without end."

While the priest prays for forgiveness of sins and in-pouring of the Spirit, the deacon chants a short litany with the people for peace, pardon, the virtue of the Cross, and unity in the Faith. The priest prays aloud, gives a blessing, and the deacon commands:

> "Let no catechumen or one of little faith or undergoing penance or anyone unclean approach these divine mysteries."

The liturgy of the faithful then begins, the choir singing:

> "The body of the Lord and the blood of the Saviour are about to be[11] before us. The heavenly powers sing unseen, saying with ceaseless voice, Holy, Holy, Holy, Lord God of Hosts."

Deacon: "Sing hymns to the Lord our God, O ye singers, spiritual hymns of sweetest sound."

Accordingly the choir sings the *hagiology*, which varies with the day. As they begin the people kneel, and the curtain

---

[11] The words "about to be" are a Catholic addition, so that the dissident form is a remarkable example of liturgico-dramatic anticipation. There are others.

is drawn across for a moment while the priest removes his crown (if a bishop, he takes off all distinctively pontifical ornaments). He then bends low and prays in a low voice that he may be made worthy to sacrifice: ". . . make me worthy to assist at this holy altar and to consecrate thy stainless body and thy precious blood. . . ."

Meanwhile the deacon has gone to the side table and brings thence the holy gifts, coming round the back of the altar, holding the chalice and paten above his head and accompanied by incense, lights, and rattling *keshotz* (the Byzantine "great entrance"). The priest receives them at the altar, incenses them, and washes his hands, saying verses 6–12 of Psalm 25; he prays in a low voice for the accomplishment and acceptance of the sacrifice and that "this cup may be a remedy of expiation for the sins of him who drinks it," while the deacon exhorts the people to pray worthily, "not with a wavering spirit, doubting in faith, but with honest actions, sincere thoughts, humble hearts and immovable faith." He then kisses the altar and the celebrant's arm and gives the kiss of peace to a layman; the people convey it in turn to one another just as the ministers the *pax* in the Latin rite, or simply bow. A series of verses and responses between *deacon* and choir lead up to the "preface" of the *anaphora* which the priest says in a low voice; the choir sings the *Sanctus*, while the celebrant says a prayer, in which the blessings and types of the old dispensation are recalled, leading up to the words of institution:

> "Then, taking bread in his holy, divine, stainless and worshipful hands, he ✠ blessed it, gave thanks, broke it and gave it to his chosen and holy disciples seated with him, saying,"

Deacon: "Sir, bless!"

The priest chants (or says) aloud: "Take, eat, *this is my Body*, which is given for you and for many for the expiation and forgiveness of sins." *All:* "Amen."

Priest (secretly): "In like manner, having taken the cup, he ✠ blessed it, gave thanks, drank, and gave it to his holy and chosen disciples seated with him, saying,"

Deacon: "Sir, bless!"

The priest chants aloud: "Drink ye all of this: *this is my Blood of the new testament, which is shed for you and for many for the expiation and forgiveness of sins.*" *All:* "Amen."

There are properly no "elevations" here, but they have been introduced into some Catholic churches, with two genuflections (instead of prostrations); some priests at "low Mass" even say all the words of institution inaudibly. The people kneel from the *Sanctus* till after the consecration.

While the choir sings, the celebrant continues in a low voice, "To do this in remembrance of him was the command," etc. He makes a "little elevation" with Chalice and Host. The invocation of the Holy Ghost, "by whose means thou hast made the consecrated bread (wine) to become truly the body (blood) of our Lord Jesus Christ," is said over each species separately and over both together.

The great intercession follows, in which the priest prays for all manner of folk (including "the weary"), for the Faithful departed, good weather and material prosperity, etc., commemorating our Lady and others. Meanwhile the deacon invokes the memory of a number of saints by name, mostly Armenian, including Thaddeus and Bartholomew the apostles, Gregory the Illuminator, Mesrop, Isaac, three Nerses, Paul the Hermit, Anthony the Abbot, Neilos, and King Abgar, the choir or people responding, "Remember them, O Lord, and have mercy on us." The celebrant prays for the peace of the Catholic and Apostolic Church and for his bishop. Then the deacon sings the Thanksgiving of Bishop Khosroes the Great "which no one shall dare to change." It praises God for the holy and deathless sacrifice and asks charity, strength, and peace for the world, the Church, "our holy pope N. . . ., and our most happy[12] patriarch M. . . ." After another short litany the choir sings the Our Father, while the deacon censes the people, the priest saying the embolism in a low voice and adding the conclusion "For thine is the kingdom," etc., aloud.

The people kneel and the celebrant (deacon: "Proskhume!")

---

[12] There is pathos in this epithet in view of the history of his people.

lifts up the Sacred Host to be seen, singing "Unto the holiness of the holy," followed by a triple blessing and an elevation of the Chalice. The priest says a prayer for worthy communion, dips the Sacred Body in the Precious Blood, then takes the Chalice and Host in either hand and turns to the people, blessing them with the holy Things and saying:

> "Let us receive holy things holily; the sacred and precious body and blood of our Lord and Saviour Jesus Christ, descended from Heaven, is distributed among us," etc.

A little curtain is now drawn which hides only the priest and the altar. While the choir sings a hymn of praise with alleluia after each strophe, the celebrant kisses the Host and breaks it into four parts of which he drops three into the chalice saying, "The fullness of the Holy Spirit"; after preparatory prayers he receives the other part and drinks of the chalice. The little curtain is now withdrawn and he turns to the people with the Blessed Sacrament in his hands.

Deacon: "Draw near with fear and faith and communicate worthily."

Choir: "Our Lord and our God hath appeared to us. Blessed be he who comes in the name of the Lord."

It is lawful for the people to receive holy Communion in both kinds but for the last hundred years or so the custom has not obtained among Catholic Armenians; instead they receive kneeling a small particle, with the words of administration just as in the Latin rite.

The choir sings a hymn of thanks while the great curtain is drawn. The celebrant resumes his crown, washes the chalice and his hands, says several prayers of thanksgiving, kisses the altar and, when the curtain is withdrawn, turns to the people with the gospel-book and asks a blessing on them and on the world, to which they reply three times: "Blessed be the name of the Lord now and for ever."

Priest: "The accomplishment of the Law and the Prophets. Thou art Christ, our God and Redeemer, who has fulfilled all the prescriptions ordained by the Father: fill us with thy Holy Spirit."

Then the priest, standing in the choir and turned to the people, reads the "last gospel," John i. 1–18—the last and most surprising ancient borrowing from the west (in Easter week it is Matt. xxviii. 16–20, and in paschal-time John xxi. 15–20). He blesses the people saying: "✠ Be blessed by the grace of the Holy Spirit; go in peace and may the Lord be with you all. Amen. (*Turning to the altar*): Lord God, Jesus Christ, have mercy on me."

He then retires with his ministers. Blessed bread (*antidoron, neshkhar*) is no longer distributed among the Catholics.

The above description is substantially the Liturgy as celebrated in all Catholic Armenian churches—with one astonishing exception. In the four Transylvanian parishes of these folk in Rumania the churches are entirely Latin in appearance, Latin vestments are worn, and the Liturgy used is that found in the 1728 edition of the Missal of the Friars of Unity of St. Gregory—that is, the Dominican use of the Latin Mass translated into old Armenian! This is the more remarkable because these friars were never established in Transylvania.

THE DIVINE OFFICE

The canonical prayer of the Armenian Church is divided into nine offices, namely, Midnight (in honour of God the Father), Matins (in honour of the risen Christ), Sunrise (in honour of the Holy Ghost), prayers of the Third, Sixth, and Ninth Hours (in honour of the descent of the Holy Ghost, of the Passion, and of the death of our Lord respectively), Vespers (in honour of the entombment), Nightfall (invoking the peace of Christ), and Bedtime (for undisturbed repose). Sunrise and Nightfall are omitted on Saturdays and the eves of certain feasts, while "first Vespers" is supposed to be always celebrated in church.

These offices consist principally of psalms, variable hymns (*kanons;* several attributed to St. Nerses Glaietsi, who died in 1173), and prayers (several attributed to St. John Mantaguni,

d. 490). The psalms are divided into seven groups, one for each day of the week.

The Song of the Three Children, *Magnificat*, *Benedictus*, *Nunc dimittis*, and a form of *Gloria in excelsis* are sung at Matins, and there are readings from the gospels on Sundays and great feasts. The so-called Prayer of Manasses (which is printed at the end of the Latin Vulgate) is recited on week days in Lent at Matins and Vespers. The last-named office should be preceded by readings from the lives of the saints or from homilies, and concluded by a procession through the church, but these observances are becoming more and more rare.

Since 1911 the daily recitation of the Divine Office has been obligatory upon all Catholic priests of this rite.

THE SACRAMENTS

Baptism is a longish ceremony, which is begun outside the baptistery. The godfather renounces Satan and his powers, and makes a profession of faith for the child. The priest reads St. Matthew's gospel, xxviii. 16–20, recites the Nicene creed with the godparent, and all go into the baptistery saying certain psalms. After four scriptural lessons and a litany the priest blesses the water and pours three drops of Chrism into it. The actual baptism is performed by the priest sitting the child in the font, facing the east, and pouring water three times on its head, saying: "The servant of God N., coming by his own will to the state of a catechumen and thence to baptism, is baptized by me in the name of the Father . . . ," etc. Then the child is immersed thrice and held in the water (which is warmed) while Matt. iii. 13–17 is read.

Confirmation is administered by the priest immediately after Baptism. He anoints the forehead, eyes, ears, nostrils, mouth, hands, breast, back, and feet of the child with Chrism, accompanied by suitable words. Then he ties round its head a string of twisted red and white threads with a small cross attached; this has been blessed before the Baptism, and is removed ceremonially after eight days. He also clothes it in a white garment and offers it to God before the altar.

Penance. Confessional-boxes are in increasing use, and absolution is given by an indicative formula very similar to the Roman one.[13]

The Eucharist. The Liturgy and the manner of receiving Communion have been described above. The faithful are expected to go to confession and to communion at least at Christmas (or Epiphany), Easter, the Assumption, the Transfiguration, and the Exaltation of the Cross; Easter only is obligatory.

Extreme Unction. The proper Armenian form for the administration of this sacrament requires the presence of seven priests and is very long. It has been disused altogether by the dissidents since the fourteenth century, while the Catholics have substituted what is practically the rite in the *Rituale Romanum*, translated into their liturgical language.

Holy Orders. With the exception of the romanized Malabarese, the Armenians, Catholic and dissident, are the only Christians of the East who have four minor and three major, or sacred, orders. Minor orders are conferred by the handing-over of the instruments of office; vesting in the distinctive vestments and laying-on of hands are added for the subdiaconate and diaconate, and anointing with Chrism for the priesthood and episcopate.

Marriage is entered into by a long and admirable ceremony which, when carried out in its entirety, begins at the bride's home, includes a crowning of both parties with wreaths of flowers and celebration of the Liturgy in church, and ends with a blessed loving-cup at the house of the groom. The contract is effected by explicit declarations by the parties, unlike most Eastern wedding-services, in which they remain implicit.

Calendar. The ecclesiastical calendar of the Armenian rite is constructed on different principles from that of any other church. Strictly, there are only seven fixed feasts, all others falling on a day of the week following a certain Sunday which depends on the date of Easter; feasts may only be celebrated on Saturdays during penitential times and not at all in some

---

[13] Among the dissident Armenians ordinarily only married priests are allowed to hear the confessions of lay people.

others, e.g., Easter to Pentecost. These rules have been somewhat modified by the Catholics, who, moreover, gradually and
unwillingly accepted the Gregorian reckoning between 1892
and 1912. Their national reckoning of years is from their
eponymous ancestor Haik, who is put at 2492 B.C.

Feasts. The restrictions on the celebration of these reduces
the number of saints' days to some 130 in the year, many of
them of Armenian saints and several observed in groups, e.g.,
the Fathers of Nicaea, the Armenian Doctors, the Universal
Doctors, the Egyptian Fathers, All Apostles. The chief fixed
feasts observed by Catholics (and on the same dates as in the
West) are Christmas,[14] Circumcision, Epiphany, Purification,
Annunciation, Birthday of our Lady, her Presentation, and
Immaculate Conception. Among the specifically Western
feasts generally adopted are Corpus Christi, Christ the King,
and Trinity Sunday; feasts special to the rite include that of
the Ark of God (i.e., the Church). There are ten holydays
of obligation, in addition to Sundays.

Penitential seasons. The canonical periods of fasting and
abstinence or of abstinence alone are Lent (except Saturdays
and Sundays), 6 days before Christmas, 5 days before the
Assumption, and 5 days "of Nineveh" or "of St. Gregory,"
most Wednesdays and Fridays of the year are days of abstinence. The details of observance required vary in different
dioceses.

General observations. Many of the Western traits referred
to above date from the time of the Crusades and are shared
equally by Catholics and dissidents. Over and above these, the
rites and observances of the Catholics have been considerably
modified in some particulars by Latin influence, due largely
to the fact that so many of the faithful have for so long looked
to France for protection and help, which has been generously
forthcoming, especially at the hands of certain religious congregations. In spite of the fact that Armenians regard their
religious rites as a concrete manifestation of their nationality,

---

[14] Non-Catholic Armenians alone in all the world still keep Christmas
and the Epiphany as one feast, on January 6.

these same congregations have found many vocations to themselves among the Armenians, which, whatever it may be for the individuals concerned, is not a good thing for the Catholics of the Armenian rite as a whole, often depriving them of the direct services of very capable men.

On the other hand, there has been for some time a movement, in which the Mekhitarist monks are prominent, for maintaining their orientalism, both of ceremonies and mentality, in greater purity. Accordingly, canon 612 of the plenary Armenian council held at Rome in 1911 declared that "devotions" are a supplementary cult in Eastern worship and should conform to the liturgy both in spirit and form. Nevertheless, such specifically Latin observances as the rosary, way of the cross, benediction with the Blessed Sacrament, scapulars, etc., seem to grow in popularity, and the blessing of candles on the feast of the Purification, of ashes, and of palms have been adopted quasi-liturgically. All Armenians, whether Catholic or not, make the sign of the cross in the Western manner.

BIBLIOGRAPHY

Issaverdentz, *Armenia and the Armenians* (Venice, 1886).

*Lynch, *Armenia, Travels and Studies* (London, 1901).

Nurikhan, *The Life and Times of ... Abbot Mekhitar* (Venice, 1915).

Tournebize, *Histoire politique et religieuse de l'Arménie* (Paris, 1910).

Weber, *Die Katholische Kirche in Armenien* (Freiburg, i.B., 1903).

Fortescue, *The Lesser Eastern Churches* (London, 1913).

Charles, *Syrie Proche-Orient* (Paris, 1929).

Issaverdentz, *The Armenian Ritual* (Venice, 1876).

Bianchini, *The Music of the Armenian Liturgy* [The melodies are made chromatic], (Venice, 1877).

Chapter IX

THE CHALDEAN RITE

THE CHALDEAN RITE

1. THE CHALDEANS

I. HISTORY AND PRESENT STATE

GENERAL ECCLESIASTICAL HISTORY

Whatever may have been the beginnings of Christianity in Mesopotamia and Persia there was a church in Edessa at the end of the second century; from that city the Faith spread eastward and another great centre was formed at Nisibis. At the beginning of the fourth century the Church in Persia was organized under his own direction by a bishop of Seleucia-Ctesiphon; and in 424 a synod of Markabta proclaimed the Persian church under its katholikos independent of the Patriarch of Antioch and the "Western fathers" generally (the hierarchical bond with Antioch through Edessa had always been tenuous). During this early period the church of East Syria and Persia produced a doctor of the Universal Church, St. Ephrem (d. 373), and it was made illustrious by the theological schools of Nisibis and Edessa and by hosts of martyrs at the hands of the Persians.

In 431 the Council of Ephesus condemned the teaching of Nestorius, Patriarch of Constantinople (see p. 6). Many of the Persian Christians and a party of the East Syrians, considerably influenced by anti-imperialist political considerations, refused to accept the condemnation, which resulted in the development of an heretical Nestorian church under the protection of the sovereigns of Persia. They probably aimed at no more than a local autonomy like that of the recognized patriarchates and were moved toward Nestorianism by their strong antagonism to its opposite, Monophysism, but by the seventh century the schism had hardened and the Mohammedan conquest of Syria and Persia confirmed their severance

from the Catholic Church and their profession of the condemned teaching.

For eight hundred years the Nestorian Church was, with
fluctuations of prosperity, a mighty organization, one whose
missionary enterprise is unsurpassed in the history of Christianity. It had 25 metropolitan sees with probably 200 bishoprics
and as many monasteries, extending to China and India; but
the time of its greatest extension was soon succeeded by utter
ruin. At the end of the fourteenth century the Mongol hordes
of Timur Leng devastated Asia, sweeping away the Nestorian
Church in a cataclysm of blood and apostasy. The remnants
of the western part of his church gathered round their katholikos in northern Mesopotamia; of the eastern part, nothing
remained (except in Malabar).

During the thirteenth century Dominican and Franciscan
friars were active among the Nestorians, and the katholikos
Yaballaha III had amiable relations with the Holy See;[1] several
individual bishops became Catholics, and in the following
century a number of Latin sees were erected, but they did
not last long.

By the middle of the fifteenth century the office of Nestorian
katholikos had become hereditary in a family, passing from
uncle to nephew (it still does), and on the succession of Simon
VIII Denha in 1551 a disaffected party elected a rival, John
Sulaka. Sulaka at once turned to the Franciscans for help;
they sent him to Rome, where he made a profession of Catholic faith and was appointed by Pope Julius III to be patriarch
of those of his rite who should follow his example.[2] It was at

---

[1] He was a Sino-Turk, born in Pekin. He sent another Mongol, the
monk Barsauma, on an embassy to Rome and the West. Barsauma received holy communion from the hands of Pope Nicholas IV, and
himself gave it to King Edward I of England in Gascony. For all that,
the profession of faith he carried was only doubtfully orthodox.

[2] On this occasion Cardinal Maffei declared to the assembly that,
"The Chaldeans seem to have had the name of Nestorians without holding any Nestorian errors." Whether or no this was true at that time,
it displays a striking difference of spirit from that of the Portugese in
Malabar a few years later (see p. 244).

His Beatitude Mar EMMANUEL THOMAS,
Patriarch-Katholikos of Babylon of the Chaldeans

THE CHALDEAN LITURGY

The Celebrant Sings the Gospel

this time that the name "Chaldean" began to be used to distinguish such people, as to call them "Catholic Nestorians" was obviously impossible. From now on there were two lines of patriarchs (or katholikoi), one Catholic, the other Nestorian.

THE CHALDEAN CATHOLICS

The successors of Sulaka all took the name of Simon (Shimun), and at times during the sixteenth century they made attempts (with the approval of the Holy See) to exercise their traditional jurisdiction over the Christians of their rite in India. But in the year 1692 Simon XIII apostatized, and from him the present line of Nestorian katholikoi is descended. They went to live in Kurdistan.

Meanwhile the line of Simon Denha had not been continuously in schism, for several of his successors (all of whom took the name of Elias) had been reconciled with Rome. Diarbekir had become a particularly Catholic centre, and in 1672 the metropolitan of this city, Mar Joseph, made his profession of faith and the Holy See allowed him to have the title of patriarch (but without specifying of where or of whom). He was succeeded by other "patriarchs" there, so that for twenty years, from 1672 till 1692, when Simon XIII lapsed, there were two Catholic patriarchs among the Chaldeans, and from 1692 till 1804 two Nestorian ones.

In 1778 Elias XIII succeeded his uncle as Nestorian patriarch at the same time that his brother John Hormizd, the metropolitan of Mosul, turned Catholic. In 1781 there was no Catholic patriarch in office, Diarbekir having become vacant by the resignation of Joseph IV, who had confided the administration of his see to his nephew, the priest Augustine Hindi. There ensued a long and rather bitter rivalry between Hormizd and Hindi, both of whom wanted to be Catholic patriarch; the Holy See was not keen on either of them, and was hoping for the submission of Elias XIII. When the last-named died in 1804 without leaving a nephew to succeed him the rivalry became worse, and there was strong temptation for his Catholic brother John Hormizd to apostatize (he was in fact under censure for a time). At length Hindi also died, whereupon in 1830 Pope Pius VIII appointed Hormizd to be patriarch at last.

The upshot of all this complication is that there has been a succession of Catholic Chaldean patriarchs ever since, who are in continuity with the original historical line of Simon Denha of the house of Mama. To avoid any chance of the assertion of the hereditary principle in the succession, the Holy See gave Hormizd a coadjutor with right of succession and the patriarchal family gracefully renounced its improper privilege.

The first successor of Hormizd was charged with maladministration before the Holy Office and resigned his see, and the next patriarch, Joseph VI Audo, had a long and stormy period of office. He was an energetic and competent prelate but ambitious, and was very anxious to recover the ancient but abolished jurisdiction of his church over the Syrian Catholics of Malabar. Twice, in 1861 and 1871, he sent bishops (Mar Thomas Rokkos and Mar Elias Mellos) thither at the request of Malabarese malcontents and caused much trouble thereby. Meanwhile, in 1869, the Holy See decided to apply the bull *Reversurus*, governing the appointment of bishops,[3] to the Chaldeans. Audo asserted that this was an infringement of Eastern rights, and made a very temperate protest before the assembled Vatican Council. The advisers of Pope Pius IX, however, took a severe view of the patriarch's general policy, and he narrowly escaped excommunication. He was eventually reconciled with the Holy See and was highly spoken of by Pope Leo XIII.

Such distressing events weakened the cause of Catholicism among the Nestorians in the nineteenth century, but it nevertheless made good progress, which would have been even better but for the activities of Anglican and Russian missions. A great cultural work was done for his countrymen by Paul

---

[3] This bull caused a schism among the Armenians (see p. 206).

Bedjan (1838–1920), a Chaldean born in Persia who became a Lazarist priest. He came to Europe and published magistral editions of their liturgical and other ecclesiastical books, as well as translations into the spoken Syriac of the *Imitation of Christ*, Lives of the Saints, etc. An English translation of his text of the mystical treatises of Isaac the Syrian (of Nineveh) by A. E. Wensinck was published at Amsterdam in 1923.

The present patriarch Mar Emmanuel II Thomas was in 1902 accorded the title of papal "delegate for the Nestorians," and he shortly after reconciled two bishops with several priests and their congregations.

During the war of 1914–18 the Chaldeans suffered equally with their neighbors from massacre and deportation. Six bishops (including the two ex-Nestorians), a score of priests, and several thousand of their people were murdered by the Turks and Kurds, and four dioceses were destroyed.

Present State

Patriarch. The Patriarch-Katholikos of Babylon of the Chaldeans lives at Mosul,[4] and he has jurisdiction over the faithful of his rite throughout the world. He is elected by a synod of all the bishops, the delegate apostolic for Mesopotamia presiding. The choice must be submitted to the Sacred Eastern Congregation for confirmation by the Pope, who sends the *pallium*. He consecrates the Chrism for his whole patriarchate but ordains and institutes bishops only as delegate of the Supreme Pontiff. He is an *ex officio* member of the senate of Irak.

Bishops. The sees are that of Bagdad and Mosul (the patriarchal diocese, comprising nearly half the faithful), Kerkuk, Akra, Amadia, Zakho, Urmia, Sena, and Mardin (others are in abeyance). All the bishops depend directly on the patriarch but the two Persian sees of Urmia and Sena are called archiepiscopal.

A vacant see is filled by choice of the patriarch and bishops

---

[4] The title "of Babylon" seems to have been first given to Joseph II of the Diarbekir line by Pope Clement XI in 1701, from the erroneous identification of modern Bagdad with ancient Babylon.

from a list of candidates recommended by the clergy and chief men of the diocese, or at will. The choice must be approved by the Sacred Eastern Congregation before the elect can be consecrated and enthroned.

There are vicariates patriarchal for Basra, Syria, Egypt, and Constantinople (13,850 faithful altogether); there are small colonies of Chaldeans, totaling about 750 members with two or three priests, in the United States.[5]

Parochial clergy. The Dominicans, who have worked for the good of the Chaldeans without a break since 1750, finally established an admirable seminary for them (and for the Antiochene Syrians) at Mosul in 1882. It is directed by the friars, with the help of secular priests of the rites concerned. A seminary for the Chaldeans of Persia was opened by French Lazarists at Khosrova in 1845; it was reconstituted after the war at Urmia, or Rezaia as it is now called. A few other students go to the Jesuit oriental seminary at Beirut or elsewhere, but facilities are inadequate for the Chaldeans and many of the clergy have made very insufficient studies. They are not bound to celibacy and about a half of them are married; they mostly live in very poor circumstances.

The rank of *chorepiskopos* is conferred as a title of honour by nomination of the patriarch; that of *archdeacon* by a liturgical ceremony.

Religious institutes. The only Chaldean monks are a small congregation of *Antonians,* called "of St. Hormisdas," founded in 1808 by Gabriel Dembo.[6] In all respects except corporate wealth they closely resemble the Maronite Antonians, with whom Dembo made his novitiate. They have 20 hieromonks and 35 monks (most of the priests serve parishes), in three monasteries, of which one is Rabban-Hormizd, near Alkosh, founded originally in the seventh century by St. Hormisdas. The number of these monks, whose life is one of considerable austerity, is rapidly growing.

---

[5] Father Gabriel Oussani, professor of ecclesiastical history and other subjects in the seminary at Dunwoodie, N. Y., was a Chaldean.

[6] He had been a prosperous merchant of Mardin. He was murdered by a Turk in 1834.

A recently formed congregation of Chaldean nuns has two schools in Bagdad.

The Faithful throughout the world total 71,650 (155 priests), nearly half of whom live in the great plain of Mesopotamia, south and west of Mosul.[7] Here a good deal of debased Syriac ("Sureth") is spoken by them; elsewhere Persian, Kurdish, or Turkish, according to the neighbourhood, and Arabic in the towns. So long ago as the middle of last century a Protestant clergyman, Mr. G. P. Badger, commented on the superior civilization, intelligence, and order of the Chaldeans in Mesopotamia, in his book *The Nestorians and their Rituals* (London, 1852, Vol. I, p. 176). This praise is, of course, relative, the Chaldeans having for many centuries been part of a shamefully oppressed and exploited people. Their present encouraging state is due in large measure to the enlightened service of the Dominicans in Mesopotamia (whose training college for school-teachers at Mar-Yakub has done great work), of the Lazarists in Persia, and of other Western institutes both of men and women.

II. LITURGY AND CUSTOMS

Chaldean *church buildings* have their own plan. The sanctuary is raised above the nave and separated from it by a solid wall reaching to the roof. This wall is pierced by a door some six feet wide, covered by a curtain to be withdrawn during the Liturgy; before it is a low wall, broken in the middle, enclosing a space for the choir. Men and women are separated and there are usually no seats. In Catholic churches the altar is against the east wall of the sanctuary, and is now of western pattern, with gradines, numerous candlesticks, and artificial flowers; the Blessed Sacrament is reserved in a tabernacle. There are

---

[7] There were no Nestorians left in these regions until post-war persecution drove them toward Mosul from the mountains of Kurdistan. They are precisely the people who, under the name of "Assyrians," recently appealed to Europe for protection against their Mohammedan governors and neighbours in Irak. They are now apparently outnumbered by the Chaldeans.

pictures and sometimes even stations of the cross but no statues in these churches.

Vestments. These are very similar to those of the Syrians, but without "cuffs": *kotina* (now generally an alb); *urara*, worn crossed just like the Latin stole; *zunara*, girdle; *phania* or *maapra*, a chasuble like a cope without a hood. Bishops have adopted the Western mitre, crozier, pectoral-cross, and ring, and have no *omophorion*. Deacons wear an ungirdled alblike garment, with a long stole. The ordinary ecclesiastical dress is a curious round turban, wide, low, and flat, black cassock (violet for bishops), and over-mantle with wide sleeves.

Liturgical books. These were formerly sixteen in number, and some of them, such as the equivalents of the *Pontificale*, are still in manuscript. The most used ones, especially the *Takhsa*, priest's mass-book, with the addition of the variable parts of the Liturgy from the *Turgama*, etc., and a pastor's manual have been accurately edited and beautifully printed by the Dominican press at Mosul, from which an Arabic Bible, Syriac dictionary, and other valuable works have been issued. Earlier editions of the Chaldean books were printed at Rome, and a definitive edition of the four books of the Divine Office (*Hudra, Gazza, Kashkul, Ktaba dakdam*) was published by Father Bedjan in Paris in 1888. The usual Liturgy is called "of the Holy Apostles" (i.e., Addai and Mari, reputed apostles of the East Syrians and Persians), and has two alternative *anaphoras*, "of Theodore the Interpreter" (of Mopsuestia) and "of Nestorius." The Catholics naturally do not use these last names but call them "the Second," used on Sundays and feasts from Advent to Palm Sunday, and "the Third Hallowings," used only five times in the year.

The Liturgy is celebrated in the evening before Christmas, Passover (i.e., Maundy Thursday), and Easter, and there is a form of Liturgy of the Presanctified for "Friday of Suffering." The Liturgy may be concelebrated when several priests or bishops are available.

Altar-vessels and bread. Catholics make use of the same altar-vessels and accessories as in the West, with the hand-cross for episcopal blessings and *ripidia* for processions. The altar-

breads are similar to Latin ones in appearance but they are
leavened and have a little salt added to the other ingredients.
The custom of baking them afresh for each celebration is
almost extinct.

Music. The Chaldean enharmonic chant is traditional to the
rite and is being studied by the Benedictines of Sharfeh and
Jerusalem, but they have not yet published any of it. The
only instruments permitted are cymbals, triangles, and so
forth, to mark the rhythm.

Liturgical language. This is the "Edessene" dialect of Syriac,
with the eastern pronunciation and characters, and with less
admixture of the vernaculars than in the western Syriac rites.

THE EUCHARISTIC LITURGY

The Liturgy, derived from that of Edessa and perhaps a
branch of the Antiochene, is called *Kurbana*, "the Offering,"
or *Kudasha*, "the Hallowing." The following is an outline of
its celebration in a Catholic church, with the anaphora of
the Holy Apostles.

The priest and ministers vest in the sacristy, go to the door
of the sanctuary, and there the celebrant begins:

> "✠ In the name of the Father and the Son and the
> Holy Ghost for ever. Glory to God in the highest (three
> times) and on earth peace and good hope to men at every
> season and for ever. Amen. Our Father . . . for thine is
> the kingdom, the power, and the glory for ever and ever.
> Amen." (The choir meanwhile sings anthems from the
> Our Father.)

Deacon: "Let us pray. Peace be with us."

Three variable sets of prayers are said, the priest standing
in the middle of the sanctuary: "of the Psalms," three of
which are recited by the celebrant and ministers (Ps. 1, 150 and
16 on ordinary days), "of the antiphon of the Sanctuary,"
and "of the 'thee, Lord,'" a chant which follows, corresponding to the Byzantine *Monogenes*. Then the priest goes up to
the altar and incenses it, and the deacon incenses the people.

The *Trisagion* is sung at the word of the deacon: "Lift up your voice, O ye people, and praise the living God."

The epistle (from St. Paul always) is chanted by the deacon from the front of the sanctuary wall; on Sundays and feasts of our Lord there are first two Old Testament lessons. Both are preceded by a prayer and a blessing and the command, "Be silent." Then the deacon sings alleluia thrice and on feasts it is taken up by the choir and a psalm-verse added; he accompanies the celebrant, bearing the gospel-book, to the door of the sanctuary. The priest prays inaudibly, then blesses incense, the deacon calls for attention, and the celebrant chants the gospel in Syriac or Arabic, according to the language of the people, who reply "Glory to Christ our Lord." While the antiphon of the gospel is being sung and the altar incensed, the deacon, before the sanctuary, recites a litany in the usual form for the Church, the clergy, the faithful, the welfare of the world, the people replying, "Our Lord, have mercy on us" and "Amen." The priest says secretly the prayer "of Imposition of Hands" for mercy and grace for all members of the Church, ending aloud, and the deacon commands: "Whosoever has not received baptism, let him go out."

Priest: "Whosoever has not received the sign of life, let him depart."
Deacon: "Whosoever has not received [these] let him depart. Go ye, hearers, and watch the doors."[8]

The priest goes to a credence table and prepares the bread and wine, washes his hands and incenses the offerings, which he carries to the altar, where he takes the chalice in his right and the bread on the paten in his left hand, crosses his forearms and offers the gifts, saying:

"May Jesus Christ in his grace and mercy accept this offering from our hands: Amen." (He strikes the paten three times against the chalice, saying each time): "By thy command, O Lord our God, we set and order these

---

[8] The dismissal of the catechumens has survived also in other rites, but the reference to the *audientes* is unique.

ARMENIAN CATHEDRAL AT BZOMMAR

CHALDEAN CHURCH AT MOSUL

RUSSIAN PRIEST

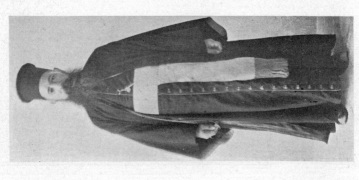

SYRIAN PRELATE

ETHIOPIAN PRIEST

glorious, most holy, life-giving and divine mysteries upon
thy absolving altar, until the second coming from Heaven
of our Lord, to whom be glory for ever and ever."

He lays the gifts on the altar, covers them with a veil, and
commemorates our Lady, the apostles, the patron of the
church, the dead, and those present. The antiphon "of the
Mysteries" is sung while the celebrant, bowing profoundly at
the foot of the altar-steps, prays for worthiness to sacrifice.
Then he intones the Nicene creed, the ministers and people
taking it up in the plural, with *Filioque* added. He returns to
the altar and says a prayer, "Praise to thee, who gathers in
the lost" and to the ministers, "Bless, O my Lord.[9] Brethren,
pray for me that this offering may be fulfilled at my hands,"
to which they reply suitably. The celebrant says secretly a
final prayer for forgiveness of sin and begins the *anaphora* of
the blessed apostles Addai and Mari.

Beginning aloud "Bless, O my Lord" (three times), he says
two prayers silently, crosses himself, and sings: "Peace be
with you." The deacon kisses the altar and the celebrant's
hand and at the door of the sanctuary a worthy layman puts
his hands in those of the deacon and then kisses his own; the
kiss of peace is thus passed on among the people. After further
prayers the priest says to the deacon: "Christ strengthen
thee always to do his will." Then, "The grace of our Lord
Jesus Christ and the love of God the Father and the fellowship of the Holy Ghost, be with us all for ever." (Amen.)
"Lift up your minds."

People: "Unto thee, O God of Abraham, of Isaac, and of
    Israel, glorious king."
Priest: "The sacrifice is offered to God, the Lord of all."
People: "It is right and just."
Deacon: "Peace be with us."

The priest kneels and prays in a low voice, then rises, lifts
up his hands and says the preface inaudibly; before the *Sanctus*

---

[9] This is not equivalent to *lube domne benedicere;* it is addressed to
God.

and *Benedictus* (where a bell is rung) he raises his voice, and bows low at the word "holy," and formulates the intention for which he offers the sacrifice. Then he recites aloud the words of institution (without genuflections or elevations).[10]

". . . And after supper of the passover of the law of Moses he took bread in his holy, spotless, and undefiled hands, and ✠ blessed and brake and ate, and gave to his disciples saying, Take eat ye all of it. *This is my body* which is broken for you for the remission of sins. (*People:* "Amen.") In like manner also he mixed the cup of wine and water, and ✠ blessed and gave thanks and drank and gave to his disciples, saying, Take drink ye all of it. *This is my blood of the new and eternal testament, the mystery of faith, which is shed for many for the remission of sins.* (*People:* "Amen.") This be ye doing. . . ." A bell is rung and the people prostrate themselves.

He continues in a low voice, praying for the Church, the Pope, the patriarch, bishop and clergy, the faithful and all humankind. Then follows the *epiklesis:*

"May thine holy spirit, O my Lord, come upon this sacrifice of thy servants, blessing and hallowing it that it may be to us for the forgiveness of sin, for the hope of the final resurrection, and for new life in the Kingdom of Heaven with all those who have been pleasing to thee; we beseech thee. . . ."

The eucharistic prayer is finished with the words: "Sending up glory and honour and confession and worship to thy living and holy and life-giving name, now, always and for ever," to which the people answer "Amen."

After prayers for peace and of thanks, followed by verses of Psalms 50 and 122, the priest raises his hands toward

---

[10] The Nestorian books have not the words of institution (unless inserted by their Anglican helpers). For a brief discussion of this, see Fortescue, *The Lesser Eastern Churches* (London, 1913), pp. 155-6, and cf. Rahmani, *Liturgies Orientales et Occidentales* (Beirut, 1929), p. 365.

Heaven three times, crosses them on his breast, kisses the altar first in the middle and then at the right and left corners, and elevates the Sacred Body, over which he makes the gesture of kissing four times, breathing in the form of a cross, saying: "Praise be to thee, O Lord Jesus Christ, and worship to thy might for ever. Amen." The breaking and commixture is a complicated rite, including the breaking of the Host into two parts and their union by touching along the line of division,[11] and the "blessing" of the Chalice with the Host and of the broken Host with the holy Blood into which a corner has been dipped; this is followed by the elevation of the Chalice. He signs himself, "✠ The grace of our Lord Jesus Christ . . ." and prays secretly for mercy, striking his breast five times, while the deacon invites to communion. The Our Father with its doxology is said aloud by the people, the priest saying its introduction aloud and its embolism inaudibly, and then, "The holy thing befits the holy."

With the chalice in his left hand and holding the Host above it he turns sufficiently to enable the people to see them and says, "O Son, who dost give us thy Body and Blood, give us also life in the kingdom." He may add if he will, "Behold the Lamb of God who takes away all the sins of the world" (three times). The choir sings the hymn "of the Altar" and the priest communicates himself. The people receive holy communion at the sanctuary-door, now usually in one kind only, but sometimes in both kinds, the Host dipped in the chalice, or even separately: "The Body of our Lord is given to the devout believer for the forgiveness of sins." The deacon invites the people to praise and thanksgiving while the celebrant cleanses the vessels and takes the ablutions. Then he says aloud the thanksgiving prayers, ending with Our Father, and, standing at the sanctuary-door, recites the conclusion of the Liturgy in a variable form and blesses and dismisses the people, who depart in peace.

---

[11] In the West this ceremony had place in the ancient Celtic rite. For some reason it gave great offence to the Portugese when they met it in Malabar.

THE DIVINE OFFICE

This consists of only three "hours," Vespers (*Ramsha*), Night Office (*Lilya*), and Matins (*Sapra*), to which the Antonian monks add the "little hours," whose text they have borrowed from their Maronite brethren. The office is made up of a considerable number of psalms (the psalter is spread over a week), with hymns (many, of course, of St. Ephrem), prayers, and litanies. The *Gloria in excelsis Deo* is sung at Matins on Sunday, after the Song of the Three Children; each office begins with the Our Father, and Vespers and Matins end with the Creed and the Angelus. After the Ascension until the beginning of November choir-office is sung in the courtyard instead of in church.

THE SACRAMENTS

Baptism. The rite of baptism is very long, being modeled on the eucharistic Liturgy, with corresponding prayers, chants, litanies, and scriptural lessons. The renunciations, profession of faith, etc., have been added from the Roman *Rituale*. There is a preface leading to an "anaphora," wherein the font is blessed, and the Holy Spirit invoked on the oil with which the child is anointed all over. The baptism proper comes at the place of the communion. The child is dipped three times in the water, with the words, "N., be baptized in the name of the Father," etc.

Confirmation follows at once, the child being anointed with Chrism between the eyes, the priest saying, "N., is signed and confirmed in the name of the Father," etc.

Eucharist. See page 239.

Penance is administered practically as in the Latin rite, and confessional boxes are now in use.

Extreme Unction consists of the Our Father, a prayer to Jesus Christ, the *Trisagion* and two psalms, with anointing of the mouth, eyes, ears, nostrils, and hands; but in some dioceses the Roman ritual has been substituted.

Holy Orders. The Chaldeans have five orders: reader, subdeacon; deacon, priest, bishop. They are conferred by the laying-on of hands, with a formula in each case analogous to the following: "N., is set apart, consecrated and ordained to the work of the presbyterate and for the office of the Aaronic priesthood, in the name of the Father," etc. There is an invocation of the Holy Ghost identical for each order, and the appropriate vestment is given. Archdeacons and archbishops are made in a similar way.

Marriage. The ceremony is called *Buraka*, "the Blessing," and includes the usual Eastern crowning of the couple (with a red, white, and blue fillet). It has other points of resemblance both to the Byzantine and Jewish rites.

Calendar. The Gregorian reckoning was adopted during the rule of Joseph Audo. The ecclesiastical year begins on Advent Sunday and is divided into three chief periods: Advent, Lent and Paschal-time, Pentecost; minor divisions are Epiphany, the Apostles, Summer, Elias, Moses, and the Dedication. These periods are of unequal length.

Feasts. There are only 66 feasts in the Chaldean calendar, of which 25 are fixed and the remainder movable, 18 of them saints' days celebrated on certain Fridays. There are several collective feasts (e.g., the Four Evangelists, the Greek Doctors, the Syrian and Roman Doctors), and some less ancient celebrations from the West—Corpus Christi, the Sacred Heart, St. Joseph. Chrism is consecrated and there is a *mandatum* on Holy Thursday; the Thursday after Pentecost is called "Golden" and kept as a memorial of the apostles' first miracle (Acts iii. 1–8).

Penitential seasons. The fast of Lent lasts seven weeks, all food, drink, and tobacco being eschewed till noon; the fast of the Apostles Peter and Paul, two days; of our Lady, five days; and of the Ninivites, three days; all Wednesdays and Fridays are days of abstinence, except from Christmas to the Epiphany and in paschal-time. The Ninivite fast is observed with special rigour, and the whole of the psalter is recited in the office on each of its days.

General observations. Despite his intransigence toward certain Roman legislation, it was the patriarch Joseph Audo who introduced several Western observances. In general, Latin influence has modified only accessories of the Chaldean rite, and encouraged private devotion by means of the rosary, scapulars, etc. The sign of the cross is made from left to right.

BIBLIOGRAPHY

Fortescue, *The Lesser Eastern Churches* (London, 1913).
Tfinkdji, *l'Eglise chaldéene* (Paris, 1913).
*Luke, *Mosul and its Minorities* (London, 1925).
*S. P. C. K., *The Liturgy of Addai and Mari* (London, 1893).

2. THE MALABARESE

I. HISTORY AND PRESENT STATE

GENERAL ECCLESIASTICAL HISTORY

Malabar is that part of the southwest coast of India which lies between Mangalore and Cape Comorin. Including the native states of Cochin and Travancore it has a large number of native Christians (Catholics of three rites, Jacobite schismatics, and Protestants of many sects), who are, however, greatly outnumbered by their pagan neighbours. They are Indo-Europeans of the dravidian family, and speak a widely used dialect called Malayalam.

These Malabar Christians call themselves as a body "Christians of St. Thomas" and are quite sure they were evangelized by that apostle, whose alleged first shrine they show on the opposite coast, at Mylapore.[12] Nevertheless, their origins are a matter of very great uncertainty. It seems certain that there were Malabarese Christians before the sixth century and it is likely that they were a fruit of the missionary activity of the East Syrian Church (it does not follow that they were always, or ever, formally Nestorian); from the earliest times their liturgy was Chaldean and its language Syriac, and their traditions are unanimous that their bishops were sent to them from "Babylon" (Bagdad).

There are certain references to these people in the records of the later mediaeval travelers and the Holy See was aware of their existence, but for practical purposes their direct contact with the West begins with the coming of the Portugese in

---

[12] The *Anglo-Saxon Chronicle* states that in 883 King Alfred the Great sent Sighelm, Bishop of Sherborne, with gifts to Rome and to "the church of the apostles Bartholomew and Thomas" in India, in fulfilment of a vow.

1498. It seems clear that the Malabarese religious leaders regarded the Portugese from the first as their brothers in religion, affirming their own communion with the Holy See and acknowledging its prerogatives (as their ancestors had done to a papal legate, the Franciscan John de Marignolis, in 1348). And at first the Portugese do not seem to have questioned their Catholicism (as St. Francis Xavier did not when he was at Cranganore in 1549), recognizing their bishop Mar Jacob and clearly holding religious communion with him. But almost at once they began to show anxiety to "latinize" the native Christians. In 1553 Pope Julius III recognized the jurisdiction of the Catholic Chaldean patriarch, John Sulaka (see p. 228), over India, and Paul IV confirmed the appointment of two Chaldean bishops for the Syro-Indians. But the Portugese, who had a Latin archiepiscopal see at Goa, were not familiar with the phenomenon of non-Latin Catholics and hardly believed it possible for right living and orthodoxy to flourish apart from specifically Roman observances; without adequate reason, they scented the Nestorian heresy everywhere among these strange native Christians.[13] There followed a period of clash and intrigue between Latins and Indians, in which the conduct of the European ecclesiastics was not uniformly edifying.[14]

When the last Chaldean bishop died, the archbishop of Goa, Alexis de Menezez, made a visitation of the Syro-Indians and

---

[13] The Indians had the Nestorian characteristic of not using holy images in their churches. "We are Christians," they said. "We do not worship idols." That attitude may be a proof of religious ignorance but it is no proof of heresy. Mar Jacob had been consecrated by the katholikos of the Nestorians at Gazerta Beit Zabdai in Mesopotamia. Several of the katholikoi had relations with Rome around this time. Things were apparently complicated by the word Nestorian being used as a racial appellation, without theological significance.

[14] There is extant a letter from Pope Gregory XIII to the King of Portugal, dated 1578, asking him to see that the viceroy in India gave fair play to one of the Chaldean bishops, Mar Abraham, "whom we hear has been greatly vexed by some." The other, Mar Joseph, was also accused of Nestorianism, but the root of his offence seems to be that he refused to ordain Indians who had been trained in a Portuguese seminary without being taught their liturgical language.

in 1599 convened a synod to deal with their affairs at Diamper (Udiamparur). The archbishop presided, assisted by Jesuit fathers, and they, together with 150 sacerdotal and 600 lay deputies of the Syro-Indians, made a profession of faith and anathematized the errors of Nestorius. Among the arbitrary changes brought about by the Portugese at this synod or about the same time were: the abolition of the jurisdiction of the Catholic Chaldean patriarch in India and the substitution of Portugese bishops for Syrians; the mutilation of the Eucharistic Liturgy, and the introduction of communion in one kind, Roman vestments, and other innovations; the abolition of the Syrian Pontifical and Ritual; the imposition of clerical celibacy; and the setting up of the Inquisition.[15]

These measures caused grave discontent. There is no serious reason to suppose that the Indians secretly hankered after Nestorianism, and there is direct evidence that they respected papal supremacy; but they disliked their Portugese masters, with their domineering ways and innovations from Europe.[16] After several vain attempts to get redress of their grievances by lawful methods, almost the whole body of Syro-Indians went into schism in the year 1653.[17]

Pope Alexander VII sent out Carmelite friars to deal with

[15] J. S. Assemani says roundly in his *Bibliotheca orientalis* that most of the acts of the Synod of Diamper were an outcome of misguided zeal, ignorance of Eastern Catholic usages, and undue attachment to those of the West. The synod has never been formally confirmed by Rome, nor could it be in its entirety for, as Mgr. Giamil notes in his *Genuinae Relationes*, p. 610, some of its acts ran clean contrary to the decrees of the Holy See. The fact is that, in addition to his "imperialism," Menezez was obsessed by his suspicion of latent Nestorianism: but some of his actions have been unjustly exaggerated or misunderstood.

[16] That Portugese policy in India was not actuated solely by concern for the good estate of the Catholic Church is shown by the *Padroado* troubles, which culminated in flat defiance of the Holy See by them in 1838.

[17] The occasion was the arrival of a Chaldean bishop from Bagdad at Mylapore, who had been sent for by the Indian leader, the archdeacon Thomas. The bishop was seized by the Portugese and the Indians alleged that he was deliberately drowned in the sea off Cochin on the way to Goa. The bishop was certainly a Catholic.

the trouble. One, Joseph Sebastiani, was made bishop and commissary apostolic and by 1662, 84 out of the 116 Indian "parishes" had returned to Catholic unity. The remainder became that schismatic body now known as the Malabar Jacobites (see p. 6). In the following year the Dutch drove all other Europeans from Cochin. Before he went, Mgr. Sebastiani consecrated bishop, as administrator for the Indians, a native priest who had led the faithful remnants of Catholics in 1653. This was Chandy Palliveetil (Alexander de Campo), and he ruled his church and consolidated the reunion for fourteen years. Before he died he welcomed the Carmelites (Italian this time) back to Malabar, but his request for a Syro-Indian successor was not granted.

Mar Shandy was followed by a succession of Carmelite vicars apostolic, who ruled till 1887, not without difficulties.[18] The Syro-Indians never ceased trying to get indigenous bishops, either by petitioning Rome or by negotiating with Catholic Chaldean prelates in Mesopotamia. One of these, Mar Elias Mellos, sent to Malabar in 1874 by the Chaldean patriarch Joseph VI Audo (who was involved in trouble with Rome) stirred up a schism which still exists: the "Mellusians" are a tiny nominally Nestorian sect in Trichur.[19]

In the words of a Belgian Jesuit, "For three centuries the European missionaries went on footling and blundering and worrying the poor Syrians with their Latin bishops, until Leo XIII got enough of it and, in the face of a strong opposition, appointed three Indian Syrian bishops" (*Catholic Herald of India*, Jan. 30, 1924). This was in 1896, when Malabar was divided anew into three vicariates apostolic; a fourth was made in 1911. Finally, in 1923, Pope Pius XI restored to the

---

[18] One of them, Miles Prendergast, was an Irishman. His career was unfortunate. He expected the secular clergy to live as strictly as mendicant friars, and he got himself so disliked that in 1831 he was recalled to Rome and asked to resign.

[19] Both the Chaldeans and Indians wanted, and a few still want, the restoration of the Chaldean patriarch's jurisdiction over the Syro-Malabarese, but the differences of race, culture, and language are against it. Audo tried to bring the question before the Vatican Council.

Syro-Indians a regular hierarchy, consisting of one archbishop
and three suffragans. During their 38 years of renewed home-
rule the Malabarese have made considerable progress in every
direction.

PRESENT STATE

Organization. The Syro-Indian province comprises the
native states of Travancore and Cochin, with British Cochin,
and depends on the Sacred Eastern Congregation through the
delegate apostolic of the East Indies. The hierarchy consists
of the Archbishop of Ernakulam, with the bishops of Chang-
anacherry, Trichur, and Kottayam; they are appointed directly
from Rome. The present archbishop and metropolitan is Mar
Augustine Kandathil, appointed in 1923.

Parochial clergy. They are mostly formed at the seminary
of Puthenpally (founded *c.* 1675 at Verapoly), directed by
Belgian Carmelites on almost exclusively European lines;
others go to Latin seminaries at Kandy, Mangalore, or Rome.
In addition to their vernacular Malayalam all Malabarese
priests are taught Latin, English, and their liturgical Syriac.
The sacerdotal standard is very high.

Subdeacons and upwards are strictly bound to celibacy.
Priests are called *kathanar* (Lord's man) and the bishops *abuna*
(our father); pastors are helped in their administrative duties
by a council of lay people.

Religious institutes. Among the Syro-Indians there is a most
remarkable number of vocations to the religious life. There is
one congregation of men, *Tertiaries of our Lady of Mount
Carmel*, founded by Fathers Thomas Palakal and Thomas
Parukara in 1831 at Mannanam. It was affiliated in 1860 to the
Order of Discalced Carmelites, whose habit is worn. Its principal work is the giving of missions and retreats, both to
Syrians and Latins, and by its pioneer efforts the Malabarese
were the first post-schism Catholic orientals to do missionary
work among the heathen (they were till recently the only ones
who had the opportunity). The prior general resides at The-
vara and there are fifteen other monasteries, with 135 priests,
107 clerics, and 55 brothers. Among their works they conduct

twelve schools and have three printing and publishing establishments.

The principal congregations of women, chiefly engaged in teaching, are the *Carmelite Tertiary Sisters* (630 members in 38 convents) and the *Franciscan Tertiary Sisters* (240 in 20 convents). There are six small "Southist" houses of Visitation nuns, and 180 Sisters of Adoration of the Blessed Sacrament.

The Faithful. There are two social castes among Malabarese Syrians, called "Northists" and "Southists." The last-named, a small minority, are exclusively found in the diocese of Kottayam and are supposed to be the descendants of some of the Syrians who, according to local tradition, came to Malabar with one Thomas Cana in the fourth (much later?) century.[20] The Northists claim to be the superior race, and even among the Catholics their mutual relations are not always what they should be. The bishops discourage distinctions based on caste with reference to low-caste converts from Hinduism.

The Malabarese have a strong taste for education; since the restoration of native bishops schools of all grades have arisen on every hand and the people have made good use of them. Their religious temper is characterized by an addiction to elaborate exterior observances and long prayers.[21] In the opinion of an apostolic delegate, Mgr. Zaleski, they are "the noblest and most intelligent race in the whole of India," but this can hardly be seriously maintained. Their real piety is weakened by a certain racial "flightiness" of character. Except for the Eucharistic Liturgy they are hardly distinguishable in their formal religious practices and outlook from Latin Catholics and their general edifyingness and the success of their institutions have been used as an argument for the latinization of orientals—by those who forget that the price of latinization in Malabar is represented today by over 400,000 souls not in communion with Rome.

---

[20] A traditional local explanation is that they are respectively the descendants of the two wives of Thomas Cana—or even of St. Thomas the Apostle!

[21] In many households evening prayers for the family last the greater part of an hour.

Early marriages are the rule, usually arranged by the parents. Northists and Southists do not intermarry.

In addition to the 532,000 Syrians (636 secular priests), there are in Malabar 458,000 Catholics of the Latin rite, fruit of European missionary efforts since the fifteenth century, and the small body of Malankara Catholics (see p. 198).

II. LITURGY AND CUSTOMS

Church-buildings. These are plain aisleless rectangles, with the roof of choir and sanctuary sometimes higher than that of the nave. The bigger and older churches have, especially on the western façade, a good deal of applied ornament and architectural features that are a curious mixture of Indian fashions with European baroque. They are furnished with stations of the cross, statues, confessional-boxes, etc., just as in the West. The sexes are separated in church, men being in front.

Vestments and altar-vessels are in the Latin forms and of the worst patterns, and the *Liturgical books* correspond to the Roman ones; they are printed in Rome by the Propaganda press and also by the local Carmelites. Clerical dress is Western, even including the biretta and shaving the beard, but priests often wear a plain gown, white or black, for ordinary dress.

Music. The liturgical chant of the Malabarese rite is Chaldean in origin but it too has undergone much Western influence, with surprising results. It has more recognizable resemblances to the plain song of the West than the music of any other Eastern rite. At the present time a system of notation is being worked out for the chant in order that it may be printed.

THE EUCHARISTIC LITURGY

This is simply the Chaldean Liturgy, with the sole anaphora "of the Holy Apostles" (SS. Addai and Mari), as revised by the Synod of Diamper; it is accordingly celebrated in Syriac. It is called *Kurbana*, the Offering, and there is a proper form of low Mass, of which the following is a brief account.

At the foot of the altar steps priest and server say the Our

Father mixed with phrases from the *Gloria in excelsis Deo*, followed by a variable prayer and by Psalms 14, 150, and 116 said antiphonally. The priest goes up to the altar, blesses incense, and verses and responses are said leading to the *Trisagion:* "Holy God, holy Strong One, holy Deathless One, have mercy on us." At the epistle side the priest says a variable prayer and reads the epistle in a clear voice. He prays silently while the book is carried across,[22] and, after blessing the people, reads the gospel. He then says the Creed, exactly as in the West but in the plural ("*We* believe").

There follows a diaconal litany; in "private Masses" the deacon's petitions are said by the server and the people's responses by the priest, thus:

Server: "Let us all stand rightly with joy and gladness (on ferias: "with sorrow and repentance"), and let us pray, saying, our Lord, have mercy on us."
Priest: "Our Lord, have mercy on us."

And so on, for peace, the harvest, the Pope and hierarchy, etc. The matter of the sacrifice is then prepared, the vessels being incensed separately and water poured into the wine, with appropriate prayers; the bread (an unleavened wafer, just like ours) is put on the paten at the gospel side. The litany is concluded, the graces of the sacrifice are asked, and a prayer of blessing said. The formula for the dismissal of the catechumens is retained, with reference to *audientes* as in the original Chaldean Liturgy.

The priest carries the host on the paten to the center, held at the level of his forehead, and offers the bread and wine together, with his hands crossed: ". . . May Christ, who was offered up for our salvation and commanded us to commemorate his passion, death, burial, and resurrection, accept this

---

[22] The moving of the book from one end to the other of the altar and the ringing of a "sanctus-bell," introduced into this and some other Eastern Liturgies, are quite meaningless ceremonies, at any rate at a solemn Liturgy, for they have arisen from the particular history of the Roman Mass.

sacrifice from our hands, through his everlasting grace and mercy. Amen."

The gifts are covered with a veil, commemoration made of our Lady and St. Thomas, the priest washes his hands, kisses the altar at either end and in the middle, and prays inaudibly for himself and the people, while the server calls on them to pray for the living and the dead and the acceptance of the sacrifice. Then the priest gives a blessing from the gospel side:

"✠ Bless us, O Lord. Brethren, pray for me that this offering may be perfected through my hands."

Similarly from the epistle side, the server or people answering each time: "May God, the Lord of all, give thee strength to sing to his glory."

The celebrant acknowledges the sins of all and asks for forgiveness, ending aloud, "And we offer thee glory and honour and praise and worship, now, always, and for ever. Amen," making a large sign of the cross slowly on himself, in such a way that his hand can be seen by the people; this is done whenever the words "now, always, and for ever" occur during the canon. At a solemn Liturgy the kiss of peace follows.

The server in a long bidding calls for the people's prayers and attention, ending:

"Let no one dare to speak; let him who prays, pray in his heart. Stand and pray in silence and fear. Peace be with us."

Priest (after uncovering the gifts and blessing incense): "The grace of our Lord Jesus Christ and the love of God the Father and the fellowship of the Holy Ghost be with us all now, always, and for ever. (Server: Amen.) Let your minds be lifted up."

Server: "To thee, God of Abraham and Isaac and Israel, king of glory."

Priest: "Sacrifice is offered to God, the Lord of all."

Server: "As is fitting and righteous. Peace be with us."

The celebrant prays for cleanness of heart before proceeding to the short invariable preface; it is said inaudibly with a raising of the voice before the *Sanctus*, which is sung by the choir or people at a sung Liturgy but otherwise said aloud by the server: ". . . Hosanna to the Son of David. Blessed is he who came and is to come in the name of the Lord. . . ." A little bell is rung here and elsewhere, as in the Roman Mass.

Most of the canon, including the words of consecration, is said in a low voice. The preface is at once followed by the great intercession, commemorations of our Lady and the saints, and the invocation of the Holy Ghost.[23] Then the celebrant censes the server, people, altar, and gifts, and proceeds to the consecration.

> "Glory be to thine holy name, O Lord Jesus Christ, and worship to thy majesty, always and for ever. Amen. Who the day before he suffered . . ."

and so on, with words and actions exactly as in the Roman Mass. At the elevation of the Host he says:

> "Truly this is the living and life-giving Bread which came down from Heaven and gives life to the whole world. Those who eat of it shall not die but shall be saved and sanctified and live for ever."

And, with outstretched hands, after the elevation of the chalice:

> "Glory to thee, O Lord (three times), for thy gift beyond price, given to us until the end of time."

The Host is at once broken and dipped in the Chalice, with the same complex rite as in the original Chaldean Liturgy. The *anaphora* is ended by II Corinthians xiii. 13, said in a loud voice, the server answering "Amen."

Then, while the celebrant says the deprecatory "Hymn of St. James," the server in a long bidding calls on the people to approach the Mysteries. The priest says three times, "Lamb of the living God, who takest away the sins of the world," and

---

[23] Whether this unusual position of the *epiklesis* is due to the Portugese revisers is not decided; Dom Connolly thinks not.

the server concludes with "Accept us, O Lord," "Hear us, O Lord," and "Have mercy on us."

After a "little elevation" the server and people say the Our Father, the priest adding the embolism. He half turns to the people and says: "Peace be with you."

Server: "And with thee and thy spirit."

Priest: "The holy thing becometh holy people in the consummation, O Lord."

Server: "One holy Father and one holy Son and one holy Spirit. Glory be. . . . Amen."

Priest: "Glory be to thee, God the Father; glory be to thee, eternal Son; glory be to thee, holy Spirit by whom all is sanctified, world without end. (He touches the server's hand on the altar). The grace of the Holy Spirit."

Server: "Be with thee and with us and with those that receive him, in the kingdom of Heaven for ever."

Priest (striking his breast): "Lord, I am not worthy," etc. (three times).

He receives the Holy Things, very much as in the Latin rite, and gives communion to the people in exactly that way, the server adding the name of Thomas to Peter and Paul in the *Confiteor;* but the words of administration are:

"May the body of our Lord Jesus Christ be to the faithful layman (or "woman," or "the chaste priest," or "the deacon of God") for the forgiveness of sins and everlasting life."

The priest then blesses the communicants and, while the server says a long variable prayer of thanksgiving, cleanses the vessels and his fingers; he then says a variable prayer aloud at the epistle side, followed by the Our Father and a special prayer over the deacon or server. Finally at the altar rails, he says, facing the people, a variable hymn.

After "low Mass" the prayers for Russia are said as in the Western church, and before leaving the sanctuary the celebrant kisses the altar and says a prayer with reference to it similar to those in the West Syrian liturgies.

Concelebration is not used by the Malabarese (except at ordinations); they have a Liturgy of the Presanctified for Good Friday only.

THE DIVINE OFFICE

This was the only rite of Malabarese worship left untouched by the Portugese; it was abridged and rearranged, and the recitation of the new edition made obligatory, in 1876. There are three "hours," *Ramsha* (Vespers), *Lilya* (Night-office), and *Sapra* (Day-office), consisting almost entirely of psalms (the psalter is spread over a fortnight), with a few hymns and prayers.

THE SACRAMENTS

These are administered according to the forms in the Roman *Pontificale* and *Rituale* as edited at Goa and translated into Syriac. Confirmation is separated from Baptism, and conferred by a bishop.

Calendar and feasts. The Malabar calendar is practically that of the Western church. Besides Sundays there are thirteen holydays of obligation, including one of their special feasts of St. Thomas, his martyrdom, on July 3.

Penitential seasons. Fasting and abstinence or abstinence only is observed in Lent (50 days, but excluding Sundays), Advent (24 days), "Ninive" (3 days), Ember days, the Roman vigils, and every Friday and Saturday.

General observations. All the Western "popular devotions" and observances, and in the same forms, are in great favour with the Malabarese. They even have "methods of hearing Mass": I have seen one taken from the works of St. Leonard of Port Maurice. But there are those among them who hope that, under the influence of the indigenous hierarchy, some of the more unhappy effects of foreign domination will be undone, in such matters as revision of the Liturgy, restoration of oriental vestments, etc.

BIBLIOGRAPHY

Mackenzie, *Christianity in Travancore* (Trivandrum, 1901).

Panjikaran, *The Syrian Church in Malabar* (Trichinopoly, 1914).

———— *Christianity in Malabar* (Rome, 1926).

Bernard, *Brief . . . History of the St. Thomas Christians* (Trichinopoly, 1924).

The Carmelite Congregation of Malabar (Trichinopoly, 1932).

Fortescue, *The Lesser Eastern Churches* (London, 1913).

Vattathara, *Un coup d'oeil sur le Malabar* (Louvain, 1930).

Palokaren, *The Syriac Mass* (Trichinopoly, 1917).

Schurhammer, *The Malabar Church and Rome* (Trichinopoly, 1934).

See also the bibliography on page 199.

Chapter X

EASTERN MONASTICISM

EASTERN MONASTICISM

To Catholics in the West nowadays monastic life means the life of monks, of friars, of canons and even clerks regular, of enclosed nuns, and of active sisters. There are different orders, with different names, different rules, different ways of life, different aims and activities. So striking are the differences between some of them, that if we are suddenly challenged to say what it is they have in common (apart from the Catholic faith), we may unthinkingly fall back on some such reply as, "Oh, er ... their monasticism." Of course that is quite wrong. Monasticism pertains to monks (and their female counterpart), and most of these people are not monks at all. The friars (e.g., Dominicans), though they retain certain monastic characteristics, or the clerks regular (e.g., Jesuits), are not monks; the Little Sisters of the Poor or the Sisters of Charity, though we may call them nuns for convenience, are not female monks. What these people have in common is that they are *regulars*, living under a rule (*regula*), or as we often say, *religious*, all following "a stable mode of life in community, whereby they undertake to observe not only the general precepts but also the evangelical counsels, by means of the vows of obedience, chastity, and poverty."

But even the monks properly so called are not homogeneous. There are great practical differences between life in a Benedictine monastery of the English or American congregations, with their educational and pastoral work, and in a monastery of the congregation of Solesmes, with its intense liturgical preoccupation and normal repudiation of activity outside the cloister walls; between the public prayer and organized agriculture of the Cistercians and the eremitical solitude of the

Carthusians. Yet these are certainly all monks, engaged in the various legitimate developments which have taken place within monastic life in the West during fourteen hundred years.

All this is strange and incomprehensible to the monk of the East. Of the regular or religious life in its extended meaning he knows nothing;[1] and within monasticism itself he knows of no distinctions equivalent to "Benedictine," "Cistercian," "Carthusian." He does not belong to any "order"; he is just a monk. There is only one "rule" (except for the so-called Antonians), that of St. Basil, drawn up in the form of question and answer for the use of his monastery in Pontus, and that does not meet the requirements of a rule as understood in the West. We call these monks Basilians, but the label is inaccurate and meaningless to those of whom we use it. There was no such thing as an Eastern "Order of St. Basil" until the Italo-Greek, Ruthenian, and Melkite monks were reformed and reorganized during the last three hundred and fifty years. St. Basil was not a legislator or maker of any systematic foundation and "his" monks do not regard him as such. "They do not belong to St. Basil's order but St. Basil belonged to theirs," as it has been well put. Although St. Pachomius made an experiment in federation six hundred years ago and there is a monastic republic at Mount Athos today, with a governing council, a traditional Eastern monk still belongs to a certain monastery and to nothing else, and each monastery (*laura*) is independent of all the others.[2]

With us Latins, a monk, with due regard for St. Benedict's prescription that nothing is to be preferred before the celebra-

---

[1] There have been experiments in some dissident Orthodox countries of recent years. I refer elsewhere to those Catholic Eastern organizations which have come about by way of development or by direct importation from the West.

[2] It is worth remembering that a Benedictine monk is professed not, like a friar, for the whole order, but for his own monastery, and the principle of individual self-governing monasteries still obtains to a considerable extent. There are even some Benedictine monks who will not make use of the expression Order of St. Benedict, but call themselves "monks of such and such an abbey."

A MARONITE MONK

A MARONITE MONASTERY

Qozhayya in the Lebanon

A BYZANTINE MONK

A BYZANTINE BISHOP
(Vested in the *Mandyas*)

BYZANTINE CHURCH AT ALEXANDRIA
(On the right a parekklesia)

tion of the Divine Office, may be engaged in many ways, in teaching, in learned studies, in agriculture or the fine arts, even in parochial work. Not so in the East. "These things," they would say, "are the concern of schoolmasters, of laymen, of *savants*, of clergy; we are monks." As such, their business is to flee from "the world," to practise penance, and to worship God. In a word, to live as much as possible like the angels; and in fact they call their life the "angelic life" and their dress the "angelic habit." The conditions and means of attaining such a way of life vary in detail, but one general result is that "an Eastern monastery is the most perfect relic of the fourth century left in the world" (Fortescue). Theoretically the day is divided into three parts: eight hours for liturgical worship, eight for work (almost entirely manual), and eight for food, sleep, and recreation. The whole of the Divine Office is sung and it takes every minute of eight hours when it is celebrated properly. The principal prescribed austerity is fasting, which in its strictness and frequency outdoes anything prescribed by any rule in the West. An American Catholic, paraphrasing Dr. Fortescue, wrote in a publication of the Catholic Students' Mission Crusade that, "Eastern monks sing very lengthy offices, pray incessantly, fast incredibly, and *that is all*" (italics mine). It is therefore not out of place to point out that these activities, without the qualifying epithets and with the addition of *manual* work (which in fact Eastern monks commonly do), are precisely the occupations of monks as envisaged by St. Benedict. As an English Benedictine abbot, the late Dom Cuthbert Butler, has written: "The real use of a monastic house lies not in its activities and usefulnesses. It lies rather in things that cannot be counted by statistics or estimated by results." A monk of the East would consider that so obvious as to be not worth saying.

The Byzantine canons are not precise on the period of probation for the monastic life, and there is no noviciate and no formula of profession as we understand them. After a few days or weeks in the monastery, the aspirant is admitted to the lowest grade of monk (*rasophore*), and he may if he wishes remain in that grade for the rest of his life, as many do. Or he may, at the end of three years, go a step higher and become a *stavrophore*, when he is tonsured again and takes four oral vows, of poverty, chastity, obedience, and stability. For this step a man must be at least twenty-five years old, and a woman forty. The maxims of St. Basil had in view only the cenobitical or community life, but the Byzantine conception of monasticism looks on the eremitical or solitary life as the end which the monk ought to have in view and for which community life is a training and preparation. When a soul has strengthened herself by obedience and austerity it is natural that she should draw nearer to God and wish so to remain in a life completely devoted to contemplation—and that, and not any special Athonite mystical theory, is the precise ordinary significance of the much abused term *hesychasm*. The third and highest grade of Eastern monk, then, renews his tonsure and his vows[3] in view of the greater asceticism of prayer, fasting, and silence that he undertakes, and lives a partly, and sometimes entirely, solitary life. Twenty or thirty years of community life are the normal preparation for this rank of *megaloskhemos*, to which only a small minority of the monks ever aim or attain. The discipline of this degree is extremely strict and penitential, and to it alone is permitted the full angelical habit. A bishop who attains to it is forbidden thereafter to exercise episcopal *or sacerdotal* functions (though a priest may celebrate the Liturgy), and if he is advanced to it in view of death but recovers his health, he must resign his see and retire to a cell. Until recently, and still as a general rule among non-Catholic orientals, bishops are chosen only from the monks, whether *rasophores* or *stavrophores* (rarely from the third grade).

There are frequently servants attached to an Eastern monastery, but there are no lay brothers, and just as St. Benedict legislated for independent, self-governing families of men not in holy orders, so it still is the exception for an Eastern monk to be a priest. But no distinction is made between the monk

---

[3] The respective vows of *stavrophore* and *megaloskhemos* are not at all equivalent to our simple and solemn profession. The whole thing is different from beginning to end.

who is a priest (hieromonk) and the monk who is not.[4] The latter may be elected abbot and rule his ordained brethren, just as a monk of the lowest degree may be made abbot and rule over those of the higher degrees. The difference between *rasophore*, *stavrophore*, and *megaloskhemos* are personal, and affect the individual life; whatever the theory of beginner and proficient, imperfect and perfect monks, they are all in fact monks. The *rasophore*, though he has taken no vows, is considered equally to have bound himself for life by entering upon the way of monastic perfection and assuming a part of the habit, and until a hundred years ago dispensations to leave the monastery were unheard of, though a monk could be expelled for misbehaviour. Even now the stricter non-Catholic canonists regard such a dispensation as opposed to the fundamental teaching of Eastern monasticism.

The *rasophore* is so called because he receives the black wide-sleeved *rason;* this he wears over a girdled tunic, with a round cap (*skouphos*) on his head. The *stavrophore* is given a small wooden cross (*stavros*) and the "little habit," i.e., the above, with a black veil over the cap and a long black cloak (*mandyas*) which may be worn instead of the *rason*. The *megaloskhemos* ("great-habiter") has in addition a cowl (*koukoulion*) to be worn in church, consisting of a conical cap covered by a black veil on which are embroidered the instruments of the passion, and the *analavos;* this is made of wool or leather, and is in shape like the Western monastic scapular (with which it is quite unconnected), embroidered or painted all over with the instruments of the passion, crosses, and other symbols: the whole represents the cross which the monk has voluntarily taken up. The classical disposition of the monastic buildings is about an open quadrilateral, as in the West—but there the resemblance ends. The main church (*katholikon*) is in the middle of the court, and the

---

[4] Except that only a hieromonk may admit a man or woman to the monastic state, and then not to a degree higher than his own. For example, an abbot who is a priest and a monk of the second degree governs *megaloskhemoi*, but he cannot admit to that degree. Bishops who are monks have plenary powers in these matters.

refectory is often opposite its west end, with a well or fountain in between. Around are grouped the guest-house, the infirmary, the workshops, and the cells of the monks; the library used generally to be above the *narthex* of the church as being more secure from fire. Needless to say this arrangement is modified at will to conform to the features of the ground, as at the monasteries on Mount Athos.

Monasticism in the past was even more influential in the East than in the West, and has left its imprint on every aspect of religious life, from the form of the Divine Office and the dress of bishops to the high ascetical standard and the fasts imposed on the laity.

The traditional Eastern monastic life (still almost the only form of monasticism, in various states of vigour or decadence, in the different dissident Orthodox churches) is practically non-existent in the Catholic Church today. In a very modified (I believe almost unrecognizable) form it may be seen at the ancient Italo-Greek abbey of Grottaferrata (see p. 73), and it has now been revived in a purer and more traditional form by Mgr. Andrew Szepticky in Galicia.

This revival is due radically to half a dozen Ukrainian peasants who wished to undertake a more perfect way of life but were considered unsuitable for acceptance by the Ruthenian Basilians. So about 1900 they began to live a common life of their own, under the direction of the parish priest of Olesko, a village near Zloszow. Here they were found by the Metropolitan Szepticky (himself a monk), who transferred them first to Vulka, near Lwów, and then to Sknilov. In 1906 he gave them some constitutions (*typikon*), in 1908 ordained the first hieromonk, and later appointed an abbot (*hegumenos*) in the person of his own brother, Father Clement (Count Casimir Szepticky), who had been trained under the Benedictines of Beuron. In 1914 there were forty of these monks, but a Polish officer denounced them as Russian partizans; so they were conscripted, interned, or deported to Hungary, and their monastery at Sknilov burned down in the Polish-Ukrainian war. After the war the metropolitan (who retains supreme authority over them as *archimandrite*) collected them together in his country-house at Univ and they began all over again.

These monks call themselves Studites, as emulating the life lived in the monastery of the Stoudion at Constantinople in the ninth century. That observance simplified and systematized the customs of St. Basil and, so far from being a particular code, was an attempt to gather up and express the spirit of all Eastern monastic legislation; it had a profound effect particularly on the monasticism of Russia. The Ruthenian Studites aim at no particular task, and accept any vocation that is not at variance with oriental ideas of monastic life. Most of the subjects at present are young peasants, used only to manual work, but even before the war Mgr. Szepticky had made the nucleus of a foundation in Lwów itself where those who were suitable could undertake intellectual pursuits. The Byzantine liturgy is carried out with great care, and the morning office with the Eucharistic Liturgy lasts from five a.m. till nine; but daily life is far less precise and ordered than in a monastery of the West, for spontaneity and freedom are among the notes of Eastern monachism.

At present the Studites have three *lauras* and three secondary houses, with 117 members (10 hieromonks, 7 hierodeacons, 100 simple monks), of whom 51 are *rasophores* and 66 *stavrophores* (the Slavonic equivalents are *ryasonosetz* and *skhimnik*). There are also three nunneries, with about a score each of *ryasonositzy* and *skhimnitzy;* they are strictly enclosed and bound to choral office, but conduct an orphanage, etc., within their precincts.

So far I have referred only to monks of the Byzantine rite, but there are others of other rites, who are commonly called Antonians, as professing the so-called "rule of St. Antony." This was put together from the oral instructions and written apothegms of the saint and was intended rather for those living a semi-eremitical life than for cenobites. It is professed by the non-Catholic Coptic monks of Egypt and Abyssinia and at the famous dissident Orthodox monastery of Mount Sinai, but the most important bodies of Antonians are among the Catholic Maronites in the Lebanon. They have preserved the Eastern prescription of three classes of monks, over and above a postulancy of one or two years, and are distinguished as "habit-wearers," "cross-bearers," and "great-habiters"; but they take the three vows of the West. Some of the Lebanese monasteries have hermitages in their neighbourhood, each occupied by two monks (one a priest); these do not normally receive visitors, keep an almost perpetual silence, fast daily, and are bound to a certain number of hours of manual work every day.

Further particulars of contemporary Catholic Eastern "regular clergy" will be found in the account of each different church.

BIBLIOGRAPHY

*Gardner, *Theodore of Studium* (London, 1905).

*Robinson, *Monasticism in the Orthodox Churches* (London, 1916).

*Hasluck, *Athos and its Monasteries* (London, 1924).

Korolevsky, "Catholic Byzantine Monasticism," in *Pax*, No. 84 (Caldey, 1927).

Chapter XI

REUNION OF THE EAST

REUNION OF THE EAST

It is impossible to conclude even so slight a work as this about the Catholics of Eastern rites without saying a word on the subject of the reunion with the Catholic Church of the millions and millions of other Eastern Christians who, fundamentally, differ from her so little in doctrine and who are nourished with the true sacraments of Jesus Christ by the hands of validly ordained bishops and priests. And the problem is the more actual and urgent because the big majority of these Christians are now within Russian soviet territory and subject to an intensive campaign of godless teaching and persecution. It is well to remember that of the hundreds of clergy and thousands of laity who during the past fifteen years have given their lives for Christ's name's sake, nearly all did so without the help of that strength and sense of solidarity which come from communion with the Apostolic See of Rome and the world-wide Catholic Church; and that when, at the command of Pope Pius XI, the vernacular prayers after low Mass are offered for Russia, 99 per cent of those for whom we pray are not visibly members of that Catholic Church: the significance of this has not yet been sufficiently recognized.

The dissident churches of the East are all churches that once were Catholic. At various dates they became definitively separated from the centre of unity either by schism or heresy: nevertheless, they all profess the Catholic faith, in a greater or less degree, almost in its entirety; they have maintained the precepts of Christian morality more or less as held by Catholics; they are governed by canon law with which that of Eastern Catholics is at least nominally identical; they worship God with liturgies and rites which they share with

Eastern Catholics and which the Church recognizes as of equal authenticity and dignity with those of Rome; with one or two local and doubtful exceptions, their orders and sacraments are valid,[1] and may indeed be resorted to by Catholics in the exceptional circumstances laid down by canon law and the acts of the Holy See. It is clear, then, that, contrary to a common misunderstanding, they are not a sort of Protestants. As ecclesiastical bodies they have maintained an organic continuity with churches that were in communion with Rome (which no Protestant body has done) and represent the authentic Catholic Christianity of the East of the first ten centuries, modified by the history of the subsequent nine hundred years during which they have been separated from, and in varying measures opposed to, the theological developments and religious life of the Western Church.

It is therefore only to be expected that, in an epoch when Christianity is more seriously opposed than at any time since the Ten Persecutions, and a united front accordingly more than ever imperatively necessary, all the popes from Pius IX onward have been especially preoccupied with the problem of Eastern reunion: and not only from the point of view of the defence of Christianity but also from that of the perfecting of Christians. Schism, separation, is one of the most appalling of evils, whether for an individual or for society. It is true that the Church teaches that those inculpably separated from her visible communion may nevertheless belong to her in an invisible way; but obviously this is not the sort of inclusion in one fold under One Shepherd, the unity, willed by our Lord, and that so many souls should be only invisibly united to his Church cannot but be a matter of the very gravest concern to his Vicar on earth.

Among the last four popes Leo XIII stands out conspicuously

---

[1] Even Penance and Confirmation (administered by a priest in the East) are in practice treated as valid by the Holy See. For a brief note on the apparent lack of jurisdiction in the one, see *Clergy Review*, Vol. IV, No. 4 (October, 1932), p. 336, and for a discussion of delegation in the other, see Deslandes in *Echos d'Orient*, No. 157 (January-March, 1930), p. 5.

for what he did on behalf of the East, both Catholic and
dissident, and after him Benedict XV. But already in the
fourteen years of a most remarkable pontificate Pope Pius XI
has eclipsed even the noble efforts of his two great predecessors. He has taken up the work with yet greater urgency,
tenacity, and more clearly defined purpose than those who
went before him, and on a wider scale than they did. Labour
for reunion of the East, he has declared, is not to be just one
of his works but his chief work, the undertaking that shall
characterize his pontificate. And in all that he does for those
orientals who are already Catholics he looks beyond them to
the serried masses of their still separated brethren.

It is impossible even to mention here a tithe of the Pope's
activities in this matter (much less the multifarious works to
which they have given rise), so numerous are they and so
wide their scope: they extend from sending in 1922 a mission
of relief (under Father Edmund Walsh, S.J.) for the starving
people of Russia to addressing the whole world on the subject
of Christian unity, from pontifical protest and diplomatic
measures against bolshevist barbarism to establishing colleges
in Rome for Russian and Rumanian seminarists. Three of
these things may be selected for special mention, because they
so clearly and consistently demonstrate the mind of the Holy
See.

In 1924 the Pope addressed a letter to Dom Fidelis de
Stotzingen, abbot primate of the Benedictines, in which, after
pointing out the special aptitude of monks "for the apostolate
of reconciliation with our separated brethren," he asked that
one abbey in every Benedictine congregation should be specially concerned with Eastern affairs and that there should be
sent to them "carefully chosen men who shall fit themselves
for the work of reunion by special study of the languages,
history, customs, mentality, and especially the theology and
liturgy of the Eastern peoples." Both by the fact of their being
monks and by the large and conciliatory spirit of their institute the Benedictines are peculiarly fitted to appeal to religious
people in the East, who have been so much influenced by
monasticism. "They alone, among all other orders," said Leo

XIII in 1893, "excite no mistrust among the Orientals"; Dom Cabrol in his Life of Cardinal Pitra tells of the respect and even reverence with which that Benedictine was received both by Russian monks and by the highest hierarchs of the Orthodox churches; and Mgr. Szepticky in writing on the restoration of Slav monachism says, "What could be finer and more useful for the East than Benedictine abbeys of the Byzantine rite?" One result of the Pope's appeal was the establishment of a special monastery at Amay in Belgium, where both the Latin and Byzantine rites are in use and the monks devote themselves to the study of Eastern, particularly Russian, affairs. During its short history this monastery has been beset with difficulties, inseparable from so new a venture, and has been subjected by some to very severe criticism; but it has also earned the deep respect of many workers for reunion, Catholic and non-Catholic. It is before long to be transferred to more commodious premises at Tancrement.

On the feast of the Epiphany 1928 Pope Pius issued his encyclical *Mortalium animos* on the means of realizing true religious unity. In this magistral document he had in view Protestants and their methods of promoting a deceptive "unity" more than the dissidents of the East, but it is a guide equally for all who are concerned with healing the wounds of Christendom and must remain their charter and direction-post for so long as conditions remain as they are today, while its underlying principles are valid for all time. On the one hand, it is a warning against rash, ill-considered, or definitely illicit methods of trying to restore Christian unity; on the other, it is a call for mutual charity, forbearance, and prayer: "There can be no doubt that if those who live separated from this Apostolic See pray humbly for the light of Heaven, they will recognize the only true Church of Jesus Christ and will at last come to join themselves with us by the ties of perfect charity."

Later in the same year the Pope sent out another encyclical, *Rerum orientalium*, which was specifically concerned with the Christian East and the need for intellectual and practical interest in it. He rapidly sketches the zeal and love for the

Pope Pius XI Presides

The Consecration

CONCELEBRATION OF THE BYZANTINE
LITURGY IN ST. PETER'S BASILICA

THE SUPREME PONTIFF OF THE UNIVERSAL
CHURCH OF CHRIST

Pronouncing a Decree of Canonization
in St. Peter's Basilica at Rome

Eastern peoples shown at all times by the Holy See and particularly by his five immediate predecessors, and its recognition of the need for centres of studies from the days of Blessed Humbert of Romans, Roger Bacon, and Blessed Raymond Lull down to the foundation of the Oriental Institute at Rome in 1917. He gives an account of the objects, methods, and needs of the Institute and appeals to the bishops of the whole world to support it and to send specially selected students to it. Once again the *inclusiveness* of the Church is emphasized, and the need for Catholics to appreciate it: "Indeed, it should not be too difficult for each theological seminary to have one professor who, together with the study of history or liturgy or canon law, can at the same time be able to explain at least the elements of those things which concern the near East. In this way not a little profit may be expected for the Church from young priests' consciousness of Eastern doctrines and rites, profit not only to Orientals but *also to the Western clergy, who will thus naturally understand Catholic theology and Latin discipline more adequately*, and be excited to a yet warmer love for the true Bride of Christ, *whose bewitching beauty in the diversity of her various rites* they would be enabled to see more clearly and impressively" (italics mine).

In words addressed to an audience of Italian undergraduates in 1927 Pope Pius XI set out once for all what should be the Catholic attitude to the non-Catholic Eastern Christians: not an attitude of patronage or pity or superiority, much less of contempt or hostility, but one of love and esteem. "Catholics," he said, "are sometimes lacking in a right appreciation of their separated brethren, and are even wanting in brotherly love, because they do not know enough about them. People do not realize how much faith, goodness, and Christianity there is in these bodies now detached from the age-long Catholic truth. *Pieces broken from gold-bearing rock themselves bear gold*. The ancient Christian bodies of the East keep so venerable a holiness that they deserve not merely respect but complete sympathy."

The cause of Eastern reunion put before us so persuasively and authoritatively by pope after pope is one that requires an infinitude of patient and loving work, on a big or the tiniest scale, by those who know that they must look for no appreciable result in their time. It is the biggest, longest, and most difficult task with which Catholics are faced. "There is a fundamental difference of religious mentality between the East as it has remained throughout the ages and the West as affected by the Renaissance, the Reformation and the Revolution. This difference narrows down very noticeably as one retraces the course of history. It fairly makes one sick at heart to see how nearly related were the two Christian civilizations of earlier times, till the line of cleavage is lost in the perfect unity of primitive Christianity," and then turn to the gulf that now divides them in fact (though not in theory). What really separates Eastern dissidents from Rome is not so much theological dogma as the events of history and that difference of mind and temperament—deep-rooted variations between Eastern and Western consciousness—which, aggravated by a thousand years of separation, causes identical doctrines to be clothed in such a way that they appear mutually and subtly opposed.

As the Easterns are apt to accuse us Westerners of "dry rationalism and profane worldliness," so are we prone to dismiss their religion as mere "yearning and sentiment" or "ceremonial superstition." We must look higher and deeper than that. "Men were made that they might love one another," wrote Cardinal Mercier. "Those who from a distance believe themselves to be antagonists often find unexpected sympathies on better acquaintance. This of course does not constitute unity, but it helps toward it. Men and groups of men who have lived for long estranged from one another in an atmosphere charged with animosities, planted in the depths of their consciousness by age-long tradition, will hardly be prepared to yield to arguments thrust upon them by their opponents, however closely reasoned they may be" (Pastoral on the "Malines Conversations," pp. 6, 7. Malines, 1924).

Throughout the whole world, especially since the calamitous discord and immeasurable catastrophe of the Great War, an intense desire for the unity of Christendom has arisen, a desire springing from an acute consciousness of how our divisions flout the will of Christ that "all may be one." It is the business of Catholics to play a leading part in this move-ment—not to stand aside and watch the struggles of others. But their efforts will be wasted if they do not act in unison with the clearly expressed mind of the Supreme Pontiff: on the one hand, with love, gentleness, and well-informed under-standing; on the other, without that particularism which seeks to make everyone conform to our Western pattern in things outside divine revelation. It is right and proper that we Westerners should value the rites and usages and traditions and glorious history of the Latin church above all others; they are our own, and they have formed western Europe and us. If we go further than that and think that they confer some theoretical and practical superiority, then in face of our brothers of the East let us at least remember the motto of our own chivalry, *Noblesse oblige*. But even that attitude, the faintest sense of superiority, is to be deplored: it is arrogant and has no basis in essential reality or the economy of the Catholic Church, and will make a thousand times more diffi-cult that reunion of the Christian East which already seems almost beyond hope. But "let not this hope be considered utopian, for that were unworthy of Christians. The promise of our Lord must be fulfilled: 'there shall be One Fold and One Shepherd.'[2] Difficulties there are, but they shall in no wise discourage our apostolical zeal and charity. It is true that rebellion and estrangement have fostered a deep-rooted dissent in men's hearts: but shall that make us give up hope? Please God, never."[3]

---

[2] Pope Leo XIII, in his allocution to the Sacred College of Cardinals on the anniversary of his coronation, March 2, 1895.

[3] The same, in his letter to the English people, *Amantissimae volun-tatis*, April 14, 1895.

APPENDIX

STATISTICAL SUMMARY OF THE EASTERN CHURCHES
GENERAL BIBLIOGRAPHY
GLOSSARY

APPENDIX

STATISTICAL SUMMARY
OF THE EASTERN CHURCHES

Catholic

(The numbers of the faithful are for the most part taken from the figures in the official Statistica.)

Alexandrian Rite:
 i. Copts 41,316
 ii. Ethiopians 29,837

Antiochene Rite:
 i. Syrians in patriarchal territory 50,018
     in U. S. A. 6,801
     in other places 7,734
                  64,553

 ii. Maronites in patriarchal territory 322,715
      in U. S. A. 38,300
      in other places ....*c.* 5,000
               366,015
 iii. Malankarese 18,000

Armenian Rite:
 In patriarchal territory 41,860
 In Rumania 36,000
 Elsewhere in Europe 16,675
 In U. S. A. and other places 4,739
 In Russia .... ?
               99,274

Byzantine Rite:

Bulgars		5,598
Greeks		3,048
Hungarians	*c.*	142,000

Italo-Greek-Albanians:

In Italy and Sicily	50,850
In U. S. A.	10,000?

60,850

Yugoslavs		41,597
Melkites in patriarchal territory	150,155	
in U. S. A.	13,559	
in other places	*c.* 2,500	

166,214

Rumanians in Rumania	1,387,025
in U. S. A.	7,932

1,394,957

Russians in Poland	18,000
elsewhere	*c.* 3,500

21,500

Ruthenians in Galicia	3,602,270
in Czechoslovakia	556,734
in Rumania	62,000
in Hungary	21,281
in U. S. A.	553,110
in Canada	*c.* 300,000
in South America	67,000

5,162,385

Chaldean Rite:

   i. Chaldeans in patriarchal territory   70,894

              in U. S. A.   748

              elsewhere .... *c.*   1,000

                                   72,642

  ii. Malabarese 532,351

The general total of the Catholics of the Eastern rites is therefore over 8,200,000 souls.

They have 6 patriarchal sees and 63 archiepiscopal and episcopal sees, and in 1932 there were in addition 34 titular bishops.

Secular clergy, in 1932, 8,250

Regular clergy in 1932 (priests and deacons): *c.* 1,380

NON-CATHOLIC

(*Statistics of some of these bodies are very difficult to obtain and doubtful when obtained.*)

The Orthodox Churches (Byzantine rite):

Patriarchate of Constantinople	150,000
of Alexandria	55,000 ?
of Antioch	174,000 ?
of Jerusalem	45,000
of Moscow (nominally)	110,000,000
of Rumania	13,000,000
of Serbia	5,600,000
Katholikate of Georgia	2,500,000 ?
Exarchate of Bulgaria	4,060,000
Church of Greece	6,000,000
The Churches of Cyprus, Sinai, Albania, Czechoslovakia, Estonia, Finland, Latvia, Lithuania, and Poland total about	3,600,000
Orthodox elsewhere in the world	2,000,000 ?

Total for the dissident Orthodox churches:

   about 147,184,000

The Monophysite Churches:

Armenians	2,500,000 ?
Copts	960,000
Ethiopians	3,000,000 ?
Syrian Jacobites	100,000 ?
Malabar Jacobites	300,000
	8,860,000

The Nestorian Church:

In Irak	60,000
In India	15,000
	75,000

General total of non-Catholic Orientals:
about 154,120,000

GENERAL BIBLIOGRAPHY

REFERENCE BOOKS

Statistica con Cenni Storici della Gerarchia e dei Fedeli di Rito Orientale (Sacra Congregatione Orientale, Roma, 1932).

Alès, *Dictionnaire apologetique de la Foi catholique.*

Vacant, etc., *Dictionnaire de théologie catholique.*

Baudrillart, etc., *Dictionnaire d'histoire et de géographie ecclésiastiques.*

Cabrol, *Dictionnaire d'archéologie et de liturgie.*

Viller, *Dictionnaire de spiritualité ascétique et mystique.*

Herbermann, etc., *The Catholic Encyclopaedia.*

Attwater, *The Catholic Encyclopaedic Dictionary.*

GENERAL

Arseniev, *Mysticism and the Eastern Church* (London, 1926).

Batiffol, *Catholicism and Papacy* (London, 1926).

Bréhier, *Le schisme oriental au xie siècle* (Paris, 1899).

———— *L'Eglise et l'Orient au moyen âge: les Croisades* (Paris, 1928).

*Byron, *The Byzantine Achievement* (London, 1929).

Congrès eucharistique international à Jerusalem, 1893. Full text of the papers read (Paris, 1896).

*Davis, *A Short History of the Near East* (New York, 1923).

Diehl, *Etudes byzantines* (Paris, 1905).

———— *Histoire de l'Empire byzantin* (Paris, 1920).

Fortescue, *The Orthodox Eastern Church* (London, 1911).

Hughes, *A History of the Church*, Vol. I (London, 1934).

*Kattenbusch, *Die orthodoxe anatolische Kirche* (Freiburg i. B., 1892).

Janin, *Les Eglises orientales et les Rites orientaux* (Paris, 1925).

de' Clercq, *Les Eglises unies d'orient* (Paris, 1935).

Orientalia Christiana. A valuable series of monographs, beginning in 1923, published by the Oriental Institute at Rome. (7 piazza S. Maria Maggiore).

*Runcenian, *The Byzantine Civilization* (London, 1933).

*Scott, *The Eastern Churches and the Papacy* (London, 1928).

Soloviev, *La Russie et l'Eglise universelle* (Paris, 1889).

Stoudion, A most valuable periodical publication in 6 volumes, ending in 1930 (12 via Vespasiana, Rome).

The following useful pamphlets may be obtained from the Catholic Truth Society of London:

Bourgeois, *Reunion with the East.*

d'Herbigny, *East and West in the Unity of Christ.*

Mann, *The Early Russian Church and the Papacy.*

Scott, *Eastern Catholics.*

Attwater, *The Eastern Churches.*

——— *The Mass: its Various Forms.*

LITURGY AND ART

Bayet, *L'Art byzantin* (Paris, 1924).

*Brightman, *Liturgies Eastern and Western,* Vol. I (Oxford, 1896).

*Dalton, *Eastern Christian Art* (Oxford, 1925).

King, *Notes on the Catholic Liturgies,* Vol. I (London, 1930).

Lesage, *La sainte Messe selon les Rites orientaux* (Avignon, 1930).

Nilles, *Kalendarium manuale utriusque Ecclesiae orientalis et occidentalis,* 2 vols. (Innsbruck, 1896–97).

Rahmani, *Les Liturgies orientales et occidentales* (Beirut, 1929).

Attwater, *Prayers from the Eastern Liturgies* (London, 1931).

THE DISSIDENT CHURCHES

*Callinicos, *The Greek Orthodox Catechism* (London, 1926).

*Constantinides, *The Orthodox Church* (London, 1931).

Duchesne, *The Churches separated from Rome* (London, 1907).

*'t Hooft, *Anglo-Catholicism and Orthodoxy* (London, 1933).

Janin, *The Separated Eastern Churches* (London, 1933).

Jugie, *Theologia dogmatica Christianorum orientalium ab*

Ecclesia Catholica dissidentium, 4 vols. (Paris, 1926–33).

Lilienfeld, *Pour l'Union*. Documents and extensive bibliographies of reunion writings (Amay, 1927).

*Zankov, *The Eastern Orthodox Church* (London, 1929).

PERIODICALS

Pax. Quarterly (Prinknash Priory, Gloucester).

Echos d'Orient. Quarterly (5 rue Bayard, Paris).

L'Unité de l'Eglise. Every two months (same address).

Irénikon. Every two months (Prieuré d'Amay-sur-Meuse, Belgium).

All these periodicals are specifically concerned with the Catholic Eastern churches and reconciliation of the dissidents.

GLOSSARY

Most of the terms noted are used and explained in the text, but are repeated and briefly defined here for convenience of reference. Liturgical terms mostly apply to the Byzantine rite. *Ar.* = Arabic, *Gk.* = Greek, *Lat.* = Latin, *Sl.* = Slavonic, *Syr.* = Syriac.

ABUNA (*Ar.*, our father). The title of the head of the dissident Ethiopic Church, and the ordinary form of address to clergy in Arabic.

AER (*Gk.*, air. *Sl.*, *vozdukh*). Large veil covering the chalice and paten.

ALEPPINES. Maronite and Melkite congregations of monks, centered at Aleppo.

AMBO (*Gk.*, a raised place). A sort of pulpit in front and to one side of the *eikonostasis* in some churches.

AMNOS (*Gk.*, lamb. *Sl.*, *agnetz*). The first and principal part cut from the *prosphora* for consecration.

ANALOGION (*Gk.*). A lectern or small table.

ANAPHORA (*Gk.*, offering). Equivalent term to "canon of the Mass," sometimes used for the whole Liturgy. Most Eastern Liturgies have several alternative *anaphoras*.

ANOINTING, HOLY (*Gk.*, *eukhelaion*. *Sl.*, *eleosvyaschenie*). The sacrament called Extreme Unction in the West.

ANTIDORON (*Gk.*, a gift [instead of holy communion]). Blessed bread.

ANTIMENSION (*Gk.*, instead of a table). A cloth with relics laid on the altar for the Liturgy to be celebrated on.

ANTONIANS. Monks of the Maronite and Chaldean rites.

APOCRISIARIUS (*Lat.*, from *Gk.*, *apokrisis*, answer). A legate or nuncio.

APODEIPNON (*Gk.*, after-supper. *Sl.*, *povecherie*). Compline.

APODOSIS (*Gk.*, conclusion). The end of a feast that has lasted more than one day.

APOLYSIS (*Gk.*, dismissal. *Sl.*, *otpust*). The conclusion of a liturgical office.

APOSTOLOS (*Gk.*). The lesson from the Epistles or Acts; the book containing them.

ARCHBISHOP. In strict Byzantine usage the head of a series of metropolitan provinces. No longer strictly so used.

ARCHIEREUS (*Gk.*, high priest). A bishop. The Pope is *Ho tes Romes Archiereus.*

ARCHIMANDRITE (*Gk.*, chief of a fold). The superior of a large monastery or of a congregation; also a titular dignitary.

ARTOKLASIA (*Gk.*, breaking of bread). Blessing of bread, wine, and oil at Vespers on a vigil.

ARTOPHORION (*Gk.*, bread-carrier. *Sl.*, *kovtcheg*). The tabernacle of an altar.

ASTERISKOS (*Gk.*, star). A metal frame to keep the veil off the host.

ATHONITE. A monk (or other inhabitant) of Mount Athos.

AUTOCEPHALOUS CHURCH. A dissident Orthodox church subject to no jurisdiction outside itself.

AUTONOMOUS CHURCH. A dissident Orthodox church that is self-governing but acknowledges the jurisdiction of a patriarch or other hierarch outside itself.

AZYME (*Gk.*, unleavened). Unleavened altar-bread.

BALADITES (*Ar.*, rustics). Maronite and Melkite congregations of monks.

BASILIANS. Improperly, Eastern monks in general; properly, certain Catholic congregations.

BEATITUDE, HIS, YOUR. The style of address and reference given to an Eastern patriarch.

BEMA (*Gk.*, step). The sanctuary of a church.

BYZANTINE. Primarily, appertaining to Byzantium (Constantinople); by extension, appertaining to all those churches using the Liturgy, etc., of Constantinople.

CAESAROPAPISM. The domination of the Church by the Prince

in the later Roman empire; not unknown in the dissident Orthodox national churches today.

"CANONS, THE." Canon law.

CHARTOPHYLAX (*Gk.*, keeper of records). A diocesan chancellor.

CHERUBIKON (*Gk.*). The "hymn of the Cherubim," intoned just before the great entrance in the Byzantine Liturgy.

CHIROTONY (*Gk.*, stretching forth of hands). The sacrament of Holy Orders; ordination or consecration.

CHOREPISKOPOS (*Gk.*, rural overseer). A title of honour in several rites, sometimes with duties attached.

CIBORIUM (*Lat.*, from *Gk.*, a cup). A canopy of wood or stone, supported by pillars, covering an altar.

CONCELEBRATION. The celebration of the Liturgy by several priests at one altar at the same time.

CREED. The creed of Nicaea-Constantinople is the only one used liturgically in any Eastern rite.

CROSS. The "Russian cross" has three bars, the top one representing the title and the bottom one (sloped from left to right) representing the footrest. The "Greek cross" is equilateral.

CROWN. The Byzantine episcopal mitre, worn also by Armenian priests.

CROWNING. The marriage rite, from its chief ceremony.

DIAKONIKON (*Gk.*, of the deacon). The part of the sanctuary to the south of the altar; a liturgical book for the deacon's use.

DIKERION (*Gk.*). A two-branched candlestick.

DIPTYCHS (*Gk.*, twice-folded). The commemoration of the living and the dead in the Liturgy, whose names were formerly written on two conjoined tablets.

DISKOS (*Gk.*, quoit). The Byzantine paten.

DISSIDENT. Non-Catholic Christian, especially of an Eastern church.

DOORS. "Holy," the central doors of the *eikonostasis;* "royal," the central doors from the narthex into the nave. The "holy doors" are sometimes called "royal."

EIKON (*Gk.*, image). A flat painted sacred picture, often covered with embossed metal except over the faces and hands.

EIKONOSTASIS (*Gk.*, picture-stand). The screen separating the nave from the sanctuary, and adorned with pictures.

EILETON (*Gk.*). A linen corporal.

EKPHONESIS (*Gk.*). A "lifting of the voice" at the last words of an inaudible prayer.

ENKOLPION (*Gk.*, that worn on the breast). An oval medallion worn on a chain round the neck.

ENTRANCE, LITTLE, GREAT. Processions, with the gospel-book and the bread and wine respectively, in the Byzantine and Armenian Liturgies.

EPARCHY (*Gk.*, province). Any episcopal diocese.

EPIGONATION (*Gk.*, *epigounis*, thigh. *Sl.*, *palitza*). A lozenge-shaped episcopal vestment, worn above the right knee. Peculiar to the Pope in the West.

EPIKLESIS (*Gk.*, invocation). A prayer that the Holy Ghost may come down upon the bread and wine and turn it into Christ's body and blood, and imploring the grace of the sacrament for the recipients. It comes in fact after the consecration.

EPIMANIKIA (*Gk.*, upon the sleeves. *Sl.*, *narukavniki*). Liturgical cuffs.

EPITRAKHELION (*Gk.*, upon the neck). The sacerdotal stole.

EUKHOLOGION (*Gk.*, prayer-book. *Sl.*, *Sluzhebnik*). A book containing the texts of the Liturgies and other offices.

EXARCH (*Gk.*, ruler). The primate of an independent church, between a patriarch and an archbishop; but more usually now a priest or bishop with a special charge. Also a title of honour.

FILIOQUE (*Lat.*, and from the Son. *Gk.*, *kai ek tou Huiou*). The phrase added to the Nicene Creed in the West which Photius in 863 declared to be a "corruption of the Faith."

GEÉZ. Classical Ethiopic, the liturgical language of that rite.

GREAT CHURCH. The official name of the Orthodox Church of

Constantinople, having reference to the Holy Wisdom church.

GYNAECEUM (*Lat. Gk., gynaikites*). The part of a church reserved for women.

HAGIA (*Gk.*, holy things). The sacred elements after consecration.

HAIKAL (*Ar.*, temple). The sanctuary of a Coptic church.

HEGUMENOS (*Gk.*, leader). An abbot.

HESPERINON (*Gk. Sl., vetchernya*). Vespers.

HESYCHASM (*Gk., hesukhia*, quiet). 1. The state of a monk in the third grade of Eastern monasticism. 2. An exaggerated theory of mysticism emanating from Mount Athos in the fourteenth century.

HEXAPTERYGON (*Gk.*, six-winged). Another name for the *ripidion*.

HIERARCH (*Gk.*, sacred ruler). Any high member of a hierarchy, but especially an archbishop or patriarch.

HIERATIKON (*Gk.*). A book containing the prayers most used by a priest, a variable compilation. Also called the *Leitourgikon* (*Sl., Sluzhebnik*) or Little Eukhologion.

HIERODEACON. A monk who is a deacon.

HIEROMONK. A monk who is a priest.

HOROLOGION (*Gk. Sl., Tchasoslov*, book of the hours). A book containing the common prayers of the Divine Office, etc.

HYPAPANTE. (*Gk.*, meeting). The feast of the Purification, when our Lord and his Mother met Simeon and Anna.

ICONOCLASM (*Gk.*, image-breaking). The campaign against the veneration of holy images and the accompanying persecution, centered at Constantinople, from *c.* 726 till 787 and from 814 till 842.

IDIORRYTHMA (*Gk.*, one's own arrangements). A type of Orthodox monastery in which the monks live alone or in groups, partly supporting themselves.

JULIAN CALENDAR. Issued by Julius Caesar in 45 B.C., corrected under Pope Gregory XIII in 1582. The Julian reckoning is now 13 days behind the Gregorian.

KAMELAUKION (*Gk., kamelos,* camel, *aukhen,* nape of the neck). The clerical hat of the Byzantine rite, at first made of camel-hair cloth.

KAMISION. The long ungirdled vestment proper to minor clerics.

KANON. A rhythmical hymn.

KARSHUNI. Arabic written in Syriac characters.

KATHOLIKOS (*Gk.,* universal delegate). The title of the heads of the Nestorian, Armenian, and Georgian churches, now equivalent to patriarch.

KONTAKION (*Gk.*). A hymn referring to the day's feast.

KUMMUS. A Coptic abbot; also a title of honour for any priest of that rite.

KOIMESIS (*Gk.,* falling asleep. *Sl., Uspenie*). The feast of the Assumption of our Lady.

LANCE, THE HOLY (*Gk., lonkhe. Sl., kopyo*). The Byzantine liturgical knife.

LAURA (*Gk.,* alley). Formerly a monastery consisting of rows of cells or huts; now any sizeable monastery.

LECTOR (*Gk., anagnostes. Sl., tchtetz*). The lower of the two lesser orders normal in the East. His chief office is to read the epistle.

LITURGY, THE (*Gk., leitourgia,* a public duty or work). The Eucharistic Sacrifice, i.e., "Mass."

MANDYAS (*Gk.*). 1. A short cloak, part of the monastic habit. 2. A sort of cope, worn by bishops.

MAR (*Syr.,* lord). Title given to saints and bishops in the Syriac rites; fem., *mart.*

MASNAPHTA (*Syr.*). A small hood worn by bishops of the Antiochene rite.

MEGALOSKHEMOS (*Gk.,* great habiter). The highest grade of Eastern monk.

MELLUSIANS. A Nestorian sect in Malabar, named after Mar Mellos and dating from 1874.

MENAION (*Gk.*, *men*, month). A liturgical book in 6 or 12 volumes, containing the proper parts of the Divine Office for fixed feasts.

MESONYKTIKON (*Gk.*, midnight. *Sl.*, *Polunoschnitza*). The night-office.

METANY (*Gk.*, penance). Great, a complete prostration; ordinary or little, a profound bow, taking the place of the Western genuflection.

METROPOLITAN. In strict Byzantine usage, equivalent to a Western archbishop. Catholics now use the title almost indifferently with archbishop.

MOLEBEN (*Sl.*). An occasional service of thanksgiving or petition.

MYRON (*Gk.*, sweet oil). The Holy Chrism, which may be blessed only by patriarchs or other primates.

MYSTERY (*Gk.*, something hidden). The ordinary word for a sacrament in the East.

NARTHEX. The western vestibule of a church.

OECUMENICAL PATRIARCH. The official title borne by the patriarchs of Constantinople since the seventh century.

OLD BELIEVERS OR OLD RITUALISTS. Russian sectaries who refused the reforms of the Patriarch Nikon of Moscow in the seventeenth century. Before the revolution they numbered, with other sects, over 30 millions, but are commonly reckoned by Westerners as members of the dissident Orthodox Church.

OMOPHORION (*Gk.*, borne on the shoulders). The large Byzantine *pallium*, worn by all bishops when celebrating the Liturgy; a smaller one is used for convenience at certain parts.

ORARION (*Gk.*). The deacon's long stole.

ORTHODOX (*Gk.*, *orthodoxos*, right believer). The name for all those who accepted the Council of Chalcedon; now usually confined as a title to the non-Catholic Eastern Orthodox Church.

ORTHROS (*Gk.*, daybreak. *Sl.*, *utrenya*). The office equivalent to Matins and Lauds.

PANAGIA (*Gk.*). "All-holy," used for the Mother of God as we say "our Lady." Also another name for the *enkolpion*.

PANNYKHIDIA (*Gk.*, all night). An office for the dead.

PANTOKRATOR (*Gk.*, all mighty). An image of our Lord ruling from Heaven, i.e., Christ the King.

PAPPAS (*Gk.*, father, i.e., pope). All Greek-speaking priests are called *pappas*, and the equivalent (*pop*) is common among the Slavs but is considered wanting in respect; they say *batiushka* "little father." "Pope" is one of the official titles of the Orthodox Patriarch of Alexandria.

PAREKKLESIA (*Gk.*, beside church). A side chapel or addition to a church.

PATRIARCH (*Gk.*, ruler of a family). A bishop who holds the highest rank after the Pope in the hierarchy of jurisdiction. A patriarch can be subject to no other prelate except the Pope. In the West the title is honorary, except for the Pope himself.

PERIODEUTES (*Gk.*, visitor. *Syr.*, *bardut*, Malayalam, *prodott*). A title of honour given to priests holding positions of responsibility in the three churches of Antiochene rite.

PHANAR, THE. Expression used for the Patriarch of Constantinople and his *curia* (cf., "the Vatican"), from the quarter of the city wherein they reside.

PHENOLION (*Gk.*). The Byzantine chasuble.

PHYLETISM (*Gk.*, *phyle*, a tribe). The name by which the Patriarch of Constantinople condemned excessive nationalism in the dissident Orthodox churches in 1872.

PRAVOSLAVIE (*Sl.*). Orthodoxy (in its particular sense).

PRESANCTIFIED, LITURGY OF THE. A Liturgy in which there is no consecration; a Host consecrated at a previous Liturgy is consumed at the communion.

PROSKOMIDE (*Gk.*, preparation). The preparatory part of the Liturgy, at which the ministers vest and the bread and wine are prepared.

PROSPHORA (*Gk.*, oblation). The Byzantine altar-bread, like a small loaf or cake.

PROTHESIS (*Gk.*, ante-deposition). The part of the sanctuary to the north of the altar, where the bread and wine are made ready.

PROTODEACON. Archdeacon or senior deacon. Archdeacons are deacons, i.e., not priests, in the East.

PROTOPOPE—PRESBYTER—PRIEST. An archpriest (distinguish from *archiereus*). In some churches protopresbyters are different from archpriests.

PROTOPSALTES (*Gk. Sl.*, *regent khora*). The chief cantor.

PROTOTHRONE. The first see of a patriarchate, after the patriarch's; or a primatial see, e.g., the see of Rome is the protothrone of the world, Constantinople of the East.

RASON (*Gk.*). The wide-sleeved gown proper to the Eastern clergy.

RASOPHORE (*Gk.*, rason-wearer. *Sl.*, *ryasonosetz*). The lowest grade of Eastern monk.

RIPIDION (*Gk.*, fan). A metal liturgical fan affixed to a pole.

ROSARY (*Gk.*, *konbologion. Sl.*, *chotki*). The Eastern rosary usually consists of 100 beads at each of which a metany is made and an ejaculatory prayer said. It is a purely monastic practice. Most Eastern Catholics use the Western rosary.

"SAINT SOPHIA." A barbarous name often given in English to the Church of the Holy Wisdom at Constantinople.

SAKKOS (*Gk.*, a sack). The principal eucharistic vestment proper to Byzantine bishops.

SKOUPHOS. The cap worn by monks under their veil and by minor clerics.

SOLEA. The step before the holy doors at which communion is given.

STAROSLAV. A rather barbarous name, given first by French writers, to Church Slavonic.

STASIDIA (*Gk.*, standing-places). The fixed seats behind the altar, in front of the *eikonostasis*, and around the walls of a Byzantine church: usually stood at rather than sat upon.

STAVROPEGION (*Gk.*, setting-up of a cross). An Orthodox monastery subject to the patriarch instead of (as is usual) to the bishop.

STAVROPHORE (*Gk.*, cross-bearer). The middle grade of Eastern monk.

STIKHARION (*Gk.*). A vestment equivalent to an alb.

SUBDEACON. A lesser order in the Eastern church, and properly having no liturgical office.

SYNAXIS (*Gk.*, assembly). 1. A feast on which are commemorated saints connected with the mystery of the previous day. 2. The council of seniors in a monastery.

SYNKELLOS. 1. A bishop's secretary. 2. An auxiliary or titular bishop.

SYNOD (*Gk.*, meeting). 1. Any ecclesiastical council. 2. The governing assembly of an Orthodox church.

SYNTHRONON (*Gk.*). The bishop's throne and stalls for clergy behind the altar in a cathedral.

TEMPLON (*Gk.*). Another name for the *eikonostasis*.

THEOTOKOS (*Gk.*, *tokos*, childbirth). The Mother of God. *Theotokion:* a hymn in her honour.

TRIKERION (*Gk.*). A three-branched candlestick.

TRISAGION, THE. The thrice-holy hymn: "Holy God, holy strong One, holy deathless One, have mercy on us."

TROPARION (*Gk.*). A generic name for the short hymns of the Byzantine rite.

TYPIKON (*Gk.*). 1. A book of the calendar and rubrics; each chief church of the Byzantine rite has one of its own. 2. A charter of monastic constitutions.

VARTAPED. A rank in the Armenian hierarchy, below the episcopate.

VICAR PATRIARCHAL. A local representative appointed by a patriarch.

VLADYKA (*Sl.*, lord, master). The Slavonic form of address to a bishop.

XEROPHAGY (*Gk.*, dry food). The stricter form of Eastern fast.

ZEON (*Gk.*, boiling). Warm water poured into the Chalice before communion.

ZONE (*Gk.*). Girdle.

INDEX